We the People
Consenting to a Deeper Democracy

By John Buck and Sharon Villines

**A Handbook for Understanding and Implementing
Sociocratic Principles and Methods**

Second Edition, Updated, and Expanded

SOCIOCRACY.INFO

WASHINGTON DC

Sociocracy.info
6827 Fourth Street NW Room 213
Washington, DC 20012

contact@sociocracy.info

ISBN: 978-0-9792827-2-0 (eBook)
ISBN: 978-0-9792827-3-7 (Softcover)

We the People: Consenting to a Deeper Democracy, A Guide to Sociocratic
Principles and Methods / by John Buck and Sharon Villines

Second edition, updated and expanded.

p.   cm.

Includes illustrations, appendices, glossary, index.

Buck, John
Villines, Sharon
Endenburg, Gerard
Boeke, Kees
Boeke, Beatrice
Ward, Lester Frank

1. Sociocracy. 2. Organizational Design. 3. Leadership.
4. Dynamic Governance. 5. Effective Management. 6. Cybernetics.

Cover Credit: Bees © by Sharon Villines

Cover Quotation from *Honeybee Democracy* by Thomas D. Seeley.

IN MEMORY OF

Kees and Betty Boeke

Anna and Gerardus Endenburg

Contents

About this Book . . . . *vii*

About the Authors . . . . *xv*

PART ONE: Revisiting Governance **17**

Chapter 1: Why We Need Another "-ocracy" 23
              by John Buck

Chapter 2: Why We Need Another "-ocracy" 29
              by Sharon Villines

Chapter 3: The Idea of a Sociocracy 37

Chapter 4: Cybernetics & Sociocracy 49

PART TWO: Rewiring Organizational Power **63**

Chapter 5: Inclusive Decision-Making 67

Chapter 6: Developing Quality 85

Chapter 7: Steering & Structure 99

Chapter 8: New Leadership Strategies 115

Chapter 9: Free & Self-Optimizing Organizations 125

PART THREE: Organizing Our Strengths **141**

Chapter 10: Circles & Implementation 145

Chapter 11: Consent & Rounds 159
              Sara's Story by Tena Meadows O'Rear *169*

Chapter 12: Electing People 175

Chapter 13: Organizing Work 183

Chapter 14: Money as Measurement 197

AFTERWORD **207**

An Invitation to Share 207

Finding Sociocratic Centers, Training, & Consultants 210

APPENDICES **213**

A. Sociocracy by Lester Frank Ward 215

B. Sociocracy: Democracy as It Might Be by Kees Boeke. 223
C. Rationale for a New Social Structure by Gerard Endenburg. 231
D. Sociocracy for One by Sharon Villines 239
E. Bylaws for a Sociocratic Business 243
F. Bylaws for a Sociocratic Nonprofit Organization 261
G. Guides for Implementing Sociocracy 285
    1. The Implementation Process. 287
    2. Circles and Officers 289
    3. The Elections Process 291
    4. Circle Meetings 293
    5. Rounds 297
    6. Policy Development 299
    7. Resolving Objections & Building Consent. 301
    8. Designing the Work Process. 303
    9. Guide for Logbooks 305

GLOSSARY. 307

BIBLIOGRAPHY. 321

INDEX. 329

Illustrations

1.1 John Buck 15

1.2 Sharon Villines 15

3.1 Auguste Comte 37

3.2 Frank Ward in Yellowstone National Park 39

3.3 Frank Ward 40

3.4 Betty Cadbury and Kees Boeke 41

3.5 Children's Community Workshop. .42

3.6 Gerard Endenburg 45

3.7 Gerard Endenburg & Sociocratische Centrum 48

4.1a Occupy Wall Street Protest 51

4.2 Norbert Weiner 53

4.3 Definitions of Cybernetic. 55s

4.3 Journal of Cybernetics & Human Knowing 56

5.1 Ford Motors Assembly Line 79

5.2 Henry Ford's Model T 71

5.3 Mary Parker Follett. 5.3

5.4 Policy Decisions and Operations Decisions. 76

5.5 A Heating System Consents 79

5.6 Consent the First Principle 80

5.7 Decision-making Methods Used in Sociocracy. 80

5.8 A Reasoned Objection and Examining the Basis 83

6.1 A Circle Meeting. 90

6.2 Circles, the Second Learning Principle. 91

6.3 Typical Topics for a Circle Meeting. .91

6.4 Producing Organization. 93

6.5 The Circular Process 95

7.1a The Third Governing Principle: Double–Links. 100

7.1b Illustrating Double–Links Between Circles 101

7.2 Types of Steering. 105

7.3 The Heavy Load on Autocratic Managers 107

7.4 Governance and Operational Structures 111

8.1 Hierarchy and Bottom-archy 119

8.2 The Art of War by Sun Tzu.................................121

9.1 Margaret Wheatley.....................................128

9.2 Definition of "Aim"...................................133

9.3 John Nash..134

9.4 We Are All in the Same Boat...........................137

9.5 Rights and Rewards of Stakeholders....................138

13.1 Producing Organization...............................185

13.2 Vision, Mission, Aim Examples........................187

13.3 The 27-Block Chart..................................190

The Story of Charles and Sociocracy

As a Decision-Maker.....................................75

Charles's Policy Decisions...............................77

Charles's Operations Decisions...........................77

Resistance and Friction in Charles's Office..............78

Charles's & Domains.....................................81

Charles's Circle Meeting................................92

Charles's and His Circle's Vision, Mission, Aim..........94

Charles's & His Circle's Production Process..............96

Charles's as a Representative...........................102

Charles's and the Circular Process......................107

Charles's and Abstraction...............................112

Illustrations 4.1, 5.1, 6.3, and 8.1 used with permission of the Sociocratisch Centrum; redrawn and digitized by Jason Forrest.

About this Book

We the People presents a method of governance that gives people the power to consent and object to the conditions under which they live and work. Like democracy, it values freedom and equality. Unlike democracy, it is not based on majority rule, voting, or autocratic leadership. Sociocracy is designed to enable groups of people to govern themselves collaboratively—sharing knowledge, problem-solving, and building consent. How it does this is the story in this book.

The name of this form of government is sociocracy, pronounced *socio-* as in *sociology* and *-cracy* as in *democracy*. In French, the language, in which it was created, *sociocratie*. The Latin root, *socio* or *socius*, means "companions." Thus, sociocracy is designed so companions or associates can govern themselves collaboratively as partners in a society.

THE HONEY BEES

The honey bees sprinkled throughout the text were inspired by an excellent study of the amazingly well-organized societies of honeybees, *Honeybee Democracy*. The author, Thomas D. Seeley, has been observing honeybees since he was a child and continued to study them as a professor at Cornell University.

In an autobiographical style with the precision and detail of a scientist, Seeley explains in *Honeybee Democracy* how honeybees work collaboratively toward a single aim, delegate tasks, and make decisions by consent. Each year as their numbers exceed the size of their hive, thousands of bees will leave the hive and swarm elsewhere—on a plant or a fence post.

A much smaller group of 400 or so bees flies off in different directions to search for a new home. They return to the swarm to discuss what they have found, They describe and argue the merits of each discovery by performing a unique dance. Then members of the group will visit the most promising prospects and return to debate. They dance and visit sites until all the arguments and inspections have been done and they have all settled on one.

HONEYBEES ARE SELF-ORGANIZING

On a daily basis they self-organize to complete all the daily tasks working in unison. There is no hierarchy. The bees take tasks according to their age and genetic makeup. Only the older bees, for example, forage for nectar and pollen. When foragers return to the hive other bees process the nectar into honey. The pollen gathered is a high energy food source for the queen, workers, and emerging bees. There are bees that care for the queen and bees that make wax. When there is a shortage of bees for one task, others develop the skills needed to do them. Young bees will grow faster, for example, in order to forage sooner if the hive needs more food.

The queen can lay 2,000 eggs a day. While she is the center of the hive's population growth, she is not a ruler as "Queen" would suggest. There is no hierarchy. In addition to the dance and fluttering of wings to communicate about a potential new hive, they are also used to indicate sources of food. Other body movements indicate other needs.

We are not saying they are behaving sociocratically, but that sociocracy is based on the study of biological systems and how they organize to sustain themselves. This study, cybernetics, is the theoretical basis of the sociocratic circle method.

By studying the natural world we have learned to design more sustainable organizations that are also self-organizing and self-governing..

WHAT IS GOOD GOVERNANCE?

The word *govern* means "to steer," as sailors steer their boats to safe harbor. Pilots steer planes. As people, we steer our governments, our leaders, and ourselves. Governance is what we do when we make decisions about our future and then implement those decisions. It is the agreements we make about how we will live and work together. Sociocratic governance is self-governance, governing of ourselves as

Bad governance is being increasingly regarded as one of the root causes of all evil within our societies.

United Nations

a society.

The quality of our governance of organizations, cities, and nations determines whether we will achieve our goals, or if we will fail. The United Nations, the International Monetary Fund, and the World Bank recognize eight characteristics of good governance:

- ◆ Participatory
- ◆ Lawful
- ◆ Transparent
- ◆ Responsive
- ◆ Consensus-oriented
- ◆ Equitable and Inclusive
- ◆ Effective and Efficient
- ◆ Accountable

Sociocratic governance is designed to implement all eight and adds an ninth: a clear and compelling sense of purpose; a well-defined aim.

As we shall see, most of these characteristics of good government depend on inclusiveness and participation.

WHO CAN USE SOCIOCRACY?

Sociocracy can be used to govern any kind or size of organization: from a single-person business to a multi-national corporation, a nursery school and a university system, a bowling league and an international sports federation.

The confusion between the words *sociocracy* and *socialism* and has led some organizations and consultants to use other descriptors, including Dynamic Governance, Dynamic Self-Governance, Consent Democracy, Direct Democracy, Circle Governance, Holacracy, Holacracy Lite, Circle Forward, Sociocracy 3.0, and others. We continue use *sociocracy*, *sociocratic governance*, and *sociocratic organization* because these words are specific, less open to confusion with other methods, and link to the almost 200-year-old tradition of sociocratic thinking. In many organizations, particularly outside the United States, sociocracy is still preferred.

Examples of the types of organizations using sociocracy include:

Sociocracy is increasingly included in college and university syllabuses and reading lists for studies in business, political science, history, and sociology.

- A plastics manufacturer in Virginia
- Professional associations and societies in North and South America, Australia, and Europe
- Homeowner associations, and cohousing and ecovillage communities in North and South America, Australia, France, Scandinavia, and the United Kingdom
- A health care facility in Vermont
- A large agribusiness in Brazil
- Software developers on several continents
- Entrepreneurs and start ups
- Montessori, Waldorf, and public schools in America and the Netherlands
- The design school of a university in California
- Non-profit service organizations in Virginia
- Cooperatives in North America and Europe
- Units of governmental organizations in Maryland
- A large engine repair business in Quebec
- Heavy electrical installations company in the Netherlands
- Christian, Muslim, and Adventist congregations, and other religious communities
- A permaculture education center in Canada
- Ecovillages and intentional communities in North America, South America, Europe, and Australia
- Permaculture associations in Canada and Scotland
- Many chapters of the international Center for Nonviolent Communications
- Divisions of Shell and Philips
- The Pakistani Society for the Advancement of Training
- The Japan Management Association (JMA)
- The Al-Futtaim Management Development Centre Dubai
- National Bank of Pakistan

Founded in 2012, the Endenburg Foundation is devoted to increasing the understanding and implementation of sociocracy internationally.

Sociocracy is increasingly included in college and university syllabuses and reading lists for studies in business, political science, history, and sociology. Examples from recent years include:

- "American Political Thought," University of Vermont
- "Systems Thinking Decision Models," Elizabethtown College, Kentucky
- "The American Constitutional Order," Graduate School of Public Policy, University of Tokyo
- "American Sociology and the Problem of Order: The Socialization of Authority," Swarthmore College
- "American Political Thought," University of Utah
- "First Nations Governance and Public Administration," School of Management, Yukon College
- "Elements of Political Theory," Rai University, India
- "Systems Thinking and Decision-Making Models," University of Vermont
- "American Political Thought," Intercollegiate Institute Studies Institute
- "Political Science," University of Utah
- On the Minecraft Game Fan Zone website as a decision-making method used by Agile software programmers.

The international organization, the Sociocracy Group, formerly the Sociocratisch Centrum, has headquarters in Rotterdam, and continues to train and oversee certification of sociocratic experts, develop training materials, and promote sociocracy. There are centers on almost every continent doing training and consulting. Founded in 2012, the Endenburg Foundation is devoted to increasing the understanding and implementation of sociocracy internationally.

Training is now being conducted in many languages including Dutch, English, Flemish, French, German, Hindi, Indonesian, Korean, Russian, Spanish, and Swedish.

EDUCATION & TRAINING

Today, there are certified trainers and consultants practicing around the world. Many consultants in the area of organizational development and management have incorporated sociocratic principles and practices into their own methods.

The Sociocracy Group has three international divisions, formed around a combination of geography and languages spoken. Each division has active programs for people working toward certification as sociocracy facilitators, trainers, or consultants, or as professionals applying the principles and methods in the context of their own field.

Training is now being conducted in many languages, including Dutch, English, Flemish, French, German, Hindi, Indonesian, Korean, Russian, Spanish, and Swedish.

THE SECOND EDITION

The 2007 edition of *We the People* was the first book to present the history and theory of sociocracy from its origins in the mid-19th century to its full development and implementation in the 21st. It was also the first to discuss sociocracy in the context of general management theory during the same period. The second edition has been completely rewritten, updated, and expanded. The rewriting was done to both add material and clarify the text. The intention was to create a more-fluid, easily read text appropriate for a wide audience and with larger print and more photographs.

Though we fear that some people will only read the sidebars and look at the pictures and diagrams, that is not the worst thing that could happen to a book or to sociocracy.

We hope the new edition of *We the People* will be an even more-helpful handbook for understanding and implementing sociocracy.

The text is arranged in four parts, each with increasing specificity, so by the end, you may be ready to implement the method in your own organizations. It was a surprise to us how many organizations were able to plunge ahead on their own. Some later have more training but understand the method perfectly well from reading the text. If you are working in a larger organization, especially a business, it would be wise to have a consultant begin with a series of workshop or even extensive in-house training.

Part I: Revisiting Governance. We explain first our personal reasons for believing that our society needs this new governance system, Then we discuss the history of sociocracy and the development of the principles on which it is based.

Chapter 4, "Cybernetics & Sociocracy," has been added to explain cybernetic principles more fully. It was the science of cybernetics that enabled sociocracy to move from relatively small social groups into high-demand production environments, and everything in between.

Part II: Rewriting Organizational Power. We explore the principles and methods as they relate to various aspects of managing organizations. The work of management experts is discussed to understand how it differs and is similar to sociocracy. Comparing and contrasting is one of the best ways to understand the similarities and differences.

Part III, Organizing Our Strengths explains in more detail how the principles of sociocracy work and why they are important. What do cybernetics and systems thinking offer? It explains the practices that ensure that the method can be applied productively.

The **Appendices** contain several types of documents:

◈ Original texts by Ward, Boeke, and Endenburg
◈ Two sets of bylaws, one as an example for businesses and one for associations and non-profit organizations. Both are adapted from legally registered corporations, one a Limited Liability Corporation (LLC), and one a charitable and educational non-profit (501(c)3).
◈ A guide for using sociocratic methods personally as an individual in any decision-making situation, and
◈ A large number of how-to guides for using the methods and practices in meetings and other decision-making situations.

This is followed by a **Glossary**, a **Selected Bibliography**, and the **Index**.

We understand that some readers will be interested in the whole story, start to finish, and others will want to jump right to the "how to" chapters in Part III and the Guides to implementation in the Appendices. Wherever you start, we hope you will return to read the early chapters so you will fully understand this deeply enriching and effective method for getting more done, more harmoniously. Understanding the theory will help you understand when something is not working and why it needs to be done the way it is described.

Although we fear that some people will only read the sidebars and look at the pictures and diagrams, that is not the worst thing that could happen to a book or to sociocracy.

ACKNOWLEDGMENTS

Since the first edition in 2007, we have learned a lot about teaching and training people to use sociocracy from interactions and feedback in workshops and from those who have implemented sociocracy in their organizations. We have tried to incorporate what we have learned into the text and are indebted to everyone who has contributed by sharing sociocracy with others.

We would particularly like to thank Gerard Endenburg, Annewiek Reijmer, Gilles Charest, Pieter van der Mechè, and the many other members of the international Sociocracy Group, an international foundation based in the Netherlands and the partners of the Sociocracy Consulting Group for sharing their technical expertise, advice, and encouragement. We would also like to again thank Ramona Buck, Gerard Endenburg, and Greg Rouillard for their tireless proofing and detailed comments that brought the first edition to completion. And Ruth Thaler-Carter for enthusiastically taking on the second.

And of course, Gerard Endenburg for bringing moderns sociocracy to life. And a big thank you to Jan Houdijk for the humorous cartoons that both clarify and enliven the subject.

We appreciate the many readers who have contributed suggestions and criticisms, and we are also indebted to them for their patience waiting for this new edition. A special recognition to the many members of the sociocracy@groups.io discussion list from all over the world who question and argue on a daily basis all the fine points about sociocracy that anyone of them can raise.

John Buck and Sharon Villines
Fall 2017

About the Authors

John Buck was the first native English-speaking consultant certified to teach and implement the Sociocratic Circle-Organization Method (SCM). After learning to read Dutch to study with Gerard Endenburg at the Sociocratisch Centrum in Rotterdam, he completed a master's degree in Quantitative Sociology at George Washington University. Using quantitative analysis to measure the effects of sociocracy on Dutch workers, he confirmed its effectiveness in increasing worker commitment and organizational productivity.

Buck has extensive experience in managing hundreds of workers in both government and corporate sectors in computer systems installation and management. He is a division director for the international organization, the Sociocracy Group, LLC. An expert in governance methods and organizational design, he serves on the boards of several organizations. The father of three children, he lives with his wife in Silver Spring, MD.

Sharon Villines is a writer and Mentor *Emeritus* at SUNY Empire State College, where she taught, among other things, arts management and small business planning, and served on numerous academic and governance policy committees. She was president and grievance chair of the AFL-CIO-affiliated faculty union. She is co-author of *Orientation to College: A Reader on Becoming an Educated Person* (Wadsworth, 2004).

With a long interest in how we organize ourselves, Villines began studying sociocracy with Buck in 2002 and now writes a blog, Sociocracy. info, and moderates an active email discussion list on sociocracy. She uses her experience in nonprofit organizations, labor unions, universities, schools, religious and political action groups, cohousing, and other cooperative enterprises as a basis for analyzing and explaining sociocracy. She lives in a cohousing community in Washington, DC.

PART I

Revisiting Governance

We the People of the United States, in Order to Form a More Perfect Union, establish Justice, insure domestic Tranquility, provide for the common defence, promote the general Welfare, and secure the Blessings of Liberty to ourselves and our Posterity, do ordain and establish this Constitution for the United States of America.

The Constitution of the United States of America is one of the most enduring documents ever written. It has withstood the test of numerous challenges and continues to serve the highly successful United States of America. When the Constitution was written, however, it was much more experimental than many of us realize. The principles on which it was based had never been tested on a such a large scale. For it to work, the founders had to unite into one nation thirteen unruly states filled with a people exhausted from war and fearful of new allegiances, who did not speak a common language, and who were still breaking links with their mother countries. It was a huge task. (Amar 2005)

For the first time, a country was formed based on the values of freedom and equality, and governed by representatives chosen by the people, not a monarchy or an aristocracy of landowners. But in time, as we shall see, it began to develop cracks.

Today, sociocracy is developing a modern and even more-effective, egalitarian governance method. Although democracy flourishes in many countries, it has two major deficiencies:

- ◆ Reliance on majority rule
- ◆ Lack of commitment to use scientific methods to measure or evaluate its actions

Today, sociocracy is developing a modern and even more effective, egalitarian governance method.

17

Majority voting, and thus rule by the majority, creates winners and losers. It encourages partisanship and political alliances, with decision-making based on politics and not on effectiveness. Because it is ineffective in ensuring high performance, democracy is generally not used in business, healthcare institutions, the military, or other organizations held accountable for measurable results.

Sociocracy shares the democratic values of freedom and equality while it avoids the negative results of majority rule by using inclusive decision-making and collaborative governance. Sociocracy is based on scientific method—testing and measurement. This ensures the most-effective decisions and actions.

What can only be asserted in democracies, as in the Declaration of Independence—that all human beings are equal and endowed with the unalienable rights of "Life, Liberty, and the pursuit of Happiness"—can be guaranteed in sociocracy, which is often described as "beyond democracy" or the "next step."

GOVERNANCE AND SCIENCE

The word *democracy* is based on *demos*, the Greek word for the common people, and means governance determined by the general population. Allowing citizens to vote on adopting laws and electing representatives was a major step forward from governance by monarchies and dictators. But general elections by the whole population are not always effective in making good legislation or choosing the best leaders—or ensuring that the people elected would educate themselves on new issues before making decisions.

Sociocracy from its conception was based on different premises from democracy. The word *sociocracy* comes from the Latin *socius*, meaning "associates" or "companions." Using *socius* in its combining form *socio-*, and *-ocracy* meaning governance, means "governance by people in association with each other." The same root, *socio-*, combined with *-ology*, meaning "the study of," was used to name sociology —the study of societies or social groups. People who shared a common aim— a common purpose.

What can only be asserted in democracies—that all human beings are equal and endowed with the unalienable rights of "life, liberty, and the pursuit of happiness"—can be guaranteed in a sociocratic society.

Sociocracy was conceived in the 1850's as a new governance method that would be based on the science of sociology. Over the next 150 years, sociocracy developed from an idea to a method that allows societies to govern themselves for the mutual benefit of all.

In the 20th century, a major step forward for sociocracy was contributed by another science: cybernetics, the science of communications and control. Cybernetics is the study of systems in nature and machines. How do they adapt or adjust to their environments, sustaining themselves in adverse and changing conditions? How do systems and parts of systems self-govern while they are also governed by the whole? Cybernetics was studying the very same dilemma as societies that sought both a unified whole and individual freedom and equality.

The development of sociocracy in the late nineteenth and twentieth centuries parallels the scientific discoveries that fundamentally altered our view of how the natural world works. The mechanical model of closed systems was replaced with a world of dynamic, ever-changing systems that could self-correct and adapt. The adult brain, thought to be steadily degrading until death, was found to have the ability to develop new synapses and neurons throughout life. Chaos, once believed to be random or purposeless, was discovered to be self-organizing and incredibly powerful and energetic.

Sociocracy today is a method of self-governance enabling us to control the conditions under which we live and work. It can be used by one person, two people, a corporation, a religious group, a neighborhood association, or a whole city. It creates inherently sustainable, self-optimizing systems.

MANAGEMENT THEORY & GOVERNANCE

There are many books about methods of improving the management of businesses and other organizations. Our experience is these books could be even more valuable if combined with sociocracy.

Why? Because while they offer valuable insights for managing work, none have a fundamental theory of governance that transforms how workers are engaged. Without a new theory of governance, of

What is missing in management texts is any concept of a governance structure that addresses the primary aim of organizing: harnessing the energy of every member to accomplish the organization's aim.

decision-making and implementation processes, new management techniques will only re-create the same fundamental problems of top-down organizations that take advantage of workers because they are neither transparent, effective, nor accountable.

Most of our organizations are still designed and managed using the mechanical models of the nineteenth century. They treat people like machine parts and try to control them, rather than develop their abilities and potential. Many do focus on leadership and inclusive decision-making, but lack a feedback system or mechanism that ensures it will always be implemented. What is missing is a governance structure that addresses the primary aim of organizing: harnessing the energy of every member to accomplish the organization's aim.

WRITING OUR OWN CONSTITUTIONS

A constitution is a set of policies granting rights and privileges, setting limits on behavior, and assigning responsibilities. We chose our title, *We the People*, deliberately because it is widely recognized as the opening phrase of the Constitution of the United States, and because sociocratic principles and practices are designed to guide us in writing our own constitutions and completing our own revolution.

Sociocracy is simultaneously conservative and revolutionary. It encourages the productivity of a market economy and at the same time is deeply supportive of the ideals of individual freedom and entrepreneurial innovation. The constitution of a sociocratic organization delegates to all its members—citizens, staff, managers, leaders, investors, etc.—the responsibility for their work. It ensures that the voices on the loading dock are as respected as those in the board room, and vice versa.

Sociocracy is as potentially revolutionary as democracy was in 1776. This time, it will be a peaceful revolution, conducted by consent. A revolution that promises to be quiet, gradual, and nurturing.

IS IT PRACTICAL?

Sociocracy is not only practical; it is easier to implement and maintain

A sociocratic organization ensures that the voices on the loading dock are as respected as those in the board room, and vice versa.

than other methods of governance because it works with nature instead of against it. It creates and directs energy, rather than attempting to harness it. It alters the oppositional labor-management and citizen-government relationships, releasing enormous energy. It supports every member in participating in leading the organization and correcting deficiencies.

Sociocracy is a better form of governance not because the theory is more complex or more complicated, but because it is based on a theory of governance that only became possible after the development of cybernetics in the twentieth century. To the democratic values of freedom and equality, sociocracy adds a balance of innovation and correction, communication, and control that ensures continuous improvement.

REVISITING GOVERNANCE

In Part I, we present the 150 years of ideas that contributed to the development of sociocracy and the reasons why, based on our experience, these principles and practices are so sensible and freeing.

In Chapters 1 and 2, *Why We Need Another -ocracy*, we each present our personal experiences with organizations that were badly governed and the reasons we believe sociocracy is revolutionary.

Chapter 3, *The History of Sociocracy*, reviews the development of sociocracy from its conception by a French philosopher in the mid-nineteenth century to its practical application, developed 100 years later by a Dutch electrical engineer.

Chapter 4, *Cybernetics & Sociocracy* closes Part 1 with a discussion of cybernetic concepts, why they are important to developing effectiveness, and how they are applied in sociocracy.

To the democratic values of freedom and equality, sociocracy adds a balance of innovation and correction, communication, and control that ensures continuous improvement.

CHAPTER ONE

Why We Need Another "-ocracy"

BY JOHN BUCK

I encountered Gerard Endenburg and the sociocratic method about 30 years ago while on a trip to Amsterdam to give a speech about computer-based training. I took my family as well, and we arranged a delightful stay with friends. One evening, I vented to our host about my frustrations with the world of business.

"I am supposed to be living in a democracy," I said, "but I spend much of my life at work in a basically feudal structure. There is a Duke of Operations, an Earl of Administration, a Baroness of Personnel, and so on. Even if those people are called managers or vice presidents, it amounts to the same thing. I am not at all enfranchised. If I think they aren't doing well, the only vote I have is with my feet, walking out the door. I have done a lot of research in management literature, but I can't find anyone who has found a way to run an effective business democratically."

"Oh, but that problem has been solved," my host replied in her accented but impeccable English. "You must talk to Gerard Endenburg. He is the president of a very successful electrical engineering company. Let's call him up."

We were soon speeding on a solid Dutch train to Rotterdam to visit Gerard. My research had prepared me to probe in-depth in my talk with him and, in a short time, I was convinced that Gerard had indeed come up with something very rare: genuinely new and ingenious ideas about how to organize. He was not just tinkering with a different angle on worker participation; he had deep and practical insight into the fundamental nature of power. This book describes those insights.

I am supposed to be living in a democracy, but I spend much of my life at work in a basically feudal structure. There is a Duke of Operations, an Earl of Administration ...

I have found that there is a real delight in using Gerard's new methods, and I have been enjoying bringing them to as many organizations as possible—businesses, schools, corporations, factories, associations, even individuals.

How did I become so impassioned about finding a job as an enfranchised citizen of a company, rather than as an employee? And to want to share this possibility with others?

I am a baby boomer who, like all members of my generation, came of age to the sounds of anti-war protests and civil rights marches. I was not a radical. In fact, I handed out literature in favor of Barry Goldwater and was a runner-up in my district for appointment to West Point. I opposed the Vietnam War not because I felt war was bad, but because I felt that particular war was an unconstitutional, presidential war. I received a safe number in the draft lottery and went to work in Seattle for Boeing as a technical writer; a conventional, proper thing to do with a liberal arts degree from an Ivy League university.

More than the war, more than civil rights inequalities, it was my experience at Boeing that shocked awake a passion for trying to change the way my country and my society were functioning. As upsetting as the anti-war and civil rights demonstrations were, they were examples of a democracy in action, correcting itself—as it was designed to do. It involved tremendous citizen energy, but life at Boeing was a different matter.

As upsetting as the anti-war and civil rights demonstrations were, they were examples of a democracy in action, correcting itself—as it was designed to do.

SERVITUDE

I was working for the Manufacturing Research and Development Division, which had no union representation, but unions wouldn't have helped. All the unions could do was negotiate the conditions of servitude. The term *public servant* is respectable, but not private servant—another name for an employee. I identified with the little boy who saw that the emperor had no clothes. I was a servant in a large room of about 200 other servants, all of us sitting at long rows of desks with phone cords hanging from the ceiling, enshrouded in a constant pall of cigarette smoke. Ironically, the cigarette smoke was the only personal gratification allowed in the room.

Before we punched out each day, we had to make sure our phones were on the back left corners of our desks so the room looked in perfect order.

My supervisor treated me well, I enjoyed my co-workers, and my job was interesting. Nothing overtly bad happened. I simply felt powerless, and something deep inside of me shredded.

MAHOGANY ROW

I learned a lot at Boeing. I saw my first systems diagram—massive flowcharts of the manufacturing process whose preparation was aided slightly by the massive mainframe computers then available. I learned that you had to expect at least a 30-to-1 return before investing in a research and development project, and I saw long-term planning in operation one day when I peeked into a temporarily vacant executive conference room on "Mahogany Row." The chart on the wall predicted a gradual reduction in the number of airplane manufacturers over the next 25 years and recommended what Boeing had to do to survive those reductions, including the layoff that was about to sweep me away. The chart, it turned out, was very accurate. Boeing is now the last major commercial airplane manufacturer in the United States.

I also learned that people could care incredibly. My first child was born the week before I was laid off. I was deeply touched when my co-worker, Jan, a woman of about 50, pleaded with the company to lay her off instead of me—to no avail. I've never been back. I do imagine the pall of cigarette smoke gone; the phone cords now tucked inside modular furniture, itself tucked into cubes, Dilbert style; and the building's inhabitants probably no longer punching time clocks—but they are still servants.

I was out of work for several months, finally finding employment on the East Coast. When not looking for work, I used the time to read deeply into organizational and management theory. I researched the history of human equality and fundamental organizational structures.

My career eventually recovered from the Boeing layoff. I gained admittance to a Federal Aviation Administration (FAA) management

My supervisor treated me well and I enjoyed my co-workers. Nothing overtly bad happened. I simply felt powerless, and something deep inside of me shredded.

intern program as a full-time employee, and continued my re-search, happily now at government expense. I attended every management course I could wheedle my way into, including a course on "Management by Objectives" taught by a then-obscure guy named Ed Deming. W. Edward Deming, as many readers know, was the father of the quality movement. A few years later, he came to prominence as his ideas about quality control fed the Japanese technology explosion and Japan dominated world markets.

Before the Internet was established, I developed a computer-based instruction system for the FAA, networking 400 terminals around the country. Only the air-traffic control system itself was bigger. I negotiated a consortium with the Army and Air Force to share mainframe computers and talked the Office of Air Traffic Control into piggybacking on their radar links so my computer system had free cross-country phone service.

In 1984, I received the highly prized Secretary of Transportation Award for Excellence. I had proven to myself that I could play the bureaucracy. I had secured my position and could have stuck around, probably to climb the FAA management ladder, but somehow that prospect didn't excite me. I realized I was bored.

> I had secured my position and could have stuck around, probably to climb the FAA management ladder, but somehow that prospect didn't excite me. I realized I was bored.

DISCOVERING SOCIOCRACY

Fortuitously, I discovered sociocracy. I was in the Netherlands to speak on computer-based training and met Gerard Endenburg. What followed was excitement mixed with numerous frustrations. I made many trips to back to Holland to learn about sociocracy in more depth. I followed Endenburg and other members of the Sociocratisch Centrum around the Dutch countryside and filled several notebooks.

I left the FAA to work in computer project management for various government contractors so I would have more flexibility to pursue my interest in sociocracy. I had a kind of parallel career while I deepened my understanding. I learned to read Dutch to gain access to the considerable literature not available in English. *We the People* incorporates the material I translated.

After I encountered Gerard Endenburg, I continued my traditional business career as a project manager. I was leading 200 people in a contract to install continually updated computer equipment and software, and giving specialized training to all US consulates around the world. I was able to use some of the principles of sociocracy, consistently received outstanding client ratings, and achieved ISO 9000 quality certification for the client. Even though I could not use all aspects of sociocracy in my work, I credit my understanding of sociocratic theory for these accomplishments.

Meanwhile, I enrolled in a master's program in quantitative sociology and wrote my thesis on the effects of sociocracy on Dutch workers. My key finding was that workers in Dutch sociocratic organizations have a statistically significant higher level of commitment to their organizations than their non-sociocratic counterparts.

Convinced that sociocracy did, in fact, yield the benefits claimed, I went through a rigorous process to become a certified sociocratic organizational adviser—the first native-English speaker to do so. I began working as a trainer and consultant and, in 2002, gratefully accepted Sharon Villines's offer to co-author first edition of this book. Without her skills, discipline, and academic experience, it would never have been written. In 2006, I formally established a consulting firm and finally abandoned my managerial career.

...workers in Dutch sociocratic organizations have a statistically significant higher level of commitment to their organizations than their non-sociocratic counterparts.

CHAPTER TWO

Why We Need Another "-ocracy"

BY SHARON VILLINES

I discovered sociocracy in 2002 at a regional workshop for cohousing communities, those hybrids of old-fashioned neighborhoods and condominiums that have been springing up across the United States since the 1980s. To write full-time, I had taken early retirement from the State University of New York and, in 2000, moved into a cohousing community in Washington, DC, but I was getting little done.

For two years, I had been either working to organize the community or trying to understand why, despite being inclusive to a fault, our group, in my view, was ineffective in meeting its own needs. From locations across the eastern United States, we had cooperatively designed and built our community of 43 townhouses and apartments. Extensive common facilities included a kids' playroom, exercise room, laundry room, dining room, large professional kitchen, and workshop. And a hot tub. It was a major accomplishment.

After move-in, however, we were suddenly managing a multi-million-dollar residential complex with almost no experience. At the same time, we were trying to be good neighbors to 60 people experiencing births, deaths, and major illnesses, along with job losses and marriages. The number of decisions that had to be made was overwhelming and, of course, when it came right down to it, we were strangers. Less so than most new neighbors, but still strangers.

Like other cohousing communities, we were using full-group consensus as our method of decision-making. That meant we were spending hours in meetings and between meetings, trying to work out this agreement or that. Rather than waiting for the consensus process to

> Despite being inclusive to a fault, our group, in my view, was ineffective in meeting its own needs.

unfold, more and more decisions were being avoided, made by default, or made by fiat. That I was one of the individuals making many of those decisions didn't make it any more acceptable. I wanted the community of equals that full-group consensus promised.

CONSENSUS

My first experience with consensus decision-making was in 1972, when I joined a group of parents to form a cooperative school for our children. We had many radical ideas about education—anti-sexist, anti-ageist, and anti-racist—anti anything that ignored the unique needs and abilities of the individual child.

It was a new idea then for parents to just go off and start their own school, and we were having great difficulty finding space. We had no public funding or grants. We had no ability to guarantee even a year's worth of rent. One building finally offered us space, but there were problems. We all believed we could work them out—except one parent who was sure this was a bad decision. We spent four hours in a parent meeting, discussing all the options. Some parents had to leave. Some only stayed because their children were already asleep on a pile of coats.

Twenty-five parents wanted to rent the space and one did not. That one woman was our only parent of color. We desperately wanted to keep her in the group and we equally desperately wanted to start the school. We believed this was our only option. It was after midnight when we quit and agreed to meet again the next night. Twenty-four of us left the room hoping the one would come around and worried about what we would do if she didn't. A few parents stayed to discuss that as the rest of us wandered home.

What happened the next night was miraculous, for each of us and for the school. Without warning, without discussion, each of the 24 walked back into the room believing the one was right. The owner's demands were unreasonable and would prevent the school from being a success. Because this young single mother on welfare had presented good arguments and stood her ground against a whole room of white

... rather than waiting for the consensus process to unfold, more and more decisions were being avoided, made by default, or made by fiat.

professionals, we avoided what could easily have been a fatal mistake. Without the requirement that each person consent, the school might never have been.

That experience created enormous satisfaction and harmony in the group and it was then difficult to settle for less. But how many people had that level of commitment? Who would sit with a decision as long as we had? To sit for however long it took? And to do it repeatedly for every decision that arose?

Other cooperative ventures I joined or started during those years did not. In the food co-op, Unitarian church committees, lobbying groups, and feminist action groups, we used a "soft consensus": We tried for consent, but if it couldn't be achieved fairly quickly, we moved on with the majority view or the will of the leader. Full-group consensus worked well in the early stages of a forming group when idealism and commitment were high, but less well when idealism faded and the daily grind of operations decisions set in.

FROM IDEALISM TO GETTING THINGS DONE

In the social upheavals of the late 1960s and early 1970s, many alternative organizations rejected majority vote. It encouraged participants to take sides rather than finding mutually beneficial solutions and allowed the majority to ignore the minority when things became difficult. I was participating in many political action and alternative organizations; consensus groups at night and a lobbying group during the day. As the groups grew in size, those using consensus floundered. We had no acceptable model for delegating decisions or learning to be leaders, or to trust leadership. We knew next to nothing about delegating tasks or measuring results or analyzing needs.

It wasn't until 1981 that the Center for Conflict Resolution published *Building United Judgment: A Handbook for Consensus Decision Making*, the first practical guide to full-group consensus decision-making. By the time it began to circulate in a dog-eared typescript, I had moved away from the groups that were organized around consensus toward the groups that were focused on political action.

> Because this single, young welfare mother had presented good arguments and stood her ground against a whole room of white professionals, we avoided what could easily have been a fatal mistake. Without the requirement that each person consent, the school might never have been.

The political action groups were not less idealistic, but they were focused on accomplishing their goals, not on process. They were using parliamentary procedure (*Robert's Rules of Order*), but to include rather than exclude. They were listening to each other as well as moving forward. They were changing the laws and changing society.

I had begun to learn parliamentary procedure in 1971 in Albany, NY, where Bella Abzug, Gloria Steinem, and Betty Friedan held workshops during the founding of the National Women's Political Caucus. I remember a key session when Bella Abzug insisted that until women understood Robert's *Rules of Order*, they could not progress in politics. "You have to know the rules and when to use them or you can't speak."

During one session, in an imposing legislative chamber, surrounded by mahogany paneling and gold leaf, the New York Radical Feminists were not able to adapt to the rules. They started a ruckus on the floor, standing on benches and chanting during the debate. Frustration was growing on all sides when the chair said, "The chair senses chaos on the floor and requests a 5-minute recess to confer." Then she marched down into the center of the rebellion. When we resumed, she pounded the gavel and recognized a speaker. The Radical Feminists presented their points in perfect form. Bella did everything but throw her hat in the air, she was so happy. And Bella happy was a sight to behold.

The Radical Feminists presented their points in perfect form. Bella did everything but throw her hat in the air, she was so happy. And Bella happy was a sight to behold.

THIRTY YEARS LATER

Thirty years later, living in cohousing, ruled by consensus again, I found myself sitting in meetings where long, impassioned, off-topic speeches and other equally impassioned but wrong-headed soliloquies were much in need of Points of Order. I respected consensus but not lack of order. I searched but was unable to find a parliamentarian who would work with me on a system based on both consensus and parliamentary procedure. Not one responded.

The formal consensus process in *Conflict and Consensus* (1991) by C. T. Butler provided a simple debate process leading to consensus, very much like parliamentary procedure, but decisions were still only made as a "committee of the whole" (Butler 1999). Organizational structures based on parliamentary procedure made it too easy to lapse into majority-vote thinking.

WHY USE CONSENSUS?

Organizations use full-group consensus for two primary reasons: inclusiveness and collective intelligence. They believe it will avoid the power struggles and social domination in organizations with autocratic hierarchies. Everyone together is viewed as being in harmony.

Historically, the Quaker "sense of the meeting" was the model for full-group consensus decision-making. Too often, however, groups use consensus expecting it to produce the feeling of unity and peace experienced in Quaker meetings, but consensus alone doesn't produce the desired result without the Quaker discipline of faith and practice, and sitting together in silence.

In flat organizations without delegation of decision-making, movement toward an aim is highly dependent on the skills and influence of meeting facilitators. The group depends on the facilitator so strongly that the result is often another form of autocracy: a *facilitocracy*. The facilitator ultimately rules because no one else has permission and the facilitator is the group's only salvation.

Full-group consensus is also about focusing the collective intelligence to make better decisions. The synergy of discussion and multiple points of view can be very powerful. But how can a group move forward with too many points of view? How do you develop leadership when the only recognized leader is a facilitator who is expected to be neutral, and rarely is?

Our cohousing group was getting larger and larger. Births and adoptions that had been postponed until the community was built and the addition of significant others had grown the community from 60 people in 2000 to 80 in 2007. In 2017, we are approaching 100.

> Too often, however, groups use consensus expecting it to produce the feeling of unity and peace experienced in Quaker meetings, but consensus alone doesn't produce the desired result without the Quaker discipline of faith and practice, and sitting together in silence.

It was not just a
theory. It was being
used in professional
associations as well
as in boardrooms,
in schools as well
as corporations,
in intentional
communities as
well as breweries.
It was giving a
voice to nursing
home attendants
and beleaguered
middle managers.
It was producing
more-responsive,
more-productive,
and happier
organizations.
It was working.

GOVERNING OURSELVES

When John Buck introduced sociocracy as a way to govern ourselves that produces inclusive, consent-based, and effective organizations, I was ready to listen. There was very little written in English on sociocracy and what was available was written by a Dutch engineer. The translations were rough, and the language of physics and mathematics and cybernetics was foreign to me. What I knew of systems thinking had come from philosophy, not the technical sciences, but I found a depth of thinking and clarity of methodology that was better than anything else I had read.

Further, *it was not just a theory*. It was a practical method of organization and decision-making that was being used in professional associations as well as boardrooms, in schools as well as corporations, in intentional communities as well as breweries. It was giving a voice to nursing home attendants and beleaguered middle managers. It was producing more-responsive, more-productive, and happier organizations. *It was working.*

What I needed to know was how? That's when this book was born—out of a search to understand how and to explain it in plain English. When I proposed a book to John, I knew he had expertise in sociocracy and management. I had an ability to explain concepts that I developed in 25 years of teaching and participating in cooperative and academic organizations, some of the most poorly structured organizations in existence. Together, I felt we might be able to produce a book that would speak to a broad audience.

In the five years it took to complete the first edition of this book, I found John to be unfailingly astute in responding to questions, applying sociocratic principles in new situations, and finding new ways to express ideas that at first fell on my ears like dumbbells. In conversations and research, I learned a lot about governance, organizational theory, systems thinking, and much about the history of management and governance. On my part, this involved translating concepts from John's Dutch-flavored vocabulary to my English vocabulary, from physics to everyday language, and from scientifically accurate terminology with negative social connotations to words that expressed both the heart and science of these new principles and practices.

In this second edition, written 15 years after I first heard of sociocracy, the writing is more relaxed and reflects my experience talking with more experts and practitioners who apply and adapt the method. It also reflects the evolution of sociocratic thought.

Unless communities are in crisis, it is very hard for an established to adopt a new governance system, thus my own community is still not using the full sociocratic structure. Many of the ideas and practices have seeped in under the doormat and helped us to be more efficient while remaining inclusive—or as inclusive as people desire to be.

The time and labor to sort out ideas and write this book was exhausting. I hope like myself, you will both enjoy and benefit from *We the People*, so you can make your own organizations more inclusive, transparent, and accountable. More deeply democratic.

CHAPTER THREE

The Idea of a Sociocracy

Understanding the melding of forces that produced first the idea of a sociocracy and then its implementation is important to understanding its multi-faceted quality. Sociocracy is a unique combination of values, social theory, and scientific method that produces harmonious, respectful, self-organizing, and self-correcting organizations.

Ironically, for a method intended to produce harmony, its first practical application was not developed in a peaceful mountain setting, untouched by political and social conflict. The first sociocratic organization was established in 1926 on the eve of impending world-wide strife. The German occupation of the Netherlands began in 1940, followed by the Great Dutch Famine of 1944, and the post-war rebuilding of a decimated economy and culture. In this chapter, we examine the historical development of sociocracy, taking a closer look at the motivations that turned an ideal into a universally applicable method of governance and organization.

AUGUSTE COMTE, PHILOSOPHER & SOCIOLOGIST

The word *sociocracy* was created in 1851 by French philosopher and sociologist Auguste Comte (1798–1857) to describe a government-based on the new science of sociology, the study of people in groups, of societies. Sociocracy would use scientific method to develop policies that would benefit all the people, rather than the people being controlled by autocrats for their own benefit.

A sociocratic society would have a government formed on the basis of knowledge and intelligence, not circumstances of birth, military prowess, or political maneuvering.

3.1 Auguste Comte, French philosopher and sociologist, known as the "Father of Sociology," the scientific study of societies. He proposed that sociology should be the basis of a new governance method—a sociocracy.

Comte was born into the economic and political upheaval that followed the French Revolution as governments all over Europe were overthrown or radically changed. The Industrial Revolution had also begun disrupting the stable centuries-old agrarian culture and challenging the aristocratic European social structure. The monarchies were then gone or stripped of power and the control of the Roman Catholic Church was beginning to crumble. Disillusionment was everywhere.

> ... people had an opportunity for the first time in history to become self-sufficient and self-determining—to fully realize their essential human nature.

SELF-SUFFICIENT AND SELF-DETERMINING

In the age of the machine and the dawn of scientific thinking, Comte believed people had an opportunity for the first time in history to become self-sufficient and self-determining—to fully realize their essential human nature. Human nature, he believed, was characterized by reason, knowing, social cooperation, and altruistic feeling, but since individuals are also products of their environment, the best of human nature could flourish only with a supportive environment.

Comte believed a better future could be found using reasoning and analysis instead of theological or metaphysical understanding. He advocated acquiring "positive knowledge": observable events that could be verified. He also emphasized the importance of using quantitative and mathematical methods to analyze the application of theory.

Comte is often considered the first philosopher of science, because his philosophy, Positivism, and his emphasis on testing theory with practice provided the foundation for the newly developing scientific method.

Comte believed that social change would come from the workers and envisioned a sociocracy as an inclusive society. Having only the experience of autocratic political structures, however, and with the lack of well-educated and literate citizens, Comte was unable to envision a society without centralized decision-making. While not controlled by a single monarch or dictator, Comte's sociocracy was to be governed by social scientists. (Comte, 1853)

Comte's optimistic view of scientific method as a firm foundation for knowledge did not account for human nature, however. By the early 20th century, disillusionment with science as the basis of understanding human society began to falter. Science could be used for good or ill.

LESTER FRANK WARD, RUGGED INDIVIDUALIST

At the end of the 18th century, American scientist and sociologist Lester Frank Ward (1841–1913) believed sociology presented an opportunity to create a government based on the strengths of what could be learned from individual human accomplishments. He blamed the political party system for the failure of democracy to produce a society in which its citizens were, in fact, free and equal. He advocated a sociocracy as the better alternative.

Frank Ward continued the thinking of Comte in conceiving of an ideal society ordered by scientific thought. Where Comte's vision placed social scientists in control, however, Ward's gave them guidance but not control. Where Comte believed human success resulted from an ideal social structure, Ward believed the successful individual, supported and enabled by the social structure, was responsible for human progress.

Figure 3.2 Frank Ward, standing next to "petrified" fossil tree trunks in Yellowstone National Park in 1887. American scientist and sociologist, extolled the rugged individual who pulled himself up by the bootstraps and took every advantage offered.

Ward extolled the rugged individual who pulled himself up by the bootstraps and took advantage of what society offered. And Ward was just such a person. He interrupted his education to serve in the Union Army during the Civil War and was injured in the historic Battle of Chancellorsville. As a disabled soldier, he petitioned Abraham Lincoln and was given an appointment as a clerk in the Treasury Department. Unable to attend college during the day, he convinced the president of what became George Washington University in

Washington, DC, to offer Saturday and evening classes. After completing graduate degrees in botany and law, he studied geography, paleontology, archeology, and anthropology; became a research scientist at the Smithsonian Institution; and accepted a prestigious appointment as a paleontologist with the U.S. Geological Survey.

In addition, while still working at the Smithsonian, Ward began studying sociology and published three classic works, including the *Psychic Factors of Civilization* (1893), in which he presented his concept of a sociocracy (see Appendix A, *Sociocracy*).

In 1902, Ward retired from government service to accept a position in the Sociology Department at what is now Brown University, where he taught advanced courses in the social sciences. He was elected the first president of the International Institute of Sociology and, in 1905, the first president of the American Sociological Society, and is now considered the father of American sociology.

Figure 3.3 Frank Ward. After retirement from his work in natural history at the Smithsonian, Frank Ward taught advanced studies in the social sciences at Brown University and became the first president of the International Institute of Sociology and of the American Sociological Association. He is often referred to as the American Aristotle and the Father of American Sociology.

Ward also updated elements of Comte's Positivism to contemporary scientific and sociological thought, influencing the Pragmatists in political theory, as well as scientists working for the government.

Rather than viewing the materialistic environment as a limiting and controlling factor as Marx did, Ward saw human society bringing material culture under its control. He spoke out strongly on the wastefulness of nature and the intelligence evident in human accomplishments. While he condemned the tyranny of the individual, Ward believed that a sociocracy based on the will and intellect of individuals could become the greatest force ever known. Individuals were what sociology should be studying. (Ward 1902)

Ward wrote extensively about education as the primary force in the progress of society and believed that the unequal distribution of knowledge was responsible for many (if not all) social problems. His philosophy was associated with social liberalism and the progressive education movement that centered around the American philosopher and educational reformer John Dewey (1859–1952).

Dewey believed that education was the key to a successful democracy and he was the driving force behind the establishment of a universal public education system in the United States.

It is in education that we see the next cornerstone in the development of sociocracy.

CORNELIUS BOEKE & BEATRICE CADBURY

From the late 19th century on, the idea of a sociocracy continued to be actively discussed in Europe and America, along with the progressive education movement and other social reforms. It remained a theory, though, until 1926, when two internationally recognized Quaker peace activists and educators, Cornelius "Kees" Boeke (pronounced Case Boo-ka; 1884–1966) and Beatrice "Betty" Cadbury Boeke (1884–1976) created the first sociocracy in the Netherlands.

Figure 3.4 Betty Cadbury and Kees Boeke in the 1960s. Confined to the Netherlands during WW II, they combined their experiences with peace work and activist organizing with the ideals of the progressive education movement to develop the first functioning sociocracy.

Using what they had learned from their practice of Quaker principles, participation in activist government reform movements, and founding a number of national and international peace and educational organizations, the Boekes established a revolutionary school in Bilthoven: the Children's Community Workshop (Werkplaats Kindergemeenschap). The Boekes were very familiar with the theories of sociocracy and progressive education and, as experienced activists and organizers, were able to put these ideas into practice.

While in England to do research for his degree in civil engineering, Boeke had become a Quaker and applied for a position as head of a Quaker school in Syria. During his interview, he met Beatrice "Betty" Cadbury, whom he later married. Betty Cadbury was a member of the prominent Quaker family that owned Cadbury Chocolate, which had long been a model workplace with many benefits for workers. In 1912, the Boekes went to Lebanon and Syria as Quaker missionaries.

Believing that education and understanding were the keys to peace, the Boekes established workshops where children of all cultures and religions could study together. When the first world war broke out in 1914, they were forced to return to England, where they became active in an international peace organizations. They both took every opportunity to speak publicly against the war and encouraged peace with everyone, including the Germans.

In 1918, when he went to Germany to meet with leading pacifists, Boeke tried to speak with Hitler to dissuade him from war and was promptly deported. He returned to England, but was again deported for his advocacy of pacifism and consideration for the Germans.

Figure 3.5 Children's Community Workshop. After meeting in homes and makeshift quarters, the first Children's Community Workshop building was designed and constructed from 1927–1929 by Frants Edvard Röntgen. As of 1968, it is no longer used as a school but stands as a prime example of Röntgen's work as an architect.

The Boekes went to Kees Boeke's native country, the Netherlands, and settled in Bilthoven, where their home became a gathering place for pacifist leaders from all over Europe. Continuing their demonstrations and protests, they were arrested and imprisoned many times.

In 1919, Boeke built a conference center and held the first international peace conference, out of which developed a succession of international peace organizations, including the organization that later became known as the International Fellowship for Reconciliation (FoR).

THE FIRST SOCIOCRACY

With eight children to educate, and confined to the Netherlands until the end of the war, the Boekes turned again to education, where new developments had sprung up after WW I. They opened the Children's Community Workshop (Werkplaats Kindergemeenschap) in 1926 in the Boekes' home, It was attended at first only by their children, but other children soon joined and the school spread to other homes and makeshift spaces.

With an educational program based on the Montessori Method, Boeke and Cadbury began adapting the Quaker "sense of the meeting" and "co-responsibility" to a secular context. In addition to helping define their educational programs, students cooked meals, cleaned the facilities, and tended the gardens. The students were treated as equals and everyone used first names, which was highly unusual. The school was called a "workshop," recalling Kees's fond memories of working as a carpenter's assistant and the Boekes' strong belief that students should be learning to work, not to be "schooled." Their job was becoming educated and learning how to be self-sufficient by maintaining the school. Students were called "workers" and both teachers and staff were called "staff." (Rawson 1956)

The guiding principles were self-direction and working with head, heart, and hands. Students were expected to work together to create a harmonious environment that was beneficial for all. To ensure equal responsibility and respect, all decisions were made by consensus:

> There are three fundamental rules underlying the system. The first is that the interests of all members must be considered, the individual bowing to the interests of the whole. Secondly, solutions must be sought which everyone can accept: otherwise, no action can be taken. Thirdly, all members must be ready to act according to these decisions when unanimously made. (Boeke 1945)

Kees Boeke said these rules were nothing more than concern for one's neighbor: "[W]here love is, there will be a spirit in which real harmony is possible."

The Boekes believed this system could be applied on a national and international scale if everyone understood that social organization was a matter of discipline and respect for the group. Similarly to Ward, they believed if groups learned self-discipline the same way an individual had to learn self-discipline, there would be no need for an executive committee or a ruling class.

They believed the political party system and majority rule

We shall be able to learn this art and acquire a tradition that will make possible the handling of more difficult questions.

Kees Boeke

accentuate disagreements and divisions in favor of nurturing domi-nance, the same faults Frank Ward had criticized. In contrast to the party system, Boeke believed that a sociocratic system "activates a common search that brings the whole group nearer together." Mutual trust and the desire to act in the best interests of the group "leads in-evitably to progress."

Boeke pointed out that there were many groups functioning this way—by soliciting common agreement rather than voting—and that if a group resorted to voting to resolve differences, it would be an in-dication that the group was not functioning well. He had personally participated in many Quaker meetings of more than 1,000 people who had reached agreement together.

Sociocracy had to be learned, but Boeke believed, "We shall be able to learn this art and acquire a tradition that will make possible the handling of more difficult questions." (Boeke 1945)

SOCIOCRACY & WAR

The Boekes were not developing sociocracy in a vacuum or in a bucolic setting. During the Nazi German occupation, they continued teaching and participated in the Resistance. They took in a group of teen-aged Jewish refugees from Poland, set up a classroom in a less-conspicuous building, and gave the students assumed names.

The Boekes hired Joop Westerweel to teach the students in their native language. Westerweel was also active in the underground and eventually responsible for smuggling 200 Jews out of Germany. There were many German inspections of the school and many close calls. At one point, Betty Boeke had to go into hiding with the Jewish students.

Then, in 1944, the school building was requisitioned by the Germans for war use. The students once again met in homes. But Westerweel was found hiding on the school property and both he and Kees, as owner of the property, were arrested. In Boeke's pocket was a draft of what became the manifesto of sociocracy, "No Dictatorship." Westerweel was executed, but Boeke was released with no reasons given. (Rawson 1956)

Behavior
is determined
by the prevailing
social structure.
Unless people are
trusted and
encouraged
to be self-organizing
and supportive
of each other,
they won't be.

Gerard Endenburg
Sociocracy: Decision-
Making by Design

In "No Dictatorship," Boeke envisioned a "community-democracy, an organization of the community by the community." Revised several times, the essay became known as "Sociocracy: Democracy as It Might Be." (See Appendix B).

The experience of the Boekes unfailing message of peace, harmony, and responsibility in the midst of the German occupation and the Great Famine, in which 18,000 people died of starvation in one winter, is remarkable. This is the context in which sociocracy developed as a practical and viable alternative to the aggressive, oppositional politics that produced two world wars.

GERARD ENDENBURG, INVENTOR & ENGINEER

Beginning in 1943, one of the Boekes' students was the Dutch inventor, entrepreneur, and electrical engineer Gerard Endenburg (1933–). Endenburg was 11 in 1944 when the school was requisitioned by the Germans, his father was taken to a concentration camp, and the Great Famine began. He left the Workshop to protect and feed his mother and young sister, foraging and stealing in the streets with a pistol, a grenade, and an automatic rifle. (Quarter, 2000) When the Canadians liberated the Dutch in May of 1945, the Workshop was returned to the Boekes—ravaged, its contents gone. Endenburg rejoined the students and staff who went out to find furniture and supplies wherever they could.

Figure 3.6 Gerard Endenburg, Dutch entrepreneur and electrical engineer, creator of the Sociocratic Circle-Organization Method, 2010.

When Endenburg finished studying at the Workshop, he attended an engineering college. He found the classrooms ruled by autocratic instructors and the students silent, sullen, and bullying. Students didn't form collaborative groups to help each other learn. After years spent in an environment in which self-direction and mutual support were the norm, this was proof of Boeke's teaching that behavior is determined by the prevailing social structure. Unless people are trusted and encouraged to be self-organizing and supportive of each other, they won't be.

In the mid 1960s, after completing his education and his military service, Endenburg was working at Philips Electronics when his parents challenged him to test his management skills in a failing electronics company they had just bought.

Anna and Gerardus Endenburg were political activists and friends of the Boekes. After World War II, to the dismay of their socialist friends, the Endenburgs established Endenburg Electric, a consumer electronics company. Although socialist parties were winning control of national governments throughout Europe, the Endenburgs believed that socialism had to prove itself economically to be successful. To reject a market economy, as socialism had, was to be trapped in "either-or" thinking. Like the Boekes, they wanted a more inclusive, "both-and" society that would simultaneously support their social ideals and build a successful economy.

ENGINEERING ORGANIZATIONS

In less than a year, Endenburg succeeded in making his parents' new company successful and it was merged with the parent company, Endenburg Electrical Engineering (Endenburg Elektrotechniek). In 1968, Endenburg became general manager. Endenburg Electrical had been founded to demonstrate socially progressive ideas and now Endenburg received a challenge from Kees Boeke: Make it sociocratic. Create a collaborative and productive workplace like the Children's Community Workshop.

Endenburg accepted the challenge. He quickly discovered, however, that the requirements of sociocracy had to be coordinated with the requirements of a competitive fast-paced manufacturing business. With his background in engineering and business, he began studying management theory. He soon discovered that the social sciences were not as clear about how things work as the physical sciences. In

Sociocracy has been found to increase productivity and, where it has been measured, to increase it by 30–40%. It also increases worker retention rates and reduces sick leave.

engineering, it was clear that if you do this, that will happen. The social sciences used many of the same words—*power, tension, measurement, resistance, capacity, stress*—but their meaning was not clearly defined. How could anyone manage an organization effectively without clear understanding of cause and effect?

Endenburg's education in physics and engineering was ultimately an advantage because he was able to analyze organizational structures and social interactions from a completely different perspective. From 1968 until 1970, Endenburg translated the principles of the physical sciences into the social sciences. If power is steered this way using electricity, what is the analogous process with people?

As his parents had used Endenburg Electric as a laboratory for demonstrating that business was not antithetical to social ideals. Endenburg reduced the size of the company to 100 employees to use it as a laboratory to demonstrate that business was not antithetical to collaboration and self-direction. After experimenting for several years, Endenburg recreated in an electrical engineering company the same environment he had experienced at the Children's Community Workshop.

He named his system for managing organizations the Sociocratic Circle-Organization Method (SCM). (Endenburg, 1981)

How that system works is the subject of this book.

The Netherlands government has amended its labor regulations to exempt sociocratic organizations from worker council requirements, because sociocratic businesses protect workers' interests as well or better.

ENDENBURG TODAY

Endenburg Electrical Engineering now does heavy electrical installations on oil rigs, ships, nuclear reactors, and large buildings, and still functions sociocratically. The company has been the subject of many research studies, doctoral theses, quality certifications, and government reviews.

SCM has been found to increase productivity and, where it has been measured, to increase it by 30–40%. It also increases worker retention rates and reduces sick leave. The Netherlands government has amended its labor regulations to exempt sociocratic organizations from worker council requirements, because sociocratic businesses protect workers' interests as well or better. Worker councils, essentially in-house labor unions, are mandatory in the Netherlands. By amending their requirements, the Dutch government is confirming that sociocracy protects workers as well as labor unions do.

As Endenburg Electric prospered, Endenburg was invited to explain

his method to other organizations and help them apply it. In 1974, he published a short pamphlet, *Sociocracy: A Reasonable Ideal.* In 1977, he founded the Sociocratisch Centrum and began teaching and implementing the Sociocratic Circle-Organization Method in companies and organizations in Europe and the Americas.

In 1981, Endenburg published *Sociocracy: The Organization of*

3.7 Gerard Endenburg in front of the new Sociocratisch Centrum in 1977.

Decision-Making and in 1997, *Sociocracy as Social Design.* In 1998, he joined the school of Economics and Business Administration at the University of Maastricht, where he held an endowed chair devoted to study of the learning organization, especially the Sociocratic Circle Organization.

Now professor emeritus, Endenburg focuses on research and development and work with the Gerard Endenburg Foundation. Founded in 2012, the foundation's mission is to contribute to "the quality of life in society by encouraging research and development in theory and practice in the field of social innovation, social cohesion, and participation of individuals, groups and sections of society to realize the vision."

The next chapter, "Cybernetics & Sociocracy," explains the principles of SCM and the reasoning Endenburg used to develop it.

CHAPTER FOUR

Cybernetics & Sociocracy

The original name for the study that became "sociology" was "social physics." Physics is the study of matter and its motion through space and time. Similarly, sociology was conceived as the study of people in groups, societies, and how these societies functioned over time. These studies, just as physics studies matter and motion, would be tested using scientific methods in the same way. Comte and Ward, both sociologists, conceptualized a "sociocracy" as a governance method based on scientific studies of effective societies.

Kees Boeke and Betty Cadbury based their implementation of sociocracy on their experience in Quaker organizations. Governance of Quaker meetings and other Quaker-influenced organizations had been developed and tested for generations before scientific methods were defined. The Boekes' implementation of sociocratic values was very successful but was limited to groups that worked closely together for years. What Endenburg needed in his business was a governance method based on sociocracy that could be implemented immediately among strangers.

The science that provided this was cybernetics. To understand how Endenburg used cybernetics to develop a governance method that could be used universally, we need to examine the tradition of governance using full-group, trust-based consensus as the Boekes did.

CONSENSUS DECISION-MAKING

The same values-based principles of consensus decision-making that Kees and Betty Boeke used in their school spread widely in the 20th century in progressive education, political reform, and alternative

> Cybernetics is
> the science
> of effective
> organization.
>
> *Stafford Beer*

living movements. Because its most direct origin is Quaker practice, governance by consensus often takes on a religious tone, a reverence, as if using consensus itself could bring peace and harmony. *Consensus* is sometimes used as "a consensus community," as if the use of consensus could create a community of one mind.

While full-group consensus has been used successfully by smaller homogeneous groups with simple objectives, it has generally failed in large organizations.

Groups using consensus typically only trust decisions made by the full group and are suspicious of delegated decisions. Full-group consensus is viewed as the only way to avoid exclusion and promote equality. Instead of recognized leaders, the consensus process relies on facilitators, who are expected to be neutral and, thus, to remain unbiased in moderating discussion.

In practice, full-group consensus hasn't always produced harmonious relationships. Like the Quaker practice on which it is based, the principles were developed in closely knit, homogeneous, caring groups that worked together over an extended period of time. These conditions do not exist in many of the groups attempting to achieve consensus before making a decision. The result has often been dissension and inefficiency, resulting from hours-long, too-often-fruitless process. This makes consensus impractical in complex, fast-paced organizations, businesses, and governments.

One recent example of trying to use facilitator-led full-group consensus to make decisions is the highly publicized Occupy Movement. The Occupy Movement began in the United States in September of 2011 with the Occupy Wall Street protest against social and economic inequality. In groups of 100 or more people, they used hand gestures to indicate questions, concerns, and objections. Rather than recognized leaders, impartial facilitators guided the process. The standard for consenting was "common sentiment," not necessarily agreement. When common sentiment could not be reached, the backup was a super-majority vote of 90%. (Occupy Wall Street 2014)

Within a month, the protests had expanded to 800 cities in the

Occupy Wall Street is typical of the evolution of many organizations attempting to govern themselves using full-group consensus decision-making alone. They overtly or covertly adopt other methods of governance, dissolve, or transform into a more conventional organization.

United States and 82 countries. To avoid being co-opted, even by Occupy itself, commitment to autonomy as individuals and as a group was a prime value. Committed to autonomy and rejecting recognized leaders, participants saw dissension grow within and between groups over conflicting strategies and aims.

> Occupy was, at its core, a movement constrained by its own contradictions: filled with leaders who declared themselves leaderless, governed by a consensus-based structure that failed to reach consensus, and seeking to transform politics while refusing to become political. (Levitin 2015)

In retrospect, Occupy movements have been credited with bringing clarity to the concentration of money and power. They changed the national discourse (Chomsky 2017), but while many smaller groups inspired by the Occupy Wall Street protests have taken effective action, the movement as a whole failed to form a powerful, focused organization to implement their aims. The Principles of Solidarity on their website do not include a commitment to consensus, although the Principles were adopted by consensus in 2011. (Chomsky 2012)

Figure 4.1 Occupy Wall Street, Day 14 of the Occupy Wall Street protest, 2011. Photo credit: David Shankbone.

Occupy Wall Street is typical of the evolution of many organizations attempting to govern themselves in leaderless groups and using full-group consensus to make decisions and advocating horizontalism. They eventually dissolve or transform themselves into more-conventional organizations. This pattern has repeated itself in many social and political reform movements striving for equality and freedom without long-term goals and lasting effective action.

MAKING SOCIOCRACY EFFECTIVE

Endenburg understood the importance of the Boekes' devotion to consensus and had experienced the harmony that it created in the

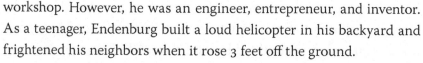

workshop. However, he was an engineer, entrepreneur, and inventor. As a teenager, Endenburg built a loud helicopter in his backyard and frightened his neighbors when it rose 3 feet off the ground.

At Philips Electronics, he invented the flat speaker that is still used in hand-held electronic devices, including cell phones. He was interested in making things work, making them work better, and making them profitable.

After completing his degree in electrical engineering, Endenburg spent his compulsory military service in Germany teaching radar technicians, among other things, cybernetics. This proved pivotal when he began developing a sociocratic company.

Cybernetics is the science that studies how effective and self-sustaining natural and mechanical systems govern themselves. Its questions are:

- How do biological systems adapt to internal and external changes?
- How do complex systems process and communicate information between all their parts?
- How do they remain functioning and coordinated in a changing and often hostile environment?
- How do they measure the effectiveness of their responses?
- How do they adapt and evolve into different forms?

Cybernetics is, thus, the science that studies the mechanisms with which systems control and communicate with all their parts—how they govern themselves.

To invent the flat speaker at Phillips, for example, Endenburg first studied vibrations in mechanical systems. He analyzed the cybernetic principles to learn how mechanical and electronic systems communicate and how they controlled vibrations. Then he applied that knowledge in designing a new system. (Endenburg 1981)

When confronted with managing Endenburg Electric, Endenburg had to answer these same questions: How could an electrical engineering business function both productively and harmoniously? How could it be less autocratic? How could it consider the interests of the individual and the company? How could it develop using the energy and creativity of all its members? And how could it meet the binding deadlines of a highly competitive ship-building industry.

Endenburg knew how to steer power in mechanical and electrical systems, but how could he steer power in human systems?

CYBERNETICS

The word *kybernetike*—cybernetics—was used by Plato in *The Republic* (~380 BCE) to compare the art of navigating or steering to that of governing a city-state. (Hunter 2012) *Governing* and *cybernetics* are both derived from the same Greek words: Cybernetics from the noun form meaning steersman, navigator, governor, pilot; *governing* from the verb form meaning steering, navigating, governing, piloting. (Dechert 1965)

Cybernetics is, thus, the science that studies the mechanisms with which systems control and communicate with all their parts—how they govern themselves. From the 18th century through WW I, these studies were conducted in many fields, including psychology, biology, and engineering. Rapid development began during WW II when the principles were applied in weapons, quality control, and work processes. The findings had not yet been recognized collectively as cybernetics and hadn't filtered out to the general population, or even to the wider scientific community. They were first unified in 1948 in the landmark work by Norbert Weiner, *Cybernetics: Control and Communication in the Animal and the Machine.*

4.2 Norbert Weiner on the cover of the first paperback edition of Cybernetics: Control and Communication in the Animal and the Machine. *MIT Press, 1948.*

Norbert Weiner (1894–1964) was a child prodigy who graduated from high school at age 11 and from Tufts College with a degree in mathematics at age 14. He entered Harvard to study zoology, then transferred to Cornell to study philosophy. Returning to Harvard, he graduated in 1912 at the age of 17 with a Ph.D. His dissertation was on mathematical logic. He then studied philosophy at Cambridge with British philosopher Bertrand Russell (1872–1970) and the University of Göttingen with German mathematician David Hilbert (1862–1943).

After serving in the army during WW I, Weiner began teaching at MIT, where he worked alongside the most advanced scientists in computing, radar, and inertial guidance technology. Weiner's broad and varied experience working with some of the greatest minds of the 20th century, in the humanities as well as the social and physical sciences, was unique and unusual. It was also perfect preparation for conceptualizing the interdisciplinary field of cybernetics.

FEEDBACK LOOPS

Cybernetics researchers discovered that biological and mechanical systems communicate and maintain their equilibrium using *feedback loops*. A feedback loop is a chain of cause-and-effect that forms a circuit or loop and "feeds back" information from the environment to the system. The system adapts in response, modifies its actions, and starts another chain of cause-and-effect that feeds back new information. The system continues to adjust and adapt as necessary to maintain optimal functioning.

A concept in cybernetics that is not present in other sciences is that of purpose or aim.

Using the human body as an example, the various organs sense and communicate information about air temperatures and adjust the responses of the sweat glands and other organs to maintain body temperature. The body continues to monitor information and adjust to the temperature as necessary while continuing to eat, breathe, talk, walk, etc. Responding to the feedback loop is how the body regulates or governs itself.

FEED-FORWARD LOOPS

Similarly, feed-*forward* loops allow organisms to take present action in anticipation of the future, based on current information and probable conditions. They enable the organism to respond to anticipated events to protect itself from danger or to optimize opportunities. Feed-forward loops are based on anticipation and preparation, and are designed to react in a certain way when a specific signal is received.

Without feedback loops to measure incoming information enabling it to change its response, a system will continue to produce the

Definitions of Cybernetics

"The science of effective organization." *Stafford Beer*

"Cybernetics is about purposiveness, goals, information flows, decision-making control processes, and feedback (properly defined) at all levels of living systems." *Peter Corning*

"Should one name one central concept, a first principle, of cybernetics, it would be circularity." *Heinz von Foerster*

"Cybernetic models are usually distinguished by being hierarchical, adaptive, and making permanent use of feedback loops." *Frank Honywill George*

"Cybernetics is the art of creating equilibrium in a world of possibilities and constraints." *Ernst von Glasersfeld*

"Cybernetics treats, not things, but ways of behaving. It does not ask, 'What is this thing?' but 'what does it do?'... It is thus essentially functional and behavioristic... " *W. Ross Ashby*

"Today's cybernetics is at the root of major revolutions in biology, artificial intelligence, neural modeling, psychology, education, and mathematics. At last there is a unifying framework that suspends long-held differences between science and art, and between external reality and internal belief." *Paul Pangaro*

"More recent work [in cybernetics] has attempted to understand how systems describe themselves, control themselves, and organize themselves. Despite its short history, cybernetics has developed a concern with a wide range of processes involving people as active organizers, as sharing communicators, and as autonomous, responsible individuals." *Stuart Umpleby*

"Narrowly defined [cybernetics] is the art of helmsmen, to hold a course by swinging the rudder to offset any deviation from that course. Helmsmen must be so informed of the consequences of their previous acts that they correct them, for the output of the helmsmen decreases the input to the helmsmen. The intrinsic governance of nervous activity, our reflexes, and our appetites exemplify this process. In all of them, as in the steering of the ship, what must return is not energy but information." *Warren McCulloch*

Figure 4.3 Definitions of Cybernetics from the American Society for Cybernetics, *2017*

programmed response without correction. To steer or govern effectively, systems have to use both feedback and feed-forward loops.

PURPOSE IN CYBERNETICS

A concept in cybernetics that is not present in other sciences is that of purpose or aim. A mathematician can use mathematics to achieve a purpose, but the study of mathematics doesn't presume a purpose other than the study of mathematics. One can study fossils to learn about biological evolution without any purpose other than gaining the knowledge. Cybernetics requires understanding the purpose; otherwise it couldn't understand why some data are responded to as feedback and other data are not.

Without an aim around which to organize, a system will respond randomly or not all, and is likely to cease to exist.

INTERDISCIPLINARY DEVELOPMENT

Cybernetics was an interdisciplinary study from its earliest development. It combined the mechanical, physical, biological, cognitive, and social study of systems in a variety of combinations. Since the mid-20th century, however, two general areas have become dominant:

- Technology, the design of computers and robotics, based in the fields of computation, regulation, and control.
- Biological and social sciences, based in autonomy, cognition, identity, purpose, and theories of self-reference.

Some scientists have been concerned with creating a more humane world and others with simply understanding the world as it is. The study of how systems communicate and control in relation to their environment is now called "first-order cybernetics" to distinguish it from "second-order cybernetics."

SECOND-ORDER CYBERNETICS

Beyond the study of systems adapting themselves to their environment, second-order cybernetics studies systems that observe themselves. It was conceptualized by Austrian American physicist and

CYBERNETICS
& HUMAN KNOWING
a journal of second-order cybernetics
autopoiesis and cyber-semiotics
10, No. 3-4, 2003

Heinz von Foerster, 1911-2002

Figure 4.3 Journal of Cybernetics & Human Knowing *is the journal of second-order cybernetics, featuring articles on how systems observe, describe, control, and organize themselves. This issue from 2003 commemorates the death of Heinz von Foerster in 2002.*

philosopher Heinz von Foerster (1911–2002) while attempting to study the cybernetics of the mind.

As a self-observing system, the human body has a more complex feedback structure than a system that only responds to the environment. It is a system that is self-observing and that can direct itself. It can function according to its own aims, independently of feedback from the environment. (Stanley-Jones 1961)

Second-order cybernetics is, thus, "cybernetics of cybernetics" and is concerned with how self-observing systems communicate control, measure, and organize themselves. Learning organizations are examples of second-order systems.

BUILDING STRONG ORGANIZATIONS

Human organizations respond to more than their environments. They respond to their internal functioning, their members, and the relationships between them. Each part of an organization—each person, each group of people—is self-aware and has aims. Their members are diverse and unlikely to have developed together the same way the parts of a frog develop together or the parts of a clock are assembled to work together. Managing a human organization, like a business, that has a collective aim as well those of each member requires a governance method that will respect and use all its human resources to achieve its purpose.

From his knowledge of cybernetics, Endenburg knew that how a system governs itself, how it communicates, and how it coordinates all its parts determines its power and predicts its longevity. He also knew that a human organization had to be a self-organizing system, one that was self-aware, self-observing. How could this be done?

The common characteristics of strong systems are:

- Resilience, the ability to rebound;
- Self-organization, the ability to transform and create new structures; and
- The ability maintain a coherent structure.

When all three characteristics are present, an organization can grow

The degree to which an organization is resilient, self-organized, and coherently structured will determine its effectiveness and its ability to achieve its aim.

and change, adapting quickly when necessary. It can recover from adversity, generate new resources, and continuously organize and re-organize itself coherently. It will be dynamic and full of energy. Capable of action.

Dynamic organizations are vigorous and forceful, but not because they have huge cash reserves, dominate a market, or hire all the top MBA graduates. They are dynamic because they are:

- prepared to respond to adversity,
- designed to develop and change without causing disruption, and
- structured coherently to be understood by all their parts.

The degree to which an organization is resilient, self-organized, and coherently structured determines its effectiveness and its ability to achieve its purpose. (Meadows, 2008) Endenburg's three principles were developed to create such organizations.

> For workers to think like entrepreneurs, there had to be a practical way for them to have meaningful control over the policies that governed their work.

THE FIRST PRINCIPLE: CONSENT

In physical systems, all parts are engaged equally. They have different tasks, but each one stands ready and responds with full energy when needed. Endenburg wanted everyone at Endenburg Electric to behave in this way. He wanted them to think like entrepreneurs, to take responsibility for innovation and operations.

Since profit and loss are important measures of a company's performance, everyone had to experience the risks and rewards so they could understand and take responsibility for them. They needed to experience the effect of their actions in the environment, the feedback from the organization as well as from the market.

Endenburg created a compensation structure that encouraged workers, managers, and investors alike to take responsibility for the success of the company. In addition to a fixed compensation based on the fair market value, or, in the case of stockholders, the amount of investment, he added a variable compensation. Variable compensation payments were directly linked to the company's, department's, and individual's performance. The result was a blurring of the distinction between investors and employees. Everyone was now subject to the financial risks of poor decisions and market fluctuations, and just as important they all benefited from the successes.

For workers to think like entrepreneurs, there had to be a practical way for them to have meaningful control over the policies that governed their work. How could workers, managers, and investors make decisions together as equal partners without paralyzing the company? In business operations, many decisions required quick responses. How could people who were hired for their technical expertise and have diverse personal values make decisions in a competitive business environment using full-group consensus? None of the other methods of making decisions—autocratic, majority vote, supra-majority vote—protected the interests of investors, managers, and worker equally. They could all be manipulated, especially under pressure.

On a personal retreat, Endenburg reviewed every step of his method and read everything he thought might lead to an answer. He finally concluded that there was no answer. He packed his bags and began loading his car. Then the answer hit him: *consent!* (Buck 2003)

In the technical sciences, all elements of a system work together in the absence of objections. If one part of a system is stressed to the point of breaking down, it sends feedback by slowing down or making a lot of noise. Ultimately it stops functioning: *It objects*. It withdraws its consent and the system stops working. (Endenburg 1981)

Endenburg had his first principle: Consent, defined as no objections, was the basis for decision-making. Any member of the organization could signal an adverse effect by objecting.

THE SECOND PRINCIPLE: CIRCLES

In daily operations, the leadership of a manager who can make moment-to-moment decisions quickly is the most efficient method of completing tasks. How could all workers function as equals if decisions were controlled by the manager? How could workers be given authority without affecting productivity? To engage everyone in taking responsibility for their work, the policies that defined their work had to be under their control.

Endenburg's solution was to create separate meetings, apart from staff meetings, in which managers, supervisors, and workers met as equals to determine the policies that would guide day-to-day operations. In these circle meetings, everyone consented to policies that defined the work process, set aims, defined and assigned roles and responsibilities, and determined how the manager would lead and how they would follow. This design engaged everyone in creating efficient operations that could be adjusted quickly as conditions changed.

THE THIRD PRINCIPLE: DOUBLE-LINKS

Distributing policy decisions to each circle according to the aim of the circle required a means of communication and coordination. Decisions that were usually made by boards of directors and high-level managers would now be made in circle meetings by those who would be affected by them. Endenburg's solution was to create a general circle of members of each specialized circle who would (1) make policies that affected multiple circles and (2) do overall planning. Who would represent circles?

In electrical engineering, one wire can't carry information in two directions. Endenburg concluded that dependable communication between circles would require two channels. The leader of operations, the "downlink," would be responsible for carrying information from the organization to the operations unit, and a second, the "uplink," would represent the operations unit and carry information up the organization.

The double links thus established feedback loops that connected and guided all units of the organization. Double-linking circles established a coherent governance structure.

TESTING THE METHOD

A now-classic story illustrates how well Endenburg's sociocratic method worked. In 1976, the Dutch shipping industry suddenly shut down, collapsing under the pressure of competition from Japan. A significant portion of Endenburg Electric's workforce was employed in

In circle meetings, everyone consented to policies that defined the work process, set aims, defined and assigned roles and responsibilities, and determined how the manager would lead and how they would follow. This design engaged everyone in creating efficient operations that could be adjusted quickly.

the shipyards, manufacturing and installing their complete electrical systems. With no shipbuilding, obviously there would be no work.

Endenburg called an emergency meeting of the board of directors (the Top Circle) to plan for layoffs. In the Netherlands, laying off workers is a complex process. Some of the directors told Endenburg that he had to set aside his sociocratic experiment because he was now confronted with a more-important business concern: saving the company.

When the drastic layoffs were announced in the shipping-related departments, a machinist who worked in electrical-cabinet fabrication called an emergency meeting of his circle. "We don't have to lay off the guys in ships," he said. "The company has built up a strategic reserve for emergencies, and this is an emergency. I propose we put coats and ties on those shipyard workers, give them some training in marketing, and send them out to get more business."

His circle supported his idea and supported him in presenting his idea to the general management circle. The general management circle, which included the operations leaders and representatives of all the production and administrative circles, made a few modifications and supported him in presenting his proposal to the top managers and directors.

After a tense discussion, two directors resigned and left the meeting, asserting that the machinist had no business even being there. To them, this was not a decision that could be made by anyone but the top levels of the organization. The other directors disagreed and, with a few more modifications, they adopted the machinist's proposal.

As a result of this move, the shipyard workers were trained to make marketing calls and within a few weeks, had brought in enough new orders that most of the layoffs were avoided. Furthermore, the company emerged from the crisis stronger because it retained its skilled workers, strengthened company morale, *and* became more diversified. (Endenburg 1981)

Endenburg now had proof that his method worked:

- ◆ It could be unusually flexible and produced highly effective and creative thinking.

Neither Endenburg Electric nor its workers were owned. The company had no strings that could control it like a puppet. It was protected from hostile takeovers and could not, along with its members, be bought or sold.

Endenburg designed a legal structure that made the organization its own owner—a free organization, one that owned itself or for which ownership had no meaning.

- It encouraged leadership to emerge and be recognized anywhere in the organization.
- It applied scientific methods, meeting the ideals of Comte.
- It allowed a complex organization to function according to the same principles of self-interest and willpower that Ward had demonstrated and praised in the individual.
- It ensured protection for all workers, as required by the Boekes, his parents, and other social reform advocates.
- It protected the interests of the investors, as well as those of the workers, as a market economy required.
- It created the harmonious working-together-productively work environment that Endenburg valued.

But there was one more condition that Endenburg wanted to correct: the fundamental question of power.

THE FREE ORGANIZATION

Consent was, in fact, not the basis of governance in Endenburg Electric, because Endenburg still owned it. At any time, he could sell, close , or take back autocratic management at any time. As long as this ultimate power existed, sociocratic governance offered no long-term security.

After numerous discussions with his lawyers and accountants, Endenburg designed a legal structure that made the organization its own owner—a free organization, one that owned itself or for which ownership had no meaning. Neither Endenburg Electric nor its workers were owned. The company had no strings that could control it like a puppet. It was protected from hostile takeovers and could not, along with its members, be bought or sold. It could consent to merge or to disband, but only if the company, in accordance with its policies, had no objections. (Endenburg 1981, 1997)

Endenburg was still a stockholder and, as CEO, had the assigned roles and responsibilities of the CEO, but he no longer had "life or death" control. He had transformed Endenburg Electric into an autonomous, self-organizing worker-manager-investor cooperative. A true sociocracy.

PART II

Rewiring Organizational Power

We the People is about how to organize power effectively to accomplish our aims, our purposes.

The word *organization* derives from the Latin *organum* and means a "tool or instrument" with a specific use or function. For example, the heart is an *organum* that accomplishes its aim of circulating blood in a body.

The suffix *-ize* means "to cause to be or to become," and the suffix *–ation* means "an action or the result of an action." Thus, *to organize* is to create a tool designed to perform a task. In human societies, people create organizations as implements with which to accomplish their social and economic purposes.

The aim of an organization might be very simple, such as watching old films together, or complex, such as influencing national tax policy. Even a simple film club, however, requires that people organize themselves enough to make decisions collectively about when, where, and how. Will they watch quietly or with commentary? Rotate homes or meet in a central location? Their ability to make these decisions is a measure of their ability to use their power effectively.

The group must also check periodically to see if everyone is enjoying themselves, since enjoyment is part of their mission. If the group has made good decisions, they will be happy. If not, they are likely to become angry, argue, and even disband. By checking periodically and making corrections if necessary, they can redirect their power from anger to improving their ability to accomplish their aim.

Very little in modern life can be accomplished without interacting with organizations. Even subsistence farming requires a goodly

In modern societies, our ability to work together and share knowledge has created powerful organizations.

number of people to plow, plant, harvest, cook, weave, and barter. To build cars or produce films—just two examples—involves complex interactions with many groups of people who specialize in intricate and interdependent technologies. National and international markets mean selling simple goods like milk and vegetables may require farmers to understand the regulations of many government agencies—local, national, and international.

Our high standard of living is a direct result of our ability to share knowledge and work together. We live much longer, with less disease and discomfort, and with many more luxuries, than at any time in history. We educate, specialize, and coordinate at a level of expertise and complexity that previous generations would have found incomprehensible. Our banks, utilities, schools, manufacturers, and hospitals are vast powerful webs of coordination.

If we were trying to accomplish everything individually—to produce our own clothes, shoes, entertainment, cars, food, etc.—we couldn't have the lifestyle we have today.

BUT WHO IS IN CONTROL?

We have improved our lives by organizing the power that each of us has to create and produce. Without good leadership and management, however, flawed and predatory policies work against our best efforts. The same organizations that bring us security, freedom, and wealth can also bring us poverty, alienation, economic collapse, and emotional imprisonment. Corporations have budgets and staffs larger than those of whole countries. Their ability to control us and our governments is enormous.

Sometimes the goals of our organizations conflict with and even replace our own. As Prince Charles, the future King of England, said, "I was about 10 when I realized I was trapped." Even a monarchy is an organization, one governed by a set of rules and expectations in exchange for its benefits. Following the rules may require us to spend our working lives fulfilling someone else's expectations.

The same organizations that bring us security, freedom, and wealth can also bring us poverty, alienation, economic collapse, and emotional imprisonment.

Just as royal families have not abdicated their privileges, though, nor are we suggesting that we abandon our comfortable lifestyles. If our organizations are not making us happy, we need to change them. To do this, we need a new method of governance.

The solution is not to destroy corporations or institutions. We need to transform them. We need to participate as full partners in determining how we live. We need better policy-making, better oversight, better enforcement, more transparency, and more accountability. We need collaboration and shared responsibility.

Our corporations, institutions, associations, and school systems control our lives, but as the financial collapse in 2008 revealed, they aren't in control of themselves.

REWIRING POWER IN OUR ORGANIZATIONS

As we discussed in Chapter 4, "Cybernetics & Sociocracy," sociocracy uses the principles of cybernetics to understand how to design organizations so they can go beyond sustainability to optimization.

Some governance systems, like communism and socialism, have attempted to correct the problems of monarchies and capitalism by removing private ownership and transferring production to the state. This hasn't worked because the state is still an autocratic system and lacks the ability to encourage self-organization in its people.

Sociocracy works within the capitalist market to develop principles and practices that support a free economy by encouraging autonomy, self-organization, and leadership. Instead of rejecting the market economy, sociocracy is a new method of managing it.

Sociocracy manages the market economy differently because it:

◆ Values equivalence, transparency, and effectiveness.
◆ Addresses the traditional concerns of managing successful organizations—good decision-making, leadership, tactical and strategic planning, quality control, and financial stability.

In the next chapters, we discuss how sociocratic principles enable organizations to value each individual as an essential participant while accomplishing the aims of the whole.

"Governance" is not the same as "the government." All organizations are governed. They all have rules and regulations about who makes the decisions. Who leads. Rules about who can say "no."

The questions we examine in Part II are:

- ◆ What is decision-making?
- ◆ What is leading?
- ◆ Why are measuring and evaluation as important as leadership?

These may seem like philosophical questions removed from daily life and work, but they are actually very practical.

**Sociocracy works within the capitalist market to develop principles and practices that support a free economy.
It encourages autonomy, self-organization, and leadership in people and their organizations.**

WHAT IS "GOVERNANCE" AND WHO GOVERNS?

All organizations have governance structures, whether formal or informal, recorded in national constitutions or implicit as in families, simple as in a small business, or complex as in corporations. "Governance" is not the same as "the government."

All organizations are governed. They all have rules and regulations about who makes the decisions. Who leads. Who can say "no." The effectiveness of the governance structure will determine how powerful an organization is or will be, and whether it will be successful.

Sociocracy is not a model for worker ownership or communal ownership; rather, it reframes the whole concept of ownership and eliminates the master-servant relationship. In doing so, it better meets investors' needs for trust in strong management and for secure long-term investments. It better meets the needs of staff for respect and true inclusion, for enfranchisement in the organization. It better meets the needs of executives and managers for cooperation, loyalty, and trust from their staff. And it strengthens leadership. How it does all that is the story of this book.

The following pages offer practical tools for bringing a truly egalitarian organization into being, achieving the highest-quality standards, contributing to the community—oh, yes, and improving the traditional bottom line: productivity and profits.

CHAPTER FIVE

Inclusive Decision-Making

Determining who makes decisions in an organization is one of the best ways to understand who has the power—who is in control. In an absolute monarchy, the royal family and those they appoint have the ultimate power. In most democracies, the majority has the power. In a business, the owner, partners, or board of directors elected by the investors. Even in employee-owned companies, the decisions are most often made by a board of directors.

If you were starting an organization or a business, would you want an autocracy with yourself as the autocrat, making all the decisions? Perhaps a benevolent autocrat using a participatory or consultative management style, but you would make the final decision—keeping the real power for yourself. What decisions would you allow your employees to make? How would you ensure that everyone follows your decisions?

In a sociocratic organization, everyone makes decisions. The board of directors, the owners, the CEO, managers, employees, and volunteers, all make decisions that affect their own work. Power is delegated to all levels of the organization. For many of us, this may feel impossible. How can an organization function with everyone sitting around making decisions and struggling over power?

The answer lies in an organizational design that nurtures and focuses the energy of each individual and each unit on the aim of the organization. Powerful organizations are characterized by commitment, by every member being aligned and working energetically toward an aim with a sense of purpose. If one person or one department becomes alienated, the whole organization will be affected.

> If you were starting an organization or a business, would you want an autocracy with yourself as the autocrat, making all the decisions?

Distributing decisions throughout the organization so they are made by the people they most affect prevents the disconnection that occurs when people are controlled by decisions they can't change or influence—when they are powerless.

While it may seem unworkable to involve everyone in decision-making, we do this daily in our families and social groups. We respect objections and seek consent when we plan holiday celebrations, decide to play poker on Tuesday nights instead of Wednesday nights, or arrange play dates for children. These are likely to be our most-pleasant experiences with decision-making because inclusiveness and fairness are assumed. We participate fully. Our voices are heard.

At work, however, managers and supervisors have power over us. The board of directors or the owner—people the workers may never see—will make the most-powerful decisions, the ones that decide layoffs or plant closings. This is why maintaining commitment in autocratic organizations is difficult: Those making decisions are often several organizational levels removed from those who are held accountable for implementing them.

Sociocracy structures decision-making and power very differently. To ensure both the quality of decisions and the commitment to execute them, decisions are made by those responsible for implementing them. Those people have right to object if a decision prevents or inhibits their ability to support or work toward the aim.

To understand the importance of consent and the right to object, we need to look at the history of power more closely.

To ensure both the quality of decisions and the commitment to execute them, decisions are made with the consent of those who are responsible for implementing them.

AUTHORITARIAN DECISION-MAKING

The first complex human organizations were theocracies in which leaders made decisions based on their interpretations of the desires of the gods. They were often considered gods themselves. A vestige of theocracy can be seen in our use of ceremony and pledges that invoke god-like status: special robes for judges, special uniforms for military officers, and special music to accompany presidential entrances and exits.

Monarchies were closely related to theocracies and some monarchs were considered divine well into the 20th century. The emperor of Japan, for example, was considered to be a direct descendant of the Shinto gods and had a priestly status that required traditional rituals. It wasn't until 1945, as part of the surrender after WWII, that references to his divinity were removed from national documents and official functions.

In the mid-16th century, revolutions began overthrowing monarchies and establishing parliamentary bodies to rule countries. Although membership was often limited to the aristocracy, citizens had more decision-making power than before. Ironically, however, autocratic rule with all the powers of the monarchy continued in the workplaces, with no consideration of human rights. After the Industrial Revolution, some citizens could vote for their government representatives but were still working 14-hour days, six days a week. Factories employed children as young as six and workers were often fed at their machines with no breaks. The authority to impose these conditions was grounded in property rights with the same effect they had as divine rights.

In 1817, in his essay: *Observations on the Effect of the Manufacturing System*, British factory owner Robert Owen advocated worker cooperatives. He proposed worker control, but his plan didn't protect the rights of investors and owners and thus was unworkable. There would be no financial investment and workers couldn't provide this themselves. The newly forming labor movement did adopt his ideas for improving work environments, but did not propose a change in the autocratic power of owners. The battles between workers and owners continued. The same freedoms that had swept into city governance got no farther than picket lines in factories.

After the Industrial Revolution, some citizens could vote on their government but were still working 14-hour days, six days a week.

EFFICIENT DECISION-MAKING

In the United States, after the Civil War ended in 1865, corporations grew in size and number. Leaders began to search for more stability, less friction, and higher profits. The focus on controlling workers intensified, largely by trying to eliminate the need for them to make decisions altogether.

American mathematician and mechanical engineer Charles Babbage (1791–1871), a pioneer in modern computing and management theory, championed objective data in guiding decisions. American mechanical engineer Frederick Winslow Taylor (1856–1915) encouraged owners and managers to collect data by measuring each of a worker's movements. He developed the time-and-motion study to reduce wasteful human variation and popularized "scientific management." For example, he measured the movements required to lay bricks and shovel coal, then designed shovels in varying sizes and shapes to carry the most-efficient load of 21 pounds of different materials.

"Taylorism" was parodied in a best-selling novel and film written by one of Taylor's children, *Cheaper by the Dozen* (1950), in which a family is organized using precise descriptions of tasks to be completed by each child in a precise amount of time.

Figure 5.1 A Ford Motors **Assembly Plant** *produced identical Model T Fords: They were all black.*

Taylor believed that a cooperative relationship between management and workers was necessary, but the role of the manager was to decide and that of the worker to follow orders. A manager who asked for workers' thoughts about their work or allowed individual human variations risked being considered weak and inviting insubordination. Since this rejection of feedback is an inherent flaw in organizational structures, Taylorism was doomed to fail. Which Henry Ford was about to prove.

American industrialist and founder of Ford Motor Company Henry Ford (1863–1947) accomplished the ultimate in efficiency by eliminating all decision-making by managers as well as by workers. He standardized both his product and his production line to produce cars in great quantities, in identical models, all black. Ford invented "minute management," in which he measured and analyzed each minute of a worker's time. Then he simplified and fragmented tasks so each worker only had to learn one small task and to repeat it all day long. To make this possible, he invented the moving assembly line. This reduced the time required to produce a car chassis from 12 hours and 28 minutes to 93 minutes.

English comedic actor and filmmaker Charlie Chaplin (1889–1977) toured the Ford plant in River Rouge, Michigan and later characterized the assembly line in his satirical film, *Modern Times* (1936). Chaplin portrays a frantic factory worker trying to keep up with a conveyor belt, failing to keep up with an assembly line moving at an ever-faster pace, and ending up in a mental hospital. In the "Job Switching" episode of the *I love Lucy* (1952) television show, the char-

acters Lucy Arnaz and Ethel Mertz attempt to wrap chocolates that pass by faster and faster. They finally start eating the candy so they appear to be keeping up, but still fail.

Ford's workers left in droves before ending up as Chaplin's character did. In 1913, the year of the first moving assembly line, the rate at which workers quit and had to be replaced was 380%: Ford had to hire 963 workers to keep 100. He had to pay so much to keep workers that his profit on each car was only $2.00.

Figure 5.2. Henry Ford's Model T. Ford's most successful early automobile, 1913.

Perhaps the most crucial mistake Ford made was limiting all decision-making to himself to reduce the chance of making mistakes. This eliminated the ability of his managers and workers to learn to innovate and discouraged them from having any creative ideas at all. When consumers began demanding more variety, Ford had no designers who could develop new models or anyone who knew how start new plants to build them such new models. To meet customer demand and remain competitive, he would have had to delegate, decentralize, or diversify. He couldn't. (Zuboff 2002)

CONSULTATIVE DECISION-MAKING

During this period, only American social worker and management theorist Mary Parker Follett (1868–1933) advocated that workers be given more responsibility. She believed creativity could flow from workers, not just managers, and that organizations also had social responsi-

bilities. She was not taken seriously until a now-famous experiment at Hawthorne Works, the Chicago factory of Western Electric, confirmed that she was right.

Hawthorne managers hired Australian American industrial psychologist and organizational theorist Elton Mayo (1880–1949) to study the lighting on its factory floor. They expected an increase in lighting to increase productivity, but would the increase offset the expense of using more electricity? Mayo conducted a series of experiments from 1924–1932 in which he first measured the existing level of productivity and then asked management to increase the lighting by a discernible increment. Productivity increased. He asked for another increase in lighting and productivity increased again, and it increased each time the lighting was increased.

With the lighting now obviously excessive, Mayo decided to double-check his results by gradually reducing it. To his amazement, productivity kept going up. When the lighting returned to the original level, productivity was substantially higher than it had been originally. Inadvertently, Mayo had confirmed that human considerations, such as concern for workers' needs, increased worker productivity. Lighting had little or nothing to do with it.

These findings supported the views that Follett had been expressing as early as 1913, and launched human relations as a recognized profession. Celebrated Austrian-American management theorist Peter Drucker (1909–2005) later honored Mary Parker Follett, calling her "the prophet of management." He told Jeffrey Krames, author of *Inside Drucker's Brain* (2008) that:

Figure 5.3 Mary Parker Follett, who maintained that more humane treatment of workers would be more productive. Managers should exercise power-with, not power-over. She was ignored and then forgotten until Peter Drucker began to praise her work in 2008.

She was totally forgotten—*totally*. She had been suppressed. Not just forgotten. She was so contrary to the mentality of the thirties, which focused on conflict and adversarial relations that her emphasis on conflict resolution was simply unacceptable.

Follett viewed organizations as "group networks" rather than hierarchical autocracies. In 1924 in *Creative Experience*, Follett introduced the concept of "power with" as opposed to "power over." Follett considered power-over to be "pseudo power" because it is coercive and creates divisions. Power-with, on the other hand, she considered integrative because it creates a whole, a unity.

> What is the central problem of social relations? It is the question of power; this is the problem of industry, of politics, of international affairs. But our task is not to learn where to place power; it is how to develop power. We frequently hear nowadays of "transferring" power as the panacea for all our ills. Transfer power to occupational groups, we are told, and all will be well; but the transference of power has been the whole course of history—power passing to priests or king or barons, to council or [elected citizens]. Are we satisfied to continue this puss-in-the-corner game? We shall certainly do so as long as we think that the transference of power is the way of progress. Genuine power can only be grown, it will slip from every arbitrary hand that grasps it; for genuine power is not coercive control, but co-active control. Coercive power is the curse of the universe; co-active power, the enrichment and advancement of every human soul. (Follett 1924)

These concepts of power-with, conflict resolution, and network-like organizations instead of autocratic hierarchies were to become central to the Boekes' and Endenburg's methods and are fundamental to sociocratic principles.

By the mid-20th century, an understanding of human potential and the use of accurate data and computer simulations were combined to analyze organizational and economic behavior. American political and social scientist Herbert Simon (1916–2001) won a Nobel Prize in economics in 1978 for his research into the decision-making process in economic organizations. Simon believed that decision-making was central to administration and that the study of cognition and choice

> Follett introduced the concept of "power with" as opposed to "power over." Follett considered power-over to be "pseudo power" because it is coercive and creates divisions.

was essential to understanding decision-making. In 1947, he published his now-classic work *Administrative Behavior: a Study of Decision-Making Processes in Administrative Organization,* in which he created the word *satisfice* to describe the daily economic decisions made by administrators. Rather than searching for the optimum decision, which they were unlikely to be able to determine or achieve, administrators accepted the choice that would "suffice" and best "satisfy" the requirements of the task, sacrificing others.

In 1954, Simon was using computer simulations to analyze problem-solving and developed his theory of "bounded rationality," presented in 1957 in *Models of Man.* Simon said decisions are not made in a search for the optimum, nor on the basis of the most rational choices, but that decision-making is limited by the cognitive abilities of the decision-maker, the information available, and the time limitations. Bounded rationality is now a central theme in behavior economics and uncertainty theory.

Following the work of Simon, Americans economist and statistician Richard Cyert (1921–1998) and organizational theorist James March (1928–), in *A Behavioral Theory of the Firm* (1963) demonstrated that decisions made in changing and unpredictable circumstances cannot be based on predetermined, standardized rules. The best decisions are made moment to moment by people who are experienced in working with each other in a particular context. Theorists began abandoning their efforts to create better and more-precise power-over systems and began studying the realities of everyday life and power-with.

This new understanding of power and decision-making supports the use of consent in decision-making and the distribution of power to those who work together as colleagues—the "socio-" in *sociocracy.*

POLICY DECISIONS VS. OPERATIONS DECISIONS

Decision-making is inherent in every action we take. Many of our actions are habits based on past decisions, but whenever circumstances change, or we become disinterested, we make new decisions. We decide what clothing to wear, how much money to spend, what price is

> The best decisions are made moment to moment by people who have experience in working with each other in a particular context.

too high or too low. We decide whether to speak to a colleague or not. To go to work or stay home. The quality of these decisions will determine our success or failure—the power we have over our lives

Some of these decisions are policy decisions because they set a standard for future behavior, such as a style of clothing. Others are made moment to moment and apply to the current situation—operations decisions. Blue suit or red?

Whether simple or complex, a decision is a choice between alternatives. Each decision has ramifications that may not be apparent in the moment. We could analyze our decisions from many perspectives, perhaps using a computer model that measures the effects of each of a range of choices. Or by doing a cost benefit study—which decision would be most beneficial for the investment of time or money? Or analyzing the effect on interpersonal effectiveness in a given social structure.

A decision can be made autocratically by an *auto-*, a "self," and *-cratic*, a "ruler." Or by a group taking a vote—a majority-rule decision. Decisions based on personal or religious beliefs are theocratic, based on a *theo-*, a "god," and "*-cratic*," a "ruler." We use all of these decision-making methods to choose between alternatives, perhaps one for this kind of decision and another for others.

Sociocracy makes a clear distinction between policy decisions, which establish the ground rules for how an organization will function until a new policy is made, and operations decisions, which are made on a daily basis and apply to the moment or to the completion of a task. Distinguishing clearly between policy and operations decisions avoids uncoordinated actions and negative results.

The consequences of operations decisions are usually apparent fairly quickly because the effects are immediate. They are made in the moment: on the factory floor, in the office

Charles as a Decision-Maker

Charles arrives at the office one morning, hangs up his coat, and sees a red message-waiting light blinking on his telephone. Knowing that he is prepared for his morning meeting, he decides he has enough time to get a cup of coffee before responding to messages. He walks to the kitchen, pours his coffee, and then decides to join a conversation with two fellow workers concerning rumors about an affair between their boss and a handsome man in the Accounting Department. After a few moments, he decides to withdraw from the conversation and go back to his desk. "I've really got to stay out of such conversations," he tells himself. "They waste so much time."

Charles as a decision-maker is mindfully making choices among possible alternatives. His choice to get coffee was mindful; his decision-making autocratic. Under other circumstances, if he had a personal religious practice related to coffee, for example, his decision would have been theocratic. If he belonged to an office coffee club, he might have voted on the flavor of coffee available, participating in a democratic, majority vote decision. Or it might have been an inclusive, sociocratic decision by choosing the brand to which no one had objections.

waiting room, in a quick staff meeting, at the desk of a colleague. They generally don't change the requirements for future decisions.

Policy decisions are likely to affect more people and more actions for a longer period of time. Approval of a department budget is a policy decision that represents many smaller decisions and has many ramifications. The purchase of a year's supply of pencils because they are on sale is an operations decision that can be easily changed with the next order.

Policy Decisions

A policy decision establishes a general principle or rule that controls or guides future decisions. Policy decisions are generally broad and remain in effect for a period of years.

Examples:

Vision, mission, and aim statements
Values statements
Allocation of financial, facilities, and human resource
Production requirements and goals
Behavioral expectations
Personnel regulations
Privacy rules

Operations Decisions

Operations decisions are made in accordance with policy decisions that govern day-to-day functioning. Operations decisions are frequent, short term, and generally limited to a specific situation.

Examples:

Responses to correspondence
Operation of machinery
Delivery of specific services
Prioritizing tasks and assigning unassigned tasks
Responses to unpredictable events
Restocking, purchasing, etc.

Figure 5.4 Policy Decisions and Operations Decisions. The distinction between a policy and an operations decision determines how and by whom it is made.

DISTRIBUTED POLICY DECISION-MAKING

Unlike autocratic organizations, sociocracy distributes policy decisions throughout the organization. When policy decisions are made by a board of directors or a top management team, they may never be well understood by the rest of the organization—most of whom may never see those directors. It is unlikely that anyone can be fully committed to a strategic plan they never see.

To avoid this disconnection, Endenburg developed a governance structure based on inclusive decision-making and transparency. Policy decisions are distributed and integrated into the work of every unit of the organization that they affect. Records of all policy decisions—budgets, salaries, roles and responsibilities, aims, etc.—are open to all members of the organization who need them to make decisions that affect their domains of responsibility. This dramatically improves the quality of decision-making, the efficiency of operations, and the development of leadership abilities. To understand how and why it does this, we need to look at the concept of power and how it relates to consent as the basis for policy decisions.

POWER IN ORGANIZATIONS

In physics, power is defined as the ability to perform work over time. A powerful car is one that can reach a high speed very quickly and maintain that speed for a great distance. Or to achieve a lower speed but maintain it for a much greater distance. Creating that motion involves managing both the accumulation of energy and the transfer of energy. All the moving parts must work together as smoothly as possible to allow the car to move forward and adjust to wind and rough roads. A car's engine can use gasoline to produce energy, but that energy must be transferred to the drive train to move the wheels. If energy is wasted in that transfer, it will negatively affect the performance of the car. If energy is required to overcome friction and resistance, less energy will be available for moving the car forward.

Charles's Policy Decisions

Charles's decision not to be involved in office gossip is a policy decision. It will probably govern his behavior in the office for some time. The effects of the decision may only become obvious much later. It might save time not to be involved in office gossip but it might also affect his job. If he did not hear about his boss's affair, for example, he might make critical remarks about his boss's lover in her presence.

Charles's Operations Decisions

Charles's first three decisions—to get a cup of coffee, to join the gossip, then to withdraw from the gossip—were one-time operations decisions that Charles made during his typical morning routine at the office. His fourth decision, the declaration to himself that he should generally stay away from gossipy conversations, was a personal policy decision.

Human organizations work the same way. Organizations are powerful when they can accumulate energy in the form of capital, skills, and motivation, and then transfer or direct that energy into accomplishing their aims. People can be energetic or passive. They can be resilient or resistant. One poorly functioning person or department will can produce so much friction that others will become less powerful as well. Their energy will be used on friction, not productivity.

But Endenburg knew that a powerful car does not depend on the driver for its power. Even excellent drivers cannot drive a car with a flat tire as well as they could drive one with four good tires. The way to make an organization more powerful wasn't in hiring and training managers, as important as those might be; it was in designing an organization so everyone's flow of energy was used in productivity and not dissipated by friction.

Resistance & Friction in Charles's Office

If Charles's boss, Susan, decides the product catalog needs to be redesigned and her staff doesn't accept that decision, they can resist, causing friction that dissipates energy, or be passive, withdrawing energy. They could sabotage Susan by following her instructions "perfectly." Since instructions can never be "perfect," energy could be wasted on overly elaborate interpretations of her instructions. Susan could fire her staff, but then she would have even less power. To produce a new catalog, she needs both their skills and their willingness to apply them.

Traditional leadership theory would focus on handling resistance by increasing Susan's personal skills as a manager, including her ability to influence and persuade others, hire the best staff, and write performance reviews that encourage her staff to work harder and to comply with her wishes. In sociocracy, however, the emphasis is on better organization and integrative decision-making to avoid triggering friction and resistance in the first place.

WHAT IS CONSENT?

A good analogy for understanding why consent, lack of objections, is important in the transfer of energy is the central heating system in Figure 5.1. The system has three elements that control its functioning: the furnace in the basement and a switch and thermometer in the thermostat on the living room wall. The thermometer measures the temperature in the room and the switch—the leader—evaluates the desired and actual room temperatures. If needed, it turns on the furnace to produce heat. When the thermometer's measurement indicates increasing room temperature, the switch compares this information to the desired temperature, and, if appropriate, turns the furnace off.

This process repeats itself as necessary. The switch tells the furnace to turn on or off, the furnace does the work, and the thermometer tells the switch how the room temperature is coming along. This is the circular process of leading-doing-measuring that creates a feedback loop, allowing the system to self-correct.

What if one element ignores limitations of another? What if the switch autocratically tells the furnace to heat the water circulating to the radiators to 120° C (248° F)? Since the water will boil at 100° C (212° F), the furnace must object because its pipes would burst, the boiler would explode, and the heating system would need costly repairs. If the switch, furnace, and thermometer decided to try making decisions by majority vote, the results would not be much better. The switch and the thermometer could vote to take the temperature higher and the furnace could vote against it. With two votes to one, the furnace would be outnumbered. As its temperature rises, it will explode again.

Only by understanding that all three elements in the heating system are of equal value in the operation of the system—that the consent of each one is necessary for the functioning of the others—can the system get the best results. The analogy to human systems is that if people cannot function, they will object and stop working or work less efficiently. This will cause friction and resistance until ultimately the group stops functioning altogether. Thus consent, defined as no objections, became Endenburg's first principle for creating a powerful organization.

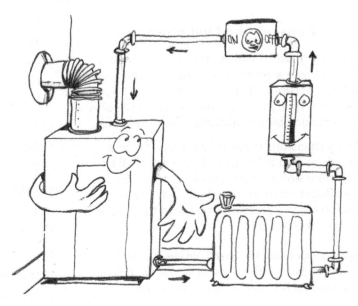

Based in both the science of cybernetics and practical experience, the principle of consent is a major paradigm shift in governance and organizational functioning. Consent as the basis of collaboration ensures that decisions will be made in ways that respect those who are affected by them.

Figure 5.5 A Heating System Consents. A conventional heating system illustrates the importance of consent in decision-making. Unless each element is able to function, the whole system will stop functioning.

CONSENT GOVERNS POLICY DECISION-MAKING

"Consent" appears prominently in the Declaration of Independence of the United States, which says the people are endowed with the rights of the governed, amongst which are "Life, Liberty and the Pursuit of Happiness." Governments are instituted to secure those rights, "deriving their just powers from the consent of the governed." When the government becomes destructive of those rights, it is the governed's duty to throw it off and provide new protections. The Declaration then gives a long list of grievances that detail the offenses of the king.

In sociocratic terms, the Declaration states that the colonies are withdrawing their consent to be considered members of the king's organization, the British Empire, and forming their own.

Sociocracy extends this same right of consent to any group of "We the People," the phrase with which the Constitution of the United States begins, to set up their own system of governance. Regardless of their level of responsibility in an organization, people should have the right to consent to the policies that determine how they will work together from day to day. These policies are called by different names depending on the type of organization: bylaws, department manual, procedures, "how we always do it," etc. Regardless of the name, these policies are the equivalent of a constitution.

Policy decisions govern the day-to-day, in the moment decisions and are usually not made by consent. Rather, the whole group will make policy decisions about how operations decisions will be made. Operations decisions are made by the operations leader according to the groups policies. For example, sociocratic teams often decide that operations leaders will make daily decisions fairly autocratically, but within the team's policies.

For some decisions, a majority vote may be appropriate and satisfactory. Religious beliefs or traditions may govern other decisions. (See Figure 5.7)

The important point is that consent governs policy decisions and policy decisions are the foundation for all other decisions. People consent to work together under specific conditions and withdraw their consent as circumstances change.

A relatively small percentage of a sociocratic

Consent, the First Principle

Consent governs policy decisions. Consent means there are no objections to a proposed policy decision. Objections are based on a person's ability to accomplish assigned roles and responsibilities and must have reasons.

Policy decisions govern future operations decisions and other policy decisions. They include vision and mission aim statements; the allocation of human, facilities, financial resources; the election of people to roles and responsibilities; etc.

Figure 5.6 Consent, the First Principle. *Consent is defined as "no objections," not as agreement. Consent only requires that one can support the decision.*

Decision-making Methods Used in Sociocratic Organizations

For Policy Decisions:

Consent (No Objections)

For Day-to-Day Operations Decisions:

Chaos ("Everyone go for it!")
Theocratic, Ideological, Magical, or other Belief Systems
Autocratic or Authoritarian
Majority Vote
Consensus
Solidarity

Figure 5.7 Decision-making Methods Used in Sociocratic Organizations. If chosen by consent, any other decision-making method may be used.

organization spends a time in consent decision-making. Consent still governs decision making, however, because the "citizens" of the organization can withdraw their consent—object with reasons.

DOMAINS OF DECISION-MAKING

Of course, not everyone has to consent to every policy—nor would they want to. Decisions are delegated to the units of an organization that they most affect and that are within its "domain of responsibility." Everyone who works together must consent to the policy decisions that govern their work. Later we will discuss how policy decisions are made that affect more than one unit.

OBJECTIONS MUST BE REASONED

Consenting to a proposed decision does not necessarily mean you agree with it. It means you have no objections. You might prefer another action or you may have no opinion at all. Consent is not an endorsement. It means you are able and willing to work with the result.

A Domain

A domain is an area of knowledge or a set of activities in which a person or team is responsible for decision-making.

Charles & Domains

When Charles ignored the message light on his phone, he was making a decision in his domain as an individual. He chose to get a cup of coffee.

When Charles decided to stop listening to gossip about his boss, he was setting a boundary for his domain in his department.

In mathematics and logic, reasoned or argued objections are the logical expression of a truth. A glass of water has physical attributes or *arguments* that can be expressed precisely, using objective parameters and measurements. You cannot stick your hand through the side of a glass of water, for example, because some of its arguments (i.e., hardness) prevent it. However, you can stick your hand over the rim into the water because the rim has different arguments. Your car consents to be driven wherever you please, but indicates that it is about to withdraw its consent with a red light on the dashboard *arguing* that low oil pressure will soon cause damage to the motor and prevent it from being driven.

This does not mean that an objection has to be stated in terms of

The requirement for objections to be reasoned and resolved before moving forward transforms decision-making from a struggle for control into a process of puzzle-solving for the ultimate benefit of all.

formal logic or mathematics, but an objection must include understandable explanations. An objection may begin as a vaguely unpleasant or heavy feeling, one that feels like depression or a closing down. The Dutch phrase is *overwegend bezwaar*. *Overwegend* is be better translated as over-weighing; *bezwaar* is a heaviness in both intellectual construct and an emotion. There is no English word to convey both the intellectual and emotional tone of an objection.

Such a feeling is acceptable as an initial statement of an objection. Other members of the circle can help explore and clarify the cause of that feeling. Ultimately, an objection has to be stated factually and explained. It might begin with "I object because I won't be able to do my job for the following reasons ..."

Unless an objection is presented clearly enough for others to understand, it can't be resolved.

OBJECTIONS AND ABILITY TO FUNCTION

An objection must also affect your ability to function in the organization. As we saw in the example of the heating system, a mechanical system's parts must always function within their limits. Beyond their limits, they will no longer function. The first squeak, clank, and clunk from the heating system is a primary objection—I can't work with this.

But people don't switch "on and off" like machines. Many things might cause resistance and friction that are not physically preventing us from working or participating. An objection has more nuance and may be based on your ability to work effectively rather than not work at all. A reasoned objection says, "Some aspect is in danger of going out of safe limits or will be unable to perform as required if this proposal is implemented." The result of the proposed decision would be "outside the range of tolerance." A person who is able to keep her equilibrium with a wide variety of people and in many social situations has a wider range of tolerance than a person who requires a more-predictable environment.

All parts of the organization must be able to express this inability to function and have their objections resolved. As we saw in our example of the central-heating system, although a switch may be delicate, the thermometer sensitive, and the heating system expensive, each element is equally important. Each is powerless without the other.

The requirement for objections to be examined and resolved before moving forward transforms decision-making from a struggle for control into a process of puzzle-solving for the ultimate benefit of all. It places the focus on the arguments for and against, rather on the personalities involved.

OBJECTION, NOT VETO

The principle of consent is not the right to veto. The Latin meaning of *veto* is "I forbid." When you are asked for consent, it is not a deferential question that gives you the right to forbid a decision. You are being asked if you have an objection. Consent means you have no objections.

Objections can normally be resolved when they are clearly stated in terms of the aims of the proposal and the circle. There are many ways to adjust a proposal to move forward and test objections in practice. For a proposal to come forward for a decision, it will have been supported by some circle members. They might have been asked by the circle to write a draft so it will already have been determined by at least some members of the circle to be a needed and appropriate action. Everyone has the right, even the obligation, to raise objections when a proposal could be modified to meet its aims better and avoid negative consequences.

The focus, however, is on moving forward and on effective action. The desire to produce a perfect solution may cause delays that also have negative consequences. Decision-making is based on measurements

A Reasoned Objection

An reasoned objection is a statement that a person's domain would be negatively affected by the proposed decision.

Examining the Basis for an Objection

Would the proposed policy decision negatively affect the circle's ability to accomplish its aim?

Would it produce new and equally troublesome difficulties?

Is the objection based on known facts or conditions, not fears or negative expectations?

Would the proposed decision conflict with other policies or bylaws that are outside the circle's domain of responsibility.

Figure 5.8 Reasoned Objections and Examining the Basis. *An objection is not a veto but rather, the beginning of an exploration.*

and testing, not on power-over withholding of consent. It is better to begin testing a reasonable decision in action, measure results, and—based on the measurements—modify the decision to improve it.

A good facilitator will seek out and welcome objections, and allow time for them to be fully expressed. If any circle members say "no objection" but have downcast looks and arms folded, the facilitator should ask whether they are still troubled by something about the proposal. If all the concerns and objections are not raised and resolved, the resulting grumbling will undermine the circle's ability to be successful. It is essential that objections be resolved.

Waiting until someone is in an exit interview before asking what they think about the organization means that there may have been months or years of negative effects on that person and on their whole unit. Consent as a means of recognizing the value of each person is a practical way of maximizing an organization's resources.

DECISION-MAKING DETERMINES BEHAVIOR

The prevailing form of decision-making determines how people will behave in organizations. If an authoritarian system prevails, behavior will include both stagnant compliance and passive aggressiveness. When majority rule prevails, behavior will include the forming of cliques who support each other's positions, a tendency to equate truth with the majority, manipulation of votes by trading favors, and anger and resistance by ignored minorities.

When consent decision-making prevails, people and organizations become cooperative and self-organizing. It creates a sense of harmony and energy.

Decision-making is based on measurements and testing, not on power-over withholding of consent.

CHAPTER SIX

Developing Quality

To understand why sociocracy produces superior quality, it is helpful to understand the history of quality control in relation to the management of work. Until the 14th century, most consumer goods were produced in artisans' workshops where the master was the judge of acceptable work. An apprenticeship was essential to gaining good training, or even any training at all, and for boys began about the age of 14. The master controlled both training and production.

This changed drastically with the Industrial Revolution, when high-speed production, as in Henry Ford's assembly line, was standardized to require as few skills as possible on the part of the factory worker. Standardization ensured a certain level of quality, but the workers had no training that would enable them to correct a problem, start a business of their own, or make the decisions required to manage it. They were parts in a machine. They had no control over quality.

Working conditions and worker-manager relationships began to change in the 1920s and 1930s, when the findings of Mary Parker Follett were confirmed by the Hawthorn experiment discussed in Chapter 5, "Inclusive Decision-Making." Workers and managers began to be included in decision-making to a greater extent, particularly on working conditions, and organizations became more inclusive.

After the recession that followed WW I ended in the 1920s, there was a boom in consumer spending. Department stores flourished and patenting new inventions was a brisk business. Large department stores allowed consumers to compare the many new products and to judge their quality before purchasing them. In choosing which products to purchase, customers began to determine acceptable standards. Quality became what the consumer wanted and would pay for.

Until the 14th century, most consumer goods were produced in artisans' workshops where the master determined the quality and was the judge of acceptable work.

Following WWII, however, an explosion of new materials and manufacturing methods and an increase in international trade made manufacturing and purchasing much more difficult. Neither businesses nor customers were able to judge their quality. In business, parts and equipment composed of different materials in different countries were unreliable and often incompatible. Customers found that products broke unpredictably or could poison those who used them.

... attention to quality standards and measurement revived the Japanese economy from the devastation of World War II to become one of the most-successful high technology manufacturers the world had ever seen.

QUALITY CONTROL

Japan is one of the best examples of how quickly attention to quality can transform a whole economy. In the 1950s, "Made in Japan" meant "junk." With the aid of American statistician Edwards Deming (1900–1993) and American engineer and quality-control expert Joseph Juran (1904–2008), and a lot of hard work by the Japanese, attention to quality standards and measurement revived the Japanese economy. Japan became a nation of successful high technology manufacturers and, by the 1970s, "Made in Japan" meant very high quality and advanced innovation at very low cost. Japanese products flooded the American market and sent business leaders into shock.

The economic success of such superior Japanese products spurred broad awareness of the importance of quality in design and production, and in meeting consumer needs.

In 1947, Deming had been working on statistical process control when he was asked to help with the upcoming Japanese census. He became so involved with Japanese culture that he was invited to speak to the Japanese Union of Scientists and Engineers (JUSE). His ideas so impressed them that in 1950, he taught hundreds of engineers, managers, and scholars statistical management control. Deming convinced them that by measuring and analyzing every aspect of their production process, including sales and consumer satisfaction, they could both produce superior quality and reduce costs. Deming's methodology became the basis of the Six Sigma quality development process developed by Motorola and used by General Motors, among many other businesses.

Independently from Deming, Juran began working in Japan in 1954. Rather than focusing on statistics as Deming did, Juran described quality from the customer's perspective. Higher quality first means a greater number of features that meet customers' needs. Second, it means "freedom from trouble." Defining quality as meeting customer needs with fewer defects resulted in an unprecedented variety of reliable, mass produced goods and services focused on the nuanced niches of customer needs.

Juran worked with the top managers of large Japanese corporations emphasizing the importance of training managers in quality control. He conceptualized the Pareto Principle, the 80-20 rule, to separate the "vital few" from the "useful many." The Pareto Principle is named after the Italian economist Vilfredo Pareto who discovered that in Italy 80% of the land is owned by 20% of the people and formulated methods of measuring and characterizing socioeconomic data. The Pareto Principle's universal application makes it one of the most useful concepts and tools in modern organizations.

By identifying the 20% of factors that were key to improving production, Juran found that a company could improve its products faster than when paying attention to everything at once. His classic work, *Managerial Breakthrough* (1964), was the first to describe a step-by-step sequence for improving the quality of goods and services.

Both Deming and Juran were influential in developing Total Quality Management (TQM), an integrated management approach that emphasizes continuous quality improvement and is implemented by all members of an organization. Its comprehensive focus includes the improvement of processes, products, services, workplace culture, and customer satisfaction.

> Defining quality as meeting customer needs with fewer defects resulted in an unprecedented variety of reliable, mass-produced goods and services focused on the nuanced niches of customer needs.

CERTIFYING QUALITY

Although Deming and Juran had proven that attention to quality control had great merit and their methods ensured quality, globalization in the mid-20th century brought new challenges. Products from different countries used different standards and measurements, so manufacturers couldn't trust that parts ordered from Germany would work in cars made in the United States. As business-to-business services grew, businesses themselves became the unhappy customers. At the same time, it became harder and harder to build a business with a reputation for high quality because rapidly increasing mobility disconnected established business and customer relationships. Both businesses and customers were "here today and gone tomorrow." With increasing globalization, manufacturers and customers were geographically separated and often did not speak the same language, but at the same time, had to convey instant quality to their ever-changing new customers.

International standards and independent certification became necessary—not only to protect customers, but to protect businesses from businesses.

The International Organization for Standardization (ISO) was formed in 1947 by delegates from 25 countries. Because its name would produce different initials in each language, it adopted the name ISO from the Greek *isos,* meaning equal. In 2015, ISO was a consortium of 165 countries and publishes quality standards for "state-of-the-art specifications for products, services, and good practices to make industry more efficient and effective." ISO has published more than 19,500 international standards in technology and business management covering both physical specifications and processes: food safety, computers, agriculture, health care, business management, etc. Several organizations conduct the certification process, which is voluntary but crucial in many industries. Many companies, for example, will only do business with those that are ISO-certified, so it is necessary ito compete internationally.

To receive ISO 9000 certification, a primary standard for quality management, companies hire consultants to examine their production processes and record-keeping. They send their managers to training sessions to learn how to do readiness audits, pre-assessment audits, document writing and review, employee training, and implementation planning. The process is exhaustive and, in and of itself, has

International standards and independent certification became necessary, not only to protect customers but to protect businesses from businesses.

sometimes led to business losses and reduced production while the company focused on certification at the cost of doing business.

The sociocratic method is based on continual measurement and evaluation of results. It involves maintaining a record of policies, measurements, evaluation of processes, financial transactions, etc. Whether an organization is a factory, nonprofit soup kitchen, law practice, or school, it will follow principles and practices designed to ensure quality control. Remarkably, because Endenburg Electric had these records, it was able to receive ISO 9000 certification *with none of the extensive preparation usually required for the certification audit*. In 1990, it was the first company in its industry in the Netherlands to receive ISO certification.

Because sociocratic methods are based on the same quality assurance processes specified by ISO 9000, all Endenburg Electric had to do was review the standards and compile the relevant reports from the records routinely kept by every department. Much of the work was simply translating these into ISO-acceptable terminology. It took about a year to accomplish the adaptation, but they did it without hiring outside consultants, undertaking any special training, setting aside time for pre-audit audits, or endangering production because they were distracted by the process.

Sociocratic organizations and businesses automatically apply the highest principles of quality control, and have the records to prove it.

Sociocratic organizations and businesses automatically apply the highest principles of quality control, and have the records to prove it.

QUALITY CONTROL & SELF-ORGANIZATION

On paper, the typical sociocratic organizational structure looks like that of most organizations, showing a hierarchy of workers, managers, and boards. There are several key differences, however, that we will discuss in the following chapters.

The first is that policy decisions usually assigned to the board of directors and top management are distributed to all levels of the sociocratic organization. In addition to traditional staff meetings led by the supervisor or manager, teams hold separate meetings in which workers or members, including the operations manager, participate as peers to make policy decisions. Although some sociocratic organizations use alternatives to a hierarchical structure, including worker-managed teams and networks, they all hold circle meetings.

Circle meetings are used to develop the policies that guide day-to-day operations, including budgets, defining and assigning roles and responsibilities, hiring and firing, work processes, and plans for the development and education of circle members.

Within the circle's assigned aim, defined domain, or area of responsibility, and the policies and processes of the larger organization, the circle has full control over its work. Together, its members determine how they will provide services or meet production and quality demands from day to day.

Figure 6.1 A Circle Meeting. Everyone in a sociocratic organization is a member of a circle that governs their day-to-day work. Circle members function as peers when deciding how their aims will be accomplished.

With the exception of sensitive proprietary information such as formulas and processes, and records involved in court cases, records are transparent and all members of a circle have access to support in making responsible policy decisions. Circle members are individually responsible for ensuring the timeliness and quality of their work.

In the last chapter, we discussed the first principle of sociocracy, Consent. The second principle is the Circle.

CIRCLES

Circles meet as often as necessary, at least every four to six weeks, to ensure that policies are current and issues are addressed. The number of members depends on the size of the organization and the organizational unit. In a small organization, one person may be assigned a distinct aim and work fairly independently, making the decisions a circle would make in a larger organization. In most cases, like teams, circles of five to 20 people might be optimal. More than 40 becomes unwieldy unless their aim is very simple, with each member doing very similar tasks.

Every member of an organization belongs to at least one circle. Everyone who is responsible for achieving the aim of the circle—managers, supervisors, heads, chairs, workers, staff, members, volunteers. Each member of a circle participates in setting the policies that govern their roles and responsibilities. Circles elect officers, including a meeting facilitator, secretary, logbook keeper, and one or more people to represent the circle in the governance of the larger organization.

Each circle member has a copy of the circle's logbook, including role and responsibility descriptions, budgets, work processes, performance history, aims, and decisions; work instructions, and any other

The Second Governing Principle

A circle is a semi-autonomous, self-organizing unit that has its own aim and domain. It makes policy decisions within its domain; delegates the leading, doing, and measuring functions to its own members; maintains its own memory system; and plans its own professional development.

Figure 6.2 Circles, the Second Governing Principle. Circle members share an aim and hold circle meetings to make policy decisions.

Typical Topics & Decisions for a Circle Meeting

Vision, mission, and aim
Policy and strategy plans
Progress of the circle toward its aim
Design of work processes
Circle's organizational design and procedures that flow from it
Role and responsibility descriptions of circle members
Election of circle members to functions and tasks
Addition or removal of a person from the circle
The circle's development plan

Figure 6.1 Typical Decisions for Circle Meetings. *In circle meetings, the circle members make decisions as equals that will govern their daily activities.*

work-related documents. Equal access to information allows each member of the circle to function as a peer. When everyone is involved in decision-making, everyone needs the information on which to base those decisions.

A circle's responsibilities include all the activities required to accomplish its aim. All the functions of leading–doing–measuring are under the control of the circle. It both "produces its organization" and "organizes its production": It decides how to use its members and resources to create products and deliver services.

In autocratic organizations, employees typically participate only in meetings that focus on operations—what they do from day to day—and are not included in decisions about what work will be done or how resources will be allocated. Even in participatory management, where workers' opinions may be solicited, managers are under no obligation to respect those opinions. In sociocratic organizations, that respect is required.

Charles's Circle Meeting

Charles, with his co-workers Abdul, Bonnie, and Susan, is organizing a technology conference. Their circle meets on the first Monday of every month. Six months ago, they elected Susan as their circle meeting facilitator and Charles as their secretary, both for one-year terms.

As secretary, Charles schedules meetings, takes notes, sends out minutes, and maintains a logbook containing all the circle's policy documents. At the last month's meeting, the circle decided the agenda would include an evaluation of their recent users conference and a review of changes they might need in their policies for organizing their next conference.

Because all members participate in both policy and operations meetings in sociocratic organizations, there are usually fewer meetings because everyone has a greater understanding of the leading-doing-measuring process and needs less day-to-day supervision.

In autocratically structured organizations, the "top" determines the policy and leaves the execution to the "bottom." Sociocracy assigns policy decisions to every level of the organization. In sociocracy, every circle determines and executes its own policy within the limits that have been set, with its consent, by the larger organization.

PRODUCING ORGANIZATION

A circle's fundamental responsibility is to realize its aim, and it organizes itself to accomplish that aim. To "produce organization," it has to understand all the steps for achieving its aim. Figure 6.4 illustrates the steps required: Define the purpose, which includes the vision, mission, and aim; and define day-to-day operations, which include the production process, a circular feedback process, and task division and delegation.

These steps are presented sequentially, beginning with the aim, but may be discussed simultaneously. Often, defining the aim is the easiest place to start, because it is normally the purpose of forming the circle and is also the tangible. The vision and mission are more abstract and the production process is more concrete. To understand the process conceptually, though, it is clearer to begin with the vision.

Producing Organization

VISION

A vision statement is a description of the future as the circle desires it to be. It inspires. It refocuses circle members when things are not going well. The vision statement might include conditions, feelings, and values, or literally be the description of a dream.

Purpose

Define Vision

Define Mission

Define Aim

Operations

Design Production Process

Design Circular Process of Feedback

Determine Task Division and Delegation

Design Program of Ongoing Development

MISSION

The word *mission* is closely related to missionary: a mission statement of how the circle will accomplish its vision. It motivates the members of the circle and defines a specific relationship to the world or the client defined in its vision. It motivates the members of the circle. Where the vision defines the desired external world, the mission looks inward and defines the responsibility in realizing that vision.

AIM

An aim describes an intended result, a product, or service that will accomplish the mission—the "what." It is tangible in that it can be

Figure 6.4 Producing Organization. The steps in creating an organization that supports the work process generally begin with the aim, because it is often easier to define, but the process requires working back and forth, revising each step until each one is complete.

delivered and received. Clients must be able to recognize the aim and differentiate it from other aims and other products or services. In fact, the circle should define its aim from the point of view of the client. It should encapsulate Juran's concept of quality as a standard that meets as many of the client's needs as possible with as few defects as possible.

The aim breathes life into the relationship with a client, or in an association or network, its members. It provides a yardstick for measuring success and a basis for evaluating arguments for or against proposed actions. Only with a well-defined aim can a circle resolve objections. A clear, well-formulated aim prevents working at cross-purposes and is a prerequisite for proper steering. We explore the aim in more detail in Chapter 13, "Organizing Work."

Charles & His Circle's Vision, Mission, Aim

The vision of Charles's communications circle is: "All the company's clients fully informed and excited about the company's products."

The mission of Charles's circle is to familiarize the company's clients with the company's products.

Their aim is to provide customized information through a variety of media channels, organize user conferences, write monthly interactive newsletters, moderate user forums online, and run an outstanding user recognition program for innovative users of the company's products.

THE PRODUCTION PROCESS

An aim is the jumping-off point for designing the production process—the doing—that describes the steps it will take to produce the tangible objects or services described in the aim.

How should a circle organize itself? Let's look more closely at the doing. In operations management, the doing has three phases: input, transformation, output. In everyday language, an agreement or contract with a client is input, producing the product or service is transformation, and delivering the goods and services to a client who is satisfied with them is the output. This completes the contract.

Involving all workers in designing the production process, combined with the next step (designing a steering process), is what gives sociocracy so many advantages in quality control. The design of production and steering processes is the core of quality control.

THE CIRCULAR PROCESS

The circle is not only responsible for doing its work. It is also responsible for measuring and evaluating the results. It organizes itself to function dynamically, as we will discuss more fully later, by using the circular process of leading-doing-measuring—a "feedback loop"—that is essential to correction and improvement.

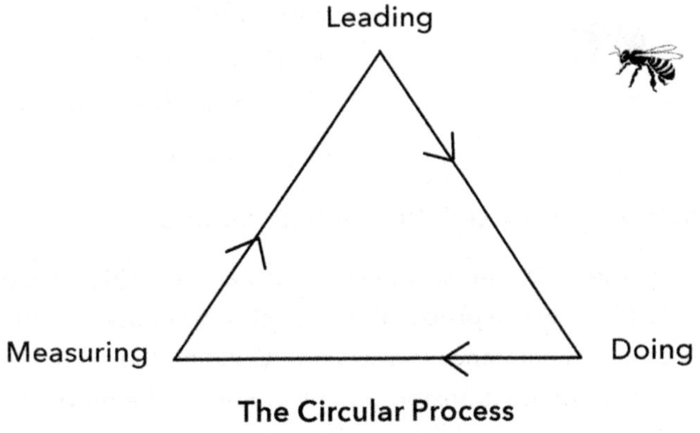

A successful team will function as a self-optimizing system that can adjust to the inevitability of unexpected change. A well-constructed leading-doing-measuring process allows each member to correct their own work, moment to moment, to accomplish the circle's aim. As a system, a circle is designed to be resilient, self-organizing, and coherently structured so it understands and has control of its vital processes.

In sociocracy, the primary responsibility for leading-doing-measuring is within the circle, in the hands of the *socius*—the associates. As we noted in discussing the research of Cyert and March in Chapter 5, "Inclusive Decision-Making," the best decisions are made in the moment by people who have experience with working with each other in a particular context.

Figure 6.5 The Circular Process. *The circular process is illustrated as a triangle because that emphasizes its three functions. The sides of the triangle represent the lines of communication between functions. This triangle, often used to represent the circle as well, has become the symbol of sociocracy.*

TASKS DEFINED AND DELEGATED

In sociocracy, roles and responsibilities are defined and delegated as policy decisions in circle meetings. Circle members may decide to give the operations leader the responsibility for allocating work autocratically, to allocate by using a sociocratic election, or even by drawing straws or rotating responsibilities. In all instances, though, the team decides in a circle meeting, using consent for which process will be used, who will be responsible for executing it, and when the assignment will be reviewed.

PROFESSIONAL DEVELOPMENT

A circle is more than a list of people assigned to a set of tasks. It is a semi-autonomous, self-organizing, organic entity that is continually developing. Circles are expected to be aware of new and competing developments that will affect their aim and to understand and evaluate new materials and processes. Development—learning, teaching, and research—is central to planning the circle's work and to its work expectations. Team members will have both a circle development plan and an individual development plan to help them respond to changing needs.

The importance of including development as one of the responsibilities of the circle became clear to Endenburg in 1979, when another of many researchers visited Endenburg Electric to study the results of implementing sociocracy. This study revealed that after nine years of operation, some workers had stopped participating in the governance process. Some circle meetings were poorly attended and some were not held at all. More was required for people to participate in governance than just informing them of the opportunity. People who had worked in organizations with implicitly or explicitly autocratic leadership needed to "undergo a phase of complete democratization before converting to sociocracy." In other words, they needed the experience of participating in governance before they could take full responsibility for governing themselves.

Charles & the Circle's Production Process

In the case of Charles's conference, the agreement phase (input) would begin with a proposal for a conference based on the needs of potential conference registrants. "Creating the service"– the second phase (transformation)–would be the production of the conference and copies of the presentations, and the third, assessing client or member satisfaction (output). Client or member acceptance might be measured through evaluation forms and sales made as a result of the conference.

Charles's circle has written instructions for each step needed to prepare and run a conference, from budgeting for the conference and developing conference themes, to publicizing and running it, to collecting and analyzing feedback forms and sales figures. Each doing step then has its own circular process for leading-doing-measuring. The measurements may produce results that lead to changes in the instructions.

Endenburg did more training and a second implementation of his method in which he made it explicit that circles were responsible for their own development—their own learning, teaching, and research.

SELF-OBSERVING ORGANIZATIONS

As discussed in Chapter 4, "Cybernetics & the Principles of Sociocracy," sociocracy creates systems that observe themselves, both people systems in circle meetings and data systems in logbooks. The pervasiveness of feedback loops in structuring the leading-doing-measuring process, for example, ensures that the data are available to guide continuous development. Because decisions are made by consent, the organization must pay attention to alerts from its members at all levels that things have gone awry or that an unexpectedly positive change is occurring.

To adjust, change, learn, and grow requires a clear process.

WHY DESIGN ORGANIZATIONS THIS WAY?

In addition to addressing the issues of quality in production and services, organizing work sociocratically has numerous benefits:

- ◆ Complex processes remain steerable.
- ◆ Processes do not become isolated from their environment.
- ◆ Circle members understand their domains (their common aim and processes).
- ◆ Circle members are responsible and held accountable for the results of their work.
- ◆ No gaps occur between processes.
- ◆ Every level in the organization follows the same general decision-making pattern, greatly simplifying understanding and problem-solving.
- ◆ The management and information systems are integral to the primary work process.
- ◆ Orientation toward the client is integral to the work process.

Sociocracy is applicable in medical practices, Scrabble clubs, nursing homes, summer camps, automotive factories, schools, sporting

People who had worked in organizations with implicitly or explicitly autocratic leadership needed to "undergo a phase of complete democratization before converting to sociocracy." In other words, they needed the experience of participating in governance before they could take full responsibility for governing themselves.

events, theater productions, associations, and networks of all kinds. In this sense, it is sometimes referred to as an "empty tool": Each organization fills in its own content.

The process for designing a sociocratic organization is always the same, for groups or individuals; only the content changes. This pattern is a fractal—common in nature—and is one of the beauties of learning the sociocratic method for designing organizations. It works universally, but it isn't a recipe. It adjusts to the organization while retaining its structure.

CHAPTER SEVEN

Steering & Structure

In physics, *dynamic* is used to describe an element that is in motion or changing. The opposite, *static*, is an element incapable of change. Both the natural and economic environments are dynamic, but many organizational structures are static. Adjusting and adapting are very difficult, even if possible. If an organization can change like a living organism does, it can respond to the environment while continuing to function. It can continue to achieve its aims regardless of what it may be confronting.

Sociocratic organizations are designed to be dynamic, which is why sociocracy is often referred to as "dynamic governance." The principles and practices build in the ability to optimize; to be responsive while managing instability. Sociocracy maintains dynamism by using the circular process of leading-doing-measuring to structure and then steer its work process. It is this incorporation of continuous feedback that enables it to change quickly while continuing operations.

DOUBLE-LINKING CIRCLES

Building feedback loops into operations management is not unusual. What is unique in sociocracy is that *feedback loops are integrated into the governance structure*. As we discussed in the last chapter, all units of the organization—the circles—are self-governing and determine their own policies. This structure, however, risks creating conflicting policy decisions. One way to avoid this is for the domain of each circle to be defined carefully so there are no overlaps. A second, one that serves many other functions as well, is to establish communications and control between circles.

If an organization can change like a living organism does, it will be able to respond to the environment without closing down, making changes, and then starting up again.

99

We've discussed how strong systems are resilient, self-organizing, and coherently structured. The structure in most organizations is a hierarchy in which each level has control of the levels below it. The obvious pitfall here is that top-down, linear, autocratic decision-making is almost inevitable. *Hierarchy* becomes synonymous with *autocratic*.

As we discussed earlier, sociocracy avoids a linear, autocratic hierarchy by establishing a *circular hierarchy* in which communications and control also move up the organization, not just down. A circular hierarchy can also be viewed as a network with a common aim. Each hub has both its own aim and functions in relation to the common aim.

The Third Governing Principle: Double-Links

A feedback loop between circles is formed by the operations leader and one or more elected representatives who are also members of the next higher circle. In the circular process of leading-doing-measuring, the operations leader serves the leading function, and the representative serves the measuring function.

Figure 7.1 The third governing principle is double-links between circles to form a feedback loop that maintains the circular process between circles.

The circular hierarchy in sociocratic organizations is established with a *double-link* between circles. The operations leader and one or more representatives elected by the circle are also members of the next higher circle. The operations leader is charged with bringing information from the organization to the circle and provides the leading function, and the representative(s) bringing information from the circle to the organization and provides the measuring function. This does not mean that either one is restricted in what they can discuss, but that they are responsible for ensuring that specific information is conveyed. This feedback loop between circles is, thus, "hard-wired."

The most well-known form of a circular hierarchy is the hand game Rock, Paper, Scissors, in which each element has equal power and can control the others.

The double-link is replicated for all circles and integrates the circular process of leading-doing-measuring into the governance structure. Because policy decisions are governed by consent, feedback must be recognized and not ignored. Double-linking prevents autocratic, top-down decision-making and keeps the whole organization coherent, as well as resilient and more capable of change. It ensures that each circle is operating with the consent of other circles and with optimum harmony.

This means that these two roles—the representative and the

operations leader—cannot be assigned to the same person. The operations link is leading on behalf of the organization and the representative is measuring the response of the circle and carrying it back to the general circle. They each have clear aims. Leading, which includes evaluation of measurements, must be separate from measuring. Using an analogy to electricity, power cannot flow in two directions at once on one wire.

REPRESENTATIVES

A circle elects one or more of its members to represent them in the next circle. They may have a representative elected for a one-year term and elect another person to represent them in a specific meeting in which issues are to be discussed that are of particular interest or on which they have expertise. In some circles, the responsibilities may be so disparate that it requires more than one person to accurately convey information about them.

The number of representatives a circle sends is flexible because decisions are not made by majority vote. The circle is not sending extra votes to manipulate a decision; only to inform it. Decisions are made on the basis of information and arguments, not the number of people for or against them or the status of those in favor of one option or another.

Any circle member, with the exception of the operations leader, may be elected to represent the circle, but the skills required are the ability to articulate the concerns of the circle and the ability to think at a higher level of abstraction to function as an equal member of the circle.

This requires both ability and interest. Perfectly competent and

Illustrating the Double Link Between Circles

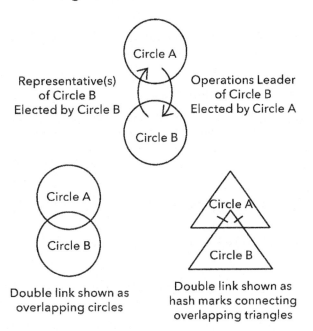

Figure 7.1b Double-Links between Circles. Double-links establish and maintain feedback and feed-forward loops between circles to complete the circular process.

intelligent people may have no interest in abstract analysis and, thus, would probably not be good representatives on an ongoing basis.

The requirement that representatives consent to decisions is important because it means their feedback cannot be ignored. Consent, in effect, hard-wires the links between the decision-making circles that form the structure in the organization.

Charles as a Representative

The Communications Division, where Charles works, reports to the Marketing Department. Susan was hired by Marketing to be director of Communications. As the operational leader, she is responsible for ensuring that any information from the Marketing Department is clearly communicated to the Communications Division.

In its circle meeting, the Communications Division has elected Charles in each of the last three years to be their representative in the Marketing Department circle meetings. His participation and consent are necessary in the Marketing Department circle meetings, as well as in the Communications circle meetings. He participated in hiring Susan to be director of Communications and had to consent before she could be hired.

Susan and Charles, thus, form a feedback loop between the Marketing and the Communications circle meetings.

OPERATIONS LEADERS

Each circle meeting includes the operations leader, who functions as an equal in those meetings. Operations leaders are responsible for directing the work of the circles. Since circles are self-organizing and semi-autonomous, the role of the operations leader is to steer them within the larger organization's policies, to ensure that they are functioning in ways that support the larger organization and are not at cross-purposes. A well-developed circle will maintain a logbook with well-organized, up-to-date policies, including procedures and instructions.

In day-to-day functioning, the operations leader works within the policies of the circle. The leader has both participated in deciding these policies and consented to their adoption. If leaders are faced with a decision that is not covered by a policy, the leader makes a decision based on his or her best judgment and reviews it at the next circle meeting. This allows the department to move forward with the best decision possible at the moment. If necessary, a special meeting of the circle could be called, but this is rare. On a daily basis, the leader functions in a more autocratic fashion.

To understand the importance of double-linking and how these links create coherent, resilient, self-organizing, and efficient organizational structures, we need to understand how positive and negative feedback loops and anticipatory feed-forward loops work.

CIRCULAR PROCESSES

Leading-doing-measuring is a circular process that forms a feedback loop so organizations can self-correct—self-optimize.

Not all systems are self-correcting. Vending machines are designed to function in a linear manner without changing until they run out of energy or break down. Without feedback or if feedback is ignored, change will be random or, at best, based on incomplete information. Feedback tells us whether we are doing well or poorly; evaluating and acting on feedback allows us to improve or change our behavior.

A good system of feedback requires knowing what we need to know and when we need to know it. The thermostat in the heating system that we discussed earlier is one part of the circular process that provides feedback to the switch so it can "know" when to turn the furnace on or off. Gauges on the panel of an airplane are providing feedback to the pilot when something is not working or needs to be adjusted.

In autocratic structures, leaders can ignore feedback. In sociocracy, double-links ensure that they cannot. The principle of consent—the first governing principle—ensures that feedback cannot be ignored *within* circles; double-linking, the third governing principle, ensures that feedback cannot be ignored *between* circles. Feedback is the basis of steering in a dynamic environment.

> In day-to-day functioning, the operations leader is governed by the policies of the circle.

TYPES OF STEERING

As shown in Figure 7.2, steering can be *passive* or *active*, and *static* or *dynamic*. Each is effective in different circumstances. Passive steering simply reacts to the environment, while active steering attempts to change in anticipation of the environment. Static steering requires no internal changes, while dynamic steering fully uses the leading-doing-measuring cycle, the circular process, to make both the internal and external changes that are necessary to remain viable.

For example, a turtle pulling into its shell is using passive-static

steering to protect itself from a threat in the environment. Since tur-
tles have been acting this way for millions of years, it is quite effective
for them. A school system that simply limits enrollments when classes
are overcrowded is using passive-static steering as well, but it is probably not effective for the community if there are no other schools to
take the children.

A textile mill that asks the government to erect trade barriers to
keep out foreign competition is asking for support for passive-static
steering in the form of protective legislation. Organizations that use
passive-static steering set up barriers between themselves and the
problem without interacting with the threatening force or making
changes internally. In the long run, simply building barriers can damage organizations and economies, and certainly doesn't make them
stronger.

Organizations using active-static steering respond to their environments by seeking new, non-threatening environments. A rabbit uses
speed to move to a new environment where there is no threatening
fox. A school system buses children from overcrowded school buildings to a neighboring school system. A clothing company lowers its
costs by building factories in another country where labor is less expensive. Actions are taken, but the system doesn't change; it escapes.

In autocratic
structures, leaders
can ignore feedback.
In sociocracy, double-
links and consent
decision-making
ensure that
they cannot.

In dynamic steering, on the other hand, the circular process is
used to change the system, not just react to or avoid the environment.
Passive-dynamic steering is a *difference-controlled process* that measures any difference between current conditions and an established
norm or criterion. The difference becomes the basis for making any
needed corrections.

The heating system in our earlier example uses passive-dynamic
or difference-controlled steering. The desired temperature is set and
the switch turns the furnace on when the room temperature falls below the set temperature. The typical inventory system also uses difference-controlled steering. When stocks of supplies fall below a set
point, an inventory clerk or a computer will initiate an order for more.
A school board that decides to build more classroom buildings when

its current classrooms reach a specified level of overcrowding is also using passive-dynamic, difference-controlled steering.

Difference-controlled steering is relatively simple, but can result in relatively large fluctuations due to lag times. If the temperature outside drops sharply, it may take awhile for the furnace to warm the room. If the school board starts building new classrooms only when overcrowding starts to occur, students may experience severe overcrowding before new classrooms are ready. A business using only difference-controlled or passive-dynamic steering might be bankrupt before it could adjust to a sudden change in the market.

An example of this is the Eastman Kodak company, which once dominated the photographic film industry with 90% of the market. In the 1990s, the company failed to adjust to the change to digital photography and didn't return to profitability until 2007.

TYPES OF STEERING

	STATIC	DYNAMIC
PASSIVE	**Hide** • Hunker Down • Limit School Enrollments	**Respond** • React to Events • Build More Classrooms
ACTIVE	**Escape** • Run Away • Bus Children Elsewhere	**Anticipate** • Forecast Events • Track Births • Build in Anticipation of Overcrowding

Figure 7.2 Types of Steering. Static organizations react to their environments and use unchanging steering methods. Dynamic organizations interact with their environments by using circular processes to build feedback and feed-forward loops that anticipate and respond to future conditions.

Clearly, while passive-dynamic steering is more adaptive than passive- static steering, it is not as adaptive as it could be if it measured the factors that would allow it to anticipate change.

In addition to feed*back* loops, systems based on anticipatory steering use feed-*forward* loops to make forecasts for the future. They create projections or models of the system and how future events might affect it. Our heating system, for example, would have been anticipatory if it had a thermometer on the outside of the building that measured outdoor air changes and could trigger the furnace to begin or stop warming in anticipation of environmental changes that would soon affect room temperatures.

In addition to feed*back* loops, systems based on anticipatory steering use feed-*forward* loops to make forecasts of the future. They create projections or models of the system and how future events might affect it.

Anticipatory steering builds a model of the future. In a heating system model, it would include the thermal conductivity of the walls (the R value) and the heat output of the furnace. This information would let the switch calculate how fast the temperature in the room would fall when the temperatures outside changed. It would know when to turn on the furnace to prevent a temperature drop inside the house or to turn it off to prevent over-warming when the sun rose. This system would greatly reduce temperature fluctuations inside the house.

A school board that watches births, forecasts of housing starts, and regional economic development to predict when it will need to build new classrooms is using active-dynamic steering. Active-dynamic steering requires a company to predict future demand and make innovations in its products to anticipate that demand.

The system models required for active-dynamic steering can be very complex and require extensive computer programming to establish and monitor them. With the heating system, for example, the thermal conductivity of the walls might vary depending on wind speed and direction, barometric pressure, and humidity. Sensors could be installed to measure these environmental conditions and feed data to an artificial intelligence program that would help the switch "learn" the effects of its on–off decisions, given these variables. Over time, it would become more sensitive and accurate because it is self-correcting. In the same way, the strategic or long-range plan of a business would be based in part on a sophisticated dynamic systems model of the future that is updated as new data become available.

FEEDBACK AND FEED-FORWARD LOOPS

When organizations begin using the circular process, specifically active-dynamic, anticipatory steering, performance improves dramatically. They take more variables into account, anticipate external changes more accurately, and make internal changes more effectively.

The drawback of anticipatory feed-forward loops, and thus of active- dynamic steering, is that predicting the future cannot be completely accurate. Models of or assumptions about the environment and other variable factors are only as good as the predictions. Feed-forward loops can dampen most fluctuations, unpredictable variables, but we can't trust that they will always keep a system within tolerable limits. For example, the school board that anticipates an influx of children might fail to anticipate an economic downturn that causes workers to move away from the area.

Thus, organizations need both feedback and feed-forward loops to balance their steering. In practical terms, circle meetings should focus on measuring current conditions, anticipating change and calculating what that might mean for their prediction model. As systems grow larger and more complex, increasingly complex measurements and technology are required to obtain the kind of sensitive and timely data that allow anticipatory changes.

Charles & the Circular Process

If Charles's circle used active-dynamic, cause-controlled steering, they would try to anticipate their users' interests months before their next user conference. They would make written predictions, plan around them, update the predictions as they get new information, and revise the plan accordingly.

STATIC & DYNAMIC

As discussed earlier, static governance is by nature autocratic. The leader determines policy, establishes strategies, and passes them along to the other end of the line. The linear command structure is a very powerful way to direct "doing."

Military organizations use it in training soldiers to follow orders quickly and exactly because it works well when no ambiguity or hesitation can be tolerated. The military's job is to create powerful groups of soldiers who can function in the worst conditions and still maintain strong bonds and allegiance to their aim. This works well when the task, however difficult and dangerous, is well-defined and can be executed quickly.

A static, linear structure, however, cannot respond well to change because it has no formal or guaranteed feedback loops. It can't accurately read or measure change, so it can't react accurately.

In linear structures, an action is conceived at one end "of the line" and executed on the other. Like the force that propels a bullet from a gun, however, energy created at one end of a trajectory dissipates as it travels toward the other end. According to the laws of thermodynamics, this is because energy transforms in only one direction—from a usable form to an unusable form. It has no ability to renew itself.

This inevitable movement toward dissipation is the negative quality of the linear leadership structure. In complex organizations, where an order must be implemented several levels away, this dissipation factor deeply undermines the positive quality of being able to direct and control action precisely. In linear structures, energy must be constantly renewed from the top. The commander can never sleep. The autocratic structure is like a ball and chain.

Another problem is the disintegration of clarity that occurs when an autocratic leader attempts to establish a policy that does not permit interpretation or adjustment. Workers must continually return for clarification because they are facing changing conditions that require the leader to tell them how to apply the policy as the leader wishes. Or as workers stray from what the leader intends, the leader must exert more effort to monitor and correct their activities.

As shown in Figure 6.3, a static, autocratic, linear structure creates a constant pressure on leaders to inspire, motivate, make more decisions, and correct more actions.

As in Fordism, leaders in an autocratic system tend to "de-skill" jobs when they centralize leadership functions, and create an organization that cannot respond to change.

Sociocracy avoids this ossification at the bottom, burnout at the top, and general dissipation of energy and information by involving everyone in steering the organization toward its aim. The network of self-organizing, semi-autonomous, double-linked circles integrates feedback and anticipatory feed-forward loops into the work process. This design creates active, dynamic, anticipatory steering at all levels of the organization. It ensures that energy and information travel "up" as well as "down" the organization's structure.

Feedback does occur in autocratic organizations, of course, but it

The linear command structure is a very powerful way to direct "doing." Military organizations use it in training soldiers to follow orders quickly and exactly because it works well when no ambiguity or hesitation can be tolerated.

is informal, undependable, and uneven. It can vary according to "who has the boss's ear this week." Feedback can also be ignored if the boss doesn't like it or chooses not to believe it. There is no requirement that it even be acknowledged.

Some leaders in autocratically structured companies have tried to correct this feedback problem. The president may step away from his or her desk for two weeks a year to have a conversation with each of the 200 people in the company. Other organizations hold meetings similar to town meetings. But this kind of feedback is not hard-wired into the formal structure of the organization. It is periodic and can be delayed or canceled when it is inconvenient. It is still focused on the leader and subject to one person's ability to listen and evaluate accurately.

Focusing on the leader instead of the work process can also mean that the personality or skills of the leader will be credited with the success or the failure of a whole company. When there are failures, a company board will simply change leaders, rather than look at the work processes. In a sociocratic organization, the successes—and failures—are shared more equitably and the focus is on the work.

DOUBLE-LINKING & DYNAMIC GOVERNANCE

As we discussed in relation to consent, the concept of hierarchy has negative connotations for many people because they equate *hierarchy* with *autocracy*; specifically, with the static autocratic governance structure of most organizations. This has obscured the importance of the hierarchy in the organizing operations. Sociocracy uses the powerful linear structure of a hierarchy in operations, the doing, to produce efficient production.

This structure, though, is controlled by the feedback processes that balance the top-down energy with a bottom-up energy of feedback and control the structure with consent decision-making. It builds "power with" rather than "power over."

Further, the autocratic hierarchy obscures the importance of identifying and locating the levels of abstraction in decision-making. The

The network of self-organizing, semi-autonomous, double-linked circles integrates feedback and anticipatory feed-forward loops into the work process.

"lower" operations levels tend to have shorter timeframes and work is more tangible, less abstract. The "higher" levels are concerned with longer timeframes and decisions based on information that is more abstract. The higher levels are generally more concerned with issues that affect several circles, rather than tasks that might concern only one circle.

Figure 7.4 is a diagram of a simple sociocratic structure with the generic names for the circles: top circle, general circle, and department circles. The number of levels and circles will differ from one organization to another, depending on both the size and the level of complexity. Some organizations will have many circles but only three levels; others, many circles and many levels. Circle names will also be determined by the organization. The generic names are useful, however, for understanding the various functions of circles in the hierarchy of work.

The department circles will be of two kinds: those responsible for:

1.   fulfilling the aim of the organization, and

2.   supporting the aim-fulfilling circles by providing the administrative functions including accounting, personnel, and facilities maintenance.

Figure 7.3 The Heavy Load of Autocratic Management. When all decisions are pushed to the top, managers feel the burden of the organization on their shoulders.

An organization fully implementing sociocracy will typically have a support circle that oversees ongoing development in the use of sociocratic governance at all levels of the organization. The general circle brings both types of department circles together to determine overall operations policy.

Department circles include members who work together functionally. In a factory, for example, they might be particular sections of an assembly line. In a large high school, they might be one academic department. In a community organization, they might be membership, programming, legislation, and events units.

The general circle includes the operations department leaders, representatives selected by the department circles, and the general

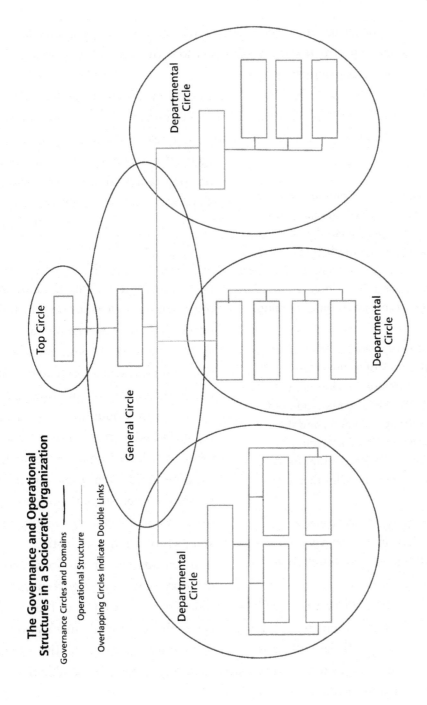

The Governance and Operational Structures in a Sociocratic Organization

Governance Circles and Domains ───────

Operational Structure ─ ─ ─ ─ ─

Overlapping Circles Indicate Double Links

Top Circle

General Circle

Departmental Circle

Departmental Circle

Departmental Circle

Figure 7.4 The Governance and Operational Structures in a Sociocratic Organization. The circle structure for governance encompasses the hierarchical structure for day-to-day operations in each domain or area of decision making.

manager or CEO. The general circle selects the operations leaders of the departments and makes decisions that affect the general policies of the departments.

The top circle (also called a board of directors) includes external experts, the general manager or CEO, and the chosen representative(s) from the general circle. The top circle selects the top executive officer (general manager or CEO) and focuses on long-range planning and relationships with external organizations.

The top circle's external experts serve as full members of the top circle and normally include a technical expert who is familiar with the aim of the organization, a social or organizational expert, a legal or governmental expert, and a financial or economics expert who can represent stockholders' interests or the interests of funding agencies or donors in a nonprofit organization. By including experts along with the CEO and elected representatives from the general circle, the top circle encompasses the interests of the organization itself, its members, its environment, and its profession or industry.

In an alliance or network of organizations, the central governing body, often called a council, has members of the top circle of the member organizations who will serve as members of the alliance's governing body. These will be the an expert member, the executive director, and/or elected representatives. In any event, the double-links are maintained.

By connecting the organization to its environment, the external members of the top circle prevent the organization from becoming a

Charles & Abstraction

In Charles's company, for example, his Communications Circle is concerned with a specific area: communication with clients about the company's products. All decisions concerning these communications are made by the circle, based also on feedback from clients and feedback from the rest of the company. The Marketing Circle looks at broader issues related to image, advertising, packaging, printing, resources, etc.

The next-higher circle, the General Management Circle, looks at issues that affect the work of all the circles in the company—marketing, software development, administration, finance, etc. The General Management Circle is responsible for long-range planning and the Marketing Circle on planning individual marketing campaigns. In Charles's Publicity Circle, the timeframe is even shorter and narrower—the next newsletter and the next user conference.

When Charles and his colleague participate in the Marketing Circle, however, their time horizon is at least three years and includes considering new products and multi-year budgets.

closed system. While the operations benefit from the control that the circular process provides in a closed system, this closed system benefits from the energy flowing from outside itself.

A top circle always includes the CEO or equivalent and representatives elected by the general circle. In many organizations, the traditional board, consisting only of outsiders, has an autocratic, controlling relationship with the CEO and all other employees. This relationship is not the case in sociocratic organizations, where not only the CEO but other members of the general circle are elected to be members of the top circle. Within the top circle, consent decision-making and the reframing of relationships through double-linking allows the CEO, elected representatives, and external experts to work together as true partners in developing policy.

HELPING CIRCLES

Another type of circle is the helping circle. The aim of a helping circle is policy preparation. Helping circles are temporary circles created as the need arises, depending on problems regarding policy or execution, marketing tasks, research assignments, etc. They are formed by people from existing circles and reinforced, if necessary, by external experts. A helping circle might be set up to prepare a marketing strategy plan for a potential new client and be composed of people from different parts of the organization. This is typical in a highly complex organization.

Helping circles do not make policy decisions, however; they recommend policies. Consenting to a policy can only be done by the circle or circles that created the helping circle.

FULL CIRCLE MEETINGS

In some organizations, it is desirable or necessary for all circles to meet together for discussion or to make decisions that affect all members. Some condominiums, for example, are required to make certain decisions in annual meetings of all owners. Intentional communities, college faculties, and religious organizations based on participation

> By including experts along with the CEO and elected representatives from the general circle, the top circle encompasses the interests of the organization itself, its members, its environment, and its profession or industry.

by all members, where the focus is on developing a sense of the community as a whole, want to meet together and make certain decisions.

Full-circle meetings serve this purpose. The top circle officers or the coordinating circle officers might serve the full-circle meeting officers, thus providing a leader, a secretary, and a facilitator. Because a full-circle meeting might occur infrequently, having a separate set of officers might not be meaningful.

If the organization does have full-circle meetings, the policy decisions they make, or recommend, should be defined in the aim of the full circle. The process of setting policy in the full-circle meeting would follow that of making policy decisions in circles.

CHAPTER EIGHT

New Leadership Strategies

When we hear *leader*, we often think of exceptional people—scientists who discover cures for deadly diseases and politicians who inspire generations of audiences. Perhaps we think of those who demonstrate extraordinary courage in unusual circumstances, like military leaders or astronauts, or charismatic, powerful people who make decisions, control money, and hire and fire other people at will. Thus, the modern CEO, like Jack Welch, has become a legend. Welch has 10 best-selling books focusing on his leadership at General Electric, including *Jack Welch on Leadership, Big Shots: Business the Jack Welch Way, Jack Welch and the 4 E's of Leadership, Jack Welch and the GE Way, The GE Way Fieldbook*, and *Winning*.

In the sociocratic organization, leadership by everyone is the responsibility of everyone, not just the exceptional person. Leadership is encouraged by both the governing principles and the organizational structure.

Studies in leadership often assume that leadership is a unique personal quality and that there is a difference in leadership between presidents and managers, managers and first-line supervisors, transformational leadership and transactional leadership, and so on. From this viewpoint, leadership is one thing for the board of directors, another for a floor supervisor, and still another for a peace activist or meeting facilitator. This approach has led to definitions of leadership as lists of specific skills. One definition lists 11 skills and another lists four. These lists of skills lead to arguments about how the pie should be sliced, but ignore the nature of the pie. In particular, they ignore the relationship between leadership and the nature of work.

Leadership by Everyone is encouraged by both the governing principles and the organizational structure.

In sociocratic organizations, leaders are not autocrats. The responsibilities of operational leaders are determined by consent, first by the circle that selects them for a leadership role, and then by the circle whose work they lead. The responsibilities of operational leaders are thus defined by everyone affected by them.

Scholars conducting research on leadership observe and conduct case studies of the most successful leaders. Since they collect their data in organizations using autocratic command structures, a structure that severely limits the nature and quality of leadership that can occur within it, these studies reflect a very narrow definition of leadership. As we have seen in the example of Henry Ford and his assembly line, authoritarian structures constrict, rather than encourage, leadership.

Sociocratic organizations approach leadership very differently. First, they distinguish between leadership roles and leadership functions. When most of us think of leadership, we think of the leadership role—the president, the boss, the person who tells everyone else what to do. In sociocratic organizations, leaders are not autocrats. The responsibilities of operational leaders are determined by consent, first by the circle that selects them for a leadership role, and then by the circle whose work they lead. The responsibilities of operational leaders are thus defined by everyone affected by them.

While operational leadership is very important in sociocracy and each working unit has an identified leader, there is more to leadership than fulfilling a role. There are leadership functions, among them the ability to stimulate themselves and others to action, to evaluate and plan, to obtain and allocate resources, to define tasks and determine the required results, to initiate ideas, and to share the risks and rewards of implementing them. These leadership functions are expected of everyone—each person is encouraged to think like a leader; to become an entrepreneur within their domains of responsibility.

An autocratic leader typically avoids expressing uncertainty for fear of looking weak. In sociocratic organizations, uncertainty is an important part of the process of seeking a solution. A leader can be both strong and uncertain.

ELECTING LEADERS

The election process applies the principle of consent is in hiring, assigning tasks, and choosing leaders. This process can be used to choose among multiple possibilities. In this process, circle members first define the responsibilities, qualifications, and terms. Nominations are made and explained, and then nominees are discussed openly with all members of the circle present. Discussion focuses on the job requirements and each nominee's ability to fulfill them. In many instances, the choice may be clear after minimal deliberation and the election leader may simply propose a choice at this point. The process is complete when everyone consents to a choice. (See Chapter 13, "Electing People" for more information.)

While foreign to most organizations, this process is highly affirming because people are openly appreciated and acknowledged for their strengths in the context of the aims of the circle and the organization. It produces a strong working group because those elected for a task know they have the full support of their colleagues and understand what their colleagues expect of them. Ensuring that everyone accepts the final selection also reduces friction and increases productivity.

The sociocratic election process has none of the winner-loser celebrations that we see in majority voting; none of the mystery that surrounds a nominating committee process; and none of the jealousy, anger, puzzlement, or despair that can arise when the boss announces an unexplained choice. The result has a positive effect on the way everyone works together and, ultimately, circle development.

LEADERSHIP AS A FUNCTION OF WORK

While sociocratic organizations extend both the rights and the responsibilities of leadership to all members of the organization, this does not mean that they eliminate the hierarchy that is typical of authoritarian organizations—rather, they use it differently. A sociocratic hierarchy is based on the requirements of the work process, not who has power over whom.

It is important to understand this distinction, because many of us reject or misunderstand the importance of the hierarchy and thus reject sociocratic ideas along with it. Hungarian British author Arthur Koestler (1905-1983), who wrote extensively on science topics,

The sociocratic election process has none of the winner-loser celebrations that we see in majority voting; none of the mystery that surrounds a nominating committee process; and none of the jealousy, anger, puzzlement, or despair that can arise when the boss announces an unexplained choice.

addressed the negative view of hierarchies that many of us hold:

> Unfortunately, the term "hierarchy" itself is rather unattractive and often provokes an emotional resistance. It is loaded with military and ecclesiastic associations, or evokes the "pecking hierarchy" of the barnyard, and thus conveys the impression of a rigid, authoritarian structure, whereas in the present theory, a hierarchy consists of autonomous, self-governing holons endowed with varying degrees of flexibility and freedom. (Koestler 1980)

Koestler's *holon* and the resultant *holarchy*, a word that Koestler coined that has been picked up by American philosopher Ken Wilber (1949–) and others, is analogous to the circle in the sociocratic organization. Circles, like holons, are semi-autonomous and self-organizing, but at the same time, are hierarchically connected and interdependent.

Producing a flower garden illustrates how the hierarchy of work and abstraction of tasks can be seen in our example of producing a flower garden. To design a garden, one must choose the colors and textures, and make budget decisions. Choosing the specific plants requires decisions about budget—will they be annuals or perennials? plants or seeds— and then finding the plants or seeds. Planning and purchasing is followed by actual planting. Planting requires coordination of plants, seeds, and workers with the weather. The soil must be prepared before the actual planting. All these steps must occur in a certain order.

Then comes the process of watering, fertilizing, and pruning, followed by preparation for the next season. Each of these steps also must occur in a particular order and the success of each is determined by how well the step before it is accomplished. This is the hierarchy of work, which forces its own hierarchy of action on the process of creating a garden. The early, abstract planning guides the manual labor of planting and tending.

Now imagine that this garden is the size of a football field—a park or a botanical garden. Each step in the process of designing and planting becomes a task involving many people, and probably several organizations. In addition, many people are involved, some of the tasks

The principle of consent is used in hiring, assigning tasks, and choosing leaders in a process called the election process, but it can be used to make any decision in which there are multiple possibilities.

might take place simultaneously—if they are well-coordinated. While one set of people is obtaining approval of the design by the city council, another set could be researching the cost of plants and seeds. Once the design is done, one group could be preparing the soil while another is procuring the plants. This requires careful planning so the plants are not ordered before the soil is ready or the budget approved.

This is why sociocratic organizations are built on a structure that, as Koestler says, is so "unattractive" to many people. The hierarchy structures communications about related tasks and controls complex tasks so they are executed efficiently.

Sociocratic organizations also include bottom-up controls, as feedback loops, that counter-balance and correct the top-down controls.

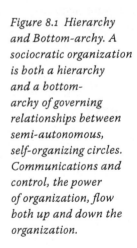

They could just as well be represented as a bottom-archy, as illustrated in Figure 8.1. In fact, a sociocratic organization is both a hierarchy and a bottom-archy.

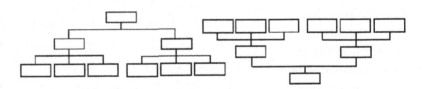

An autocratic hierarchy based on top-down decision-making can easily damage itself, because there are few mechanisms to ensure accurate feedback. Leadership becomes associated with charisma and gaining power. Without feedback related to the actual work being done, turf battles begin to take precedence over performance and productivity declines.

In *Good to Great* (2001), Jim Collins (1958–) discusses the factors that enabled good companies to become great companies. When General Electric, led by Jack Welch, outperformed the market by 2.8 times over the 15 years, it was considered to be the best-managed corporation in America. The great companies, however (most with leaders you have never heard of), outperformed the market by 6.9 times as they tipped from good to great. The leaders of these great companies were more concerned with performance than with anything else. They were not about themselves:

The good-to-great leaders never wanted to become larger-than-life

Figure 8.1 Hierarchy and Bottom-archy. A sociocratic organization is both a hierarchy and a bottom-archy of governing relationships between semi-autonomous, self-organizing circles. Communications and control, the power of organization, flow both up and down the organization.

heroes. They never aspired to be put on a pedestal or become unreach-able icons. They were seemingly ordinary people quietly producing ex-tra-ordinary results. (Collins 2001)

This focus on performance and results exemplifies the kind of leadership that each person is encouraged to display in sociocratic organizations.

STRATEGIC PLANNING & THE ART OF WAR

Sociocratic methods are both highly conceptual and fundamentally practical. They appeal to those who appreciate complex theoretical principles, as well as those who appreciate direct and efficient action. Both require good strategic planning.

By emphasizing top-down decision making, an autocratic hierarchy can easily damage itself because there are few mechanisms to ensure accurate feedback.

But what is a strategic plan?

Military theorists have written many of the works on strategic plan-ning. The earliest in Western cultures was the prominent Prussian military theorist and educator Carl von Clausewitz (1780–1831), who published a famous treatise on strategic planning in 1832, *On War*. It is still one of the most influential works on military strategy. In the first framework for formulating strategic plans, he distinguished be-tween short-term tactics, which can change from day to day, and long-term strategies, which do not. The purpose of day-to-day operations is to execute the short-term tactical decisions that fulfill the long-term strategies.

Strategic planning, Clausewitz said, should include:

- ◆ a clear overall objective
- ◆ rational estimations of resources that will be required and are currently available
- ◆ contingency plans to account for practicalities
- ◆ assurance of good sources of information
- ◆ identification of good leaders

He emphasized that strategy includes planning for all foreseeable events and identifying sufficient resources to cope with the unforeseeable.

Here, we clearly see leadership as a function, not as a role. Although Clausewitz, who was familiar only with autocratic methods of organization, would have limited these functions to the person filling the leadership role, we can see that each person must include such planning at the level of their own work and understand how their work fits into the planning of the larger organization if they are to function most effectively.

In Clausewitz, there are also startling similarities to modern nonlinearity and complexity theory, some of the same theories that Endenburg used in developing the principles for sociocratic organizations. Clausewitz said building the strength of an organization means developing its human capital, not in teaching people to perform repetitive tasks as Henry Ford was later to do in designing his assembly line.

... the use of war analogies is flawed because viewing success as a struggle to defeat an enemy places the focus on defeat instead of accomplishment.

Since the world changes from moment-to-moment, knowing specific techniques is of little long-term value. People must understand the underlying principles so they can produce new technologies as these become necessary. Good information is key, but strategic planning skills are greater predictors of ultimate success.

In the 1970s, when the Japanese suddenly burst forth in world markets with superior and much cheaper technology, Sun Tzu's *The Art of War*, written in 500 BC, was cited as their inspiration. It quickly became required reading in management programs and students were all encouraged to become samurai.

Sun Tzu (544–496 BC) praised subtlety and swift action with as little loss as possible. He advised against physical violence. "Why destroy," he asks, "when you can win by stealth and cunning? To subdue the enemy's forces without fighting is the summit of skill." He counsels that the effective general undermines the enemy's alliances, morale, and economic foundations. Physical

*Figure 8.2 **The Art of War** by Sun Tzu has been reproduced in thousands of editions.*

force is not the best weapon, Sun Tzu said, nor destruction the best value. Organization and leadership require more skill and cunning.

DEFICIENCIES OF THE WAR ANALOGY

While both Clausewitz and Sun Tzu were excellent theorists and their ideas have been applied very successfully, the use of war analogies is flawed because viewing success as a struggle to defeat an enemy places the focus on defeat instead of accomplishment. Even though the focus of war in Sun Tzu's terms is more subtle (to acquire without destroying), the emphasis is still on power over others, not on excellence as a standard apart from "others." As Collins discovered in his research, the great companies focused internally on measures of their own performance, continually improving without reference to what others were doing. Their leaders' names were often unknown in the competitive business media.

Military leaders, particularly those who are successful wartime leaders, are not necessarily successful leaders in other kinds of organizations. For example, Ulysses S. Grant (1822–1885) was a business failure both before the Civil War and after his presidency. Yet, he was by far the North's best military strategic thinker, bringing the ferocious and brilliant tactician Robert E. Lee (1807–1870) to submission.

Military organizations are highly structured, with clearly defined aims and often a captive minimally compensated workforce. Their world-view is black and white; they polarize to focus energies and emphasize the all-important battle. War is literally life or death and very immediate.

If war leaders are to be emulated, then an enemy has to be identified. While nonprofit charitable organizations may naturally focus on a disease, human rights, or poverty, for businesses, the only enemy in sight is usually the competition. Destroying the competition may become more important than serving the best interests of the consumer or the client. Even associations that are formed to serve their members may fall into this trap. The American Federation of Teachers (AFT) and the National Education Association (NEA), for example,

People must understand the underlying principles so they can produce new technologies as these become necessary. Good information is key, but strategic planning skills are greater predictors of ultimate success.

spend great sums of money challenging each other for the right to represent teachers in school districts that are already unionized. Their focus becomes the internal desire to build the largest organization, not education or the status of teachers and the teaching profession. As a strategy, this places the emphasis on the competitor, not the still under-paid and under-respected teacher, or the under-served students.

THE STRATEGIC PLANNING PROCESS

Sociocratic organizations seek leaders who understand both aim—the delivery of a product or service to a customer or client—and strategy, the planning required to achieve that aim. Many strategic planning schedules are possible. One begins with a top circle retreat, moves to the general circle, and then to each of the department circles.

The process begins in the top circle with an examination of the organization's aim. "Are we providing exactly what our clients now want?" Since the top circle includes outside experts, this process includes a variety of perspectives provided by people with an intimate knowledge of the company. While the top circle examines the aim and the associated strategy in the most abstract terms, the strategy becomes more concrete and more focused on the work process and general operations as the process moves down the hierarchy.

... transparency is essential if each person is to be expected to assume the responsibility of leadership and participate equivalently in decision-making.

Each circle adjusts its aim to align with the new overall aim. The departmental or team circles plan the tasks required in day-to-day operations to achieve the aim.

Just as important in sociocratic organization is that the planning also moves back up the organization as each circle and each person reviews the plan and suggests corrections and additions. The plan may look very good at an abstract level, but not be possible for some units to implement. Changes may have to be made in the more abstract goals so the more tangible goals can be met. The strategic plan is subject to consent, just like other policy decisions.

Based on the comments of the circles above and below, each circle in turn adjusts its written strategy and reformulates its work process.

After the adjustments in the circles are completed, each person revises their own strategy, including what they would like to achieve in their job, how to accomplish that, and how to allocate their own time and resources. Then a round of elections begins. Each circle elects or reaffirms current operational leaders. The circles reassign their members to new tasks that reflect the new aims. And they reaffirm or elect new representatives.

Everyone records the decisions made during this process in their personal logbooks. These logbooks also contain the organization's working documents: the budget, the strategic plan, etc. Everyone has direct access to all policy documents and any other records relating to their work. This transparency is essential if each person is to be expected to assume the responsibility of leadership and participate equivalently in decision-making.

The double-linked circle structure enables the strategic planning process to link long-term strategic planning directly to short-term tactical planning and day-to-day operations. Leaders are chosen in the context of the strategic plan and the defined aim. This places the focus of electing leaders on their ability to help achieve the aim.

CHAPTER NINE

Free & Self-Optimizing Organizations

One of the major contributions of sociocracy to the operation of effective and fair organizations is a structure that allows the organization to control its own future. It can't be bought, sold, disbanded, or merged without its permission. The importance of corporation self-ownership requires a look at the history of corporations—both profit and nonprofit—and how it has influenced the power of organizations in society.

When the United States gained freedom from the British in 1783, charters for corporations were granted by state governments for a limited number of years and for limited purposes. If corporations exceeded these purposes, states could withdraw their charters at any time and states were not required to, and did not automatically, renew them. Local governments decided whether a corporation was in the best interests of the community. In 1886 one event began a process that changed state's control over corporate behavior.

The event that laid the ground for the vast power that corporations have today came as a result of the case of *Santa Clara County v. Southern Pacific Railroad,* in which the county attempted to collect property taxes from a railroad at a special corporate rate. The summary written by a court reporter that preceded a decision on this unrelated issue stated that the justices were "of the opinion" that corporations were protected by the 14th Amendment to the Constitution, which forbids a state from denying any person equal protection under the law:

> All persons born or naturalized in the United States and subject to the jurisdiction thereof, are citizens of the United States and of the State wherein they reside. No State shall make or enforce any law which shall abridge the privileges or immunities of citizens of the United States; nor shall any State deprive any person of life, liberty, or property, without due process of law; nor deny to any person within its jurisdiction the equal protection of the laws.

That corporations were "persons under the law" was not the subject of the case and may only have been the opinion of Chief Justice Waite, but it became a legal precedent that stands today.

The court's application of the 14th Amendment has continued, in subsequent decisions, to further extend the power of corporations to conduct business and reduced government intervention or oversight. In 2010, in *Citizens United v. Federal Election Commission* (FEC), the Supreme Court held that the First Amendment prevented the government from restricting corporate political contributions. Subsequently, this right has been extended to nonprofit corporations, labor unions, and membership associations. In 2014, in *Burwell v. Hobby Lobby Stores*, the court ruled that a closely held corporation could refuse to implement a feature of the Affordable Care Act (2010) if the owners have objections based on religious beliefs.

Unfortunately, the ability and power of corporations to inflict damage and hide the effects of their actions is much greater than an individual person or even of a most cities.

Today, neither individuals nor local governments have the resources to conduct civil litigation against large and wealthy corporations, even though they are required to treat them as if they were people. Unfortunately, the ability and power of corporations to inflict damage and hide the effects of their actions is much greater than an individual person or even of most cities. This was clearly exposed in the lawsuits against the major tobacco companies that had intentionally withheld negative information and publicly denied the harmful effects of their highly profitable tobacco products. The Tobacco Master Settlement Agreement (MSA) in 1998 between the major tobacco companies and 46 states, however, could only prohibit their deceptive marketing practices and require payment of certain health costs caused by smoking. It did not prevent the sale of tobacco products. The ability to restrict even marketing practices is rare and takes years of litigation that is far beyond the means of an individual citizen.

SOCIAL RESPONSIBILITY

Eliminating corporations would end their domination, but would also eliminate many products and services that bring great benefit to us every day. By attracting the capital investments of many, they are able to develop and produce consumer goods in a quantity and cost that would not be possible for small local businesses. While corporations are identified as the most egregious violators of public trust and welfare governments, school systems, public interest associations, and charities have all shown similar unethical behavior.

We need a new structure to ensure that such large organizations will serve the best interests of society .

Sociocratic organizations behave in the best interests of society because they have a structure based on a set of principles and checks and balances that give power to everyone in the organization and all its stakeholders. The sociocratic structure is more effective in protecting society than laws and their enforcement because it engages self-interest at the source.

To understand how, we must first look at the concepts of profit and compensation.

PROFIT & MONEY AS MEASUREMENTS

Like *competition*, the word *profit* has assumed negative connotations for some and become an obsession for others. It has become so emotionally charged that one of its main properties is under-appreciated: its ability to convey information and measure the effectiveness of the organization and produce the ability to continue to grow and develop. In both for-profit businesses and nonprofit organizations, profit is the income left over after the employee salaries and costs have been met.

Profit is the amount available for growth and reinvestment in

In the new theories of evolution and order, information is a dynamic element, taking center stage. It is information that gives order, that prompts growth, that defines what is alive. It is both the underlying structure and the dynamic process that ensures life.

Margaret Wheatley

research, expansion of services, and the development of products and employees. The difference between for-profit and nonprofit organizations is that for-profits operate by providing products and services for which they earn money, and use part of their profits to pay interest to their investors. For-profits that are not incorporated pay profits to their owners. Nonprofit organizations operate for educational and charitable purposes that benefit the public, but do not distribute their profits to their members or to the foundations, donors, or government agencies that provide their income. All profits in a nonprofit go to developing the organization and increasing its ability to provide services to the public.

If businesses and organizations had no profit, they couldn't build savings to cover crises, invest in new equipment or facilities, conduct research, expand services, or raise salaries. Profit is the "value-added" that determines what an organization can do in the future.

DYSFUNCTIONAL COMMUNICATIONS

The most common problem organizational development consultants are asked to address is not the ability to produce profit, but what is characterized as "lack of communication"—the transfer of information. Either no information is being shared or it is shared so poorly that no information would be better or simply, that the necessary information doesn't exist. American management consultant Margaret Wheatley (1944–) addresses this in *Leadership and the New Science*:

Figure 9.1 Margaret Wheatley, American writer and organizational development consultant, has worked with a wide range of organizations from Boy Scout troops to top Army officers. Her focus is how a common human desire to find ways to live together more harmoniously, more humanely, so more people may benefit.

Why is there such an epidemic of "poor communications" within organizations? In every one I've worked in, employees have ranked it right at the top of major issues. Indeed its appearance on those lists became so predictable that I grew somewhat numb to it. Poor communications was a superficial diagnosis, I thought, that covered up other, more specific issues. I was wrong. What we were all suffering from, then and now, is a fundamental mis-perception of information: what it is, how it works, and what we might expect from it. The nub of the problem is that we've treated information as a "thing," as an inert entity to disseminate.

Things are stable; they have dimensions and volume. In the new theories of evolution and order, information is a dynamic element, taking center stage. It is information that gives order, that prompts growth, that defines what is alive. It is both the underlying structure and the dynamic process that ensures life. (Wheatley 1992)

Sharing information, moving it from one person to the next, from one department to another, between divisions of multi-national corporations, is very difficult. A good example of the effects of "lack of communications" is the Deepwater Horizon oil spill in the Gulf of Mexico in 2010. The worst environmental disaster the United States had ever experienced polluted hundreds of miles of shoreline in four states, killing vegetation and wildlife, and causing mutations in fish and animals that are still appearing.

Investigations have characterized the failure as the inability to communicate the seriousness of specific safety conditions on the oil rigs in the Gulf of Mexico with BP Global management a continent and several cultures away. In addition to cost-cutting practices, the U.S. government investigation faulted systemic communications deficiencies.

BP is headquartered in elegant St. James's Square in London, with its exclusive gentleman's clubs and terraced townhouses. A reporter for CBS News characterized the divide this way:

When money is the only measurement used, the information can be misleading. Profit is not just about money. Profit includes all measures of success.

> Some distances can't be bridged. St. James's Square in London is the heart of gentleman's clubland... Next door is the London Library founded by Carlyle. Thackeray was its first auditor and Dickens, George Eliot, Kipling, Shaw, Henry James, and T.S. Eliot among its members. It's a very long way from the sulphur-scented streets of Texas City or the storm-tossed waters of the Deepwater Horizon rig. But St. James's Square also houses the headquarters of BP. It is impossible to stand in St. James's Square and imagine the life of Gulf oil workers, impossible to appreciate their world view or life circumstances. Such distance forces the question: Are some companies too big to manage? Has our love of complexity in engineering and in management taken us beyond the limits of our ability? (Heffernan 2010)

What is the organization gaining from being in business—not just income but in ability to change the environment, to develop, to sustain itself.

The fourth-largest company in the world, BP has operations in more than 80 countries. In addition, they outsource production in many locations to national and local companies. Each of these locations and each of these companies has a different culture and many speak completely different languages. The investigation of the oil spill required sorting through a tangle of overlapping and contradictory contracts with many companies. While BP was legally responsible, the complexity of the contractual relationships added to the inability to communicate the risks involved. It also allowed each party to ignore any information about risk because another company or division could be held responsible.

As we discussed in Chapter Seven, "Steering & Structure," this complex structure was further doomed to failure because it didn't include feedback loops that required corrections. If the oil rig workers, who had repeatedly reported problems, had been included in the decision-making process, the Deepwater Horizon failure might never have happened. The workers could have insisted that the top levels of the organization listen to them.

In 2015, five years after the destructive failure of its oil rig, BP settled the suit brought by the Gulf Coast states and the United States federal government for $18.7 billion to compensate for damages. The organizational dysfunction was incredibly expensive for all concerned.

In our increasingly interdependent global economy, the ability to ignore essential communications will increase unless we adopt more-effective structures and practices. The structural inability at BP to ensure attention to feedback from workers in the field would have been prevented if it had been organized according to sociocratic principles.

COMMUNICATIONS, MEASUREMENT, FEEDBACK

For communications to be effective, information misinterpretation and distortion must be minimized. If a piece of information can be described as a number, it is least likely to be misinterpreted. Numerical measurements, properly defined and reported, are a highly accurate form of feedback and easily communicated. The primary measurement used by businesses and organizations is profit because it conveys the ability to change the environment, to develop, and to sustain itself.

In the circular process of leading-doing-measuring, profit is a measurement that gives feedback. It conveys information. As we have discussed, feedback in the form of measurement is necessary for steering. The accuracy, appropriateness, and timeliness of feedback determines the ability of the leading function to evaluate and direct operations effectively.

Measurement as information can give insight into:

◆ how well an organization is performing,
◆ how well individuals are able to perform,
◆ whether competitors are achieving better results,
◆ whether compensation adequately recognizes achievement, and
◆ the degree to which the organization is sustainable.

It can also give information about whether problems previously addressed still exist.

When money is the only measurement used, however, the information can be misleading. Profit is not just about money. Profit includes all measures of success. This is particularly clear in nonprofit organizations. If the organization's aim is the elimination of land mines, for example, money may be one measure, since money may be needed to support communications, staff, and volunteer coordination. But the organization would also need to pay attention to other measurements of profit, such as the number of governments that are allowing inspectors into their countries, the number of mine fields cleared, the number of new mine fields discovered, the number of countries that have agreed not to use land mines, etc.

An organization might show a very high monetary profit in terms of donations and grants from foundations, but if the other measures do not show growth, the organization would not be fulfilling its mission and it would not be sustainable, socially or financially. A nonprofit organization must be accomplishing its aim so donors will keep donating, legislatures will keep funding, and volunteers will keep volunteering. This non-monetary measurement of profit is more difficult

> An organization that measures itself only with monetary data from business operations, such as buying, selling, market position, production method, etc., is not fully measuring its relationship with society. Measuring a corporation's success by the price of its stock is equally short-sighted.

to define and quantify, but to create and manage a dynamic organization, measuring it is essential.

Improperly defined measurements, however, can make an organization dysfunctional. For example, Deming found that one of his clients, the Veteran's Administration (VA) hospitals, was defining and measuring success in terms of "patient bed days" delivered. This encouraged hospitals to avoid releasing a patient until another patient was available to fill the bed. VA hospitals, thus, had a terrible reputation because their hospital stays were much longer than in other hospitals.

Deming convinced the VA to change the measure of success to the number of "patients made healthy." "Healthy" was then defined as a patient who did not return to the hospital for at least 30 days after discharge. As a result, the behavior of the staff changed and the reputation of the hospitals improved. The interaction between the hospital and the patients was then focused appropriately on the aim of producing healthy veterans.

A business that measures itself only with monetary data from business operations, such as buying, selling, market position, production method, etc., is not fully measuring its relationship with society. Measuring success by the price of its stock is equally short-sighted. True, a business makes a contribution to society in the form of taxes, but it also has a number of non-monetary effects that ultimately affect its overall profitability. These include its effect on environmental resources, the welfare of employees, and conditions in nearby neighborhoods. Some accountants may attempt to place a monetary value on these factors, calling them "goodwill," but in most respects, there is no attempt to fully measure the social impact of an organization on a community, certainly not the negative ones.

For both corporations and nonprofit organizations, the failure to measure non-monetary profits (and losses) is as self-defeating as failure to measure monetary profits (and losses). It undercuts the trust and respect needed to retain customers.

Improperly defined measurements, however, can make an organization dysfunctional.

EXCHANGE PROCESSES

An organization makes "exchanges" with society. It gives products or services in exchange for receiving money or acknowledgment. The effect of these exchanges on environmental resources, employees, and nearby neighborhoods can be a positive or negative.

We all make these exchanges. We exchange money for shoes rather than making them ourselves. House cleaners and doctors exchange services for money. We exchange our own goods or services with others for money, or we trade without using money. This is called the "exchange process."

Definition of "Aim"

An aim is a product or service, differentiated from other aims, and defined from the point of view of the client.

Figure 9.2 Definition of "Aim." The aim is central to the formation of an organization.

Goods and services are the "basis for the exchange." We determine what we want and how much we will exchange for it. In business, what we create or give is our aim. Whether it is chocolates or window cleaning, it is what a customer purchases. In a nonprofit organization, the person who pays and the person who receives the service are often not the same person. A foundation or an agency may supply the money because they like your aim, while a person needing a service receives it. This often places nonprofit organizations in an awkward exchange situation in which what people will pay for may not be what other people need. In both businesses and nonprofits, establishing and maintaining an ongoing exchange process is the measure of success. If a negative exchange is not corrected, the organization will go out of business.

An aim is what establishes the basis for an exchange. It creates a connection between supply and demand. A company and a customer. A service and a client. A good exchange is one that is beneficial to all participants. If my aim is to make shoes and your aim is to make shirts, we can exchange shirts and shoes. We have both profited because we are both better off than we were before the exchange. My shirts and your shoes were successful aims.

"Nonprofit" organizations are misnamed because they would not

Self-optimization requires continual measuring, using the circular process of leading-doing-measuring. It is a continuous and active search for a better way of reaching an aim.

exist unless they obtained more money than they spent. It is more accurate to say that they are "indirect client" organizations because their source of income is different from the one they serve. A shelter for the homeless serves the homeless, but its income is from the agency or foundation that funds it. A bakery is a "direct client" business because it sells bread directly to the same person who pays for it: its source of profit.

In the need to balance the exchange process, there is no difference between for-profit and nonprofit organizations. Each type of organization should be measuring its exchanges and its profit from those exchanges. Without this information, good steering is impossible.

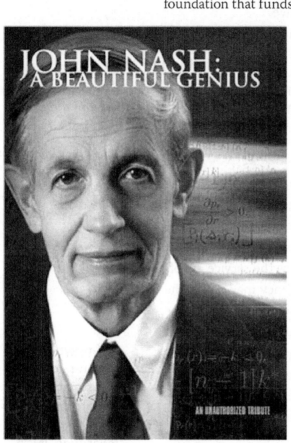

SELF-OPTIMIZATION

Why do we work? Is it our desire to satisfy our physical needs or perhaps a fear of scarcity? The work of American mathematician and Nobel Prize winner John Forbes Nash (1928-2015), the subject of the film, *A Beautiful Mind*, (2001) assumes there is basic "economic motive" in the fact of our being alive, one that is a greater sense of economy than money. It is a natural drive toward optimization or improvement of our resources. The drive to optimize might center on one's skill in body painting, the number of people one can make laugh, or the number of songs one can sing. Based on Nash's work, sociocracy is designed to create organizations that function with continuous self-optimization.

Figure 9.3 John Nash on the DVD cover on the documentary about Nobel Prize-winning American mathematician John Forbes Nash, John Forbes Nash: A Beautiful Genius, *published in 2002 by Trinity Home Entertainment.*

All exchange processes are self-optimizing, regardless of whether they are purposely constructed or naturally occurring. If they cease to be self-optimizing, it is because their aim has changed or is gone. Self-optimization requires continual measuring using the circular process of leading-doing-measuring. It is a continuous and active search for a better way of reaching an aim. A shortage of resources required for production, for example, need not result in a mindset of scarcity and an unthinking reduction in productivity.

Lack of organization is essentially the same thought that John Stuart Mill (1803-1876) expressed when he observed that society's problems of scarcity were not due to lack of wealth but to inadequate distribution of resources.

TRANSPARENCY

Because all levels of the sociocratic organization participation in decision-making, access to the information used for measurement is vital to everyone in the organization. If everyone is participating in leadership activities and policy decision-making, they need full information to make good decisions in their domains of responsibility. Sociocratic financial reporting systems are available to all members, including both the figures for the company as a whole and the team and individual contributions. Some information, including proprietary formulas and competitive information, is protected but can be available if it is relevant to a team's decisions. Over time, the fear that data will be manipulated and used against workers diminishes in sociocratic organizations for several reasons: the safety guaranteed by consent decision-making, the guaranteed base wage, and the transparency of operations.

In an autocratically structured company, only the owners or shareholders, and sometimes the top management (in the form of bonuses), "experience the measurement" of profits. In a sociocratically structured organization, all participants share in profits or losses through a unique compensation structure.

> Because the compensation structure ensures that all participants in a sociocratic organization share in profits or losses, the distrust and competition between employer and employee, senior or junior, no longer has a reason to exist. Everyone, in the same boat.

COMPENSATION AS MEASUREMENT

As we discussed earlier, in addition to money, profit may be reported in any terms that are relevant to the organization: the number of refugees resettled, reading levels increased, consumer complaints reduced, monetary surplus, etc. For purposes of the following discussion about the distribution of profit, however, we will focus on money since that is the most easily exchanged form of profit.

In most organizations, there are two kinds of participants:

- day-to-day, labor-providing participants and
- shareholders, or for nonprofits, donors or sponsors.

Both categories are equally important to the existence and success of the organization. In sociocratic organizations, both labor and share-holders are guaranteed compensation in the form of a Guaranteed Base Wage (GBW). For labor, this guaranteed payment is based on the market value of each person's functions and tasks, and on the ability of the organization to sustain these payments. The GBW is not related to profit distribution. In the literal Dutch translation, it is an "existence possibility guarantee." The equivalent for investors or donors, their GBW, is a guaranteed basic return on investment. For donors or sponsors, this guaranteed basic return might be delivery of a basic level of service to target populations.

In addition to the GBW, each participant in the organization, whether wage earner or investor, receives variable or "measuring" payments that bring the circular process of leading-doing-measuring into the wage/share structure. The specific structure of measurement payments, which are based on the wage/share ratios, is recorded in the bylaws of the organization. Everyone has access to reports on the organization's profits and losses and the variable payments made.

If variable payments are made too infrequently, participants might not get enough feedback. Annual payments in December might not give good information about efforts made early in February, nor distinguish between the efforts made in February and those made in August. Measurements have to be received in a more direct and timely manner to be reliably used for accurate measurement. Therefore, sociocracy uses a two-part variable payment measurement: a Long-Term Measurement (LTM) and a Short-Term Measurement (STM).

Depending on the industry or services provided, the STM may cover the duration of a single project or, in the case of a longer-term project, after a particular milestone. The amount paid is the difference between the originally estimated profits and the actual result. If the result is lower than projected, there is no STM payment, and furthermore, the shortfall must be recovered before more STM or LTM payments can be made. (See Chapter 13, "Money as Measurement," for more information.)

This variable payment system is not the same as piecework, where people are paid for each piece of work completed. They are different in two ways. Firstly, the GBW is paid without reference to the STM and LTM payments, and second, this compensation system applies, without exception, to everyone, from shareholders to board members to mail room employees. It is a steering device only.

Figure 9.4 We Are All in the Same Boat. In a sociocratic organization, everyone is in the same boat in terms of compensation based on profits and losses, the rewards and risks.

Because the compensation structure ensures that all participants in a sociocratic organization share in profits or losses, they share a deep common interest. Everyone benefits, or suffers, when profit falls. This also means that their responsibilities are more consciously experienced in relation to each other, and the distrust and competition between employer and employee, senior or junior, no longer has a reason to exist. Everyone is in the same boat.

INVESTORS & INVESTMENT CAPITAL

But if everyone shares in the profits of the organization, how do businesses attract investors? How do they finance start-up and expansion?

In principle, the various choices for attracting investors who will provide capital for growth and development remain the same in a sociocratic organization as in a traditional autocratic organization. A sociocratic organization can attract the capital it needs in the traditional way: loans, credit, mortgages, bonds, shares, and all other possibilities. Providers of capital participate through their representatives in the top circle and receive the equivalent of the GBW.

In autocratic organizations, for-profit or not-for-profit, the board of directors is the governing body and it approves policies. The shareholders, sponsors, or donors influence policy through the board of directors, but neither the staff nor other members of the organization have an established means of influence.

In a sociocratic organization, where all members of the organization participate in setting policy, the top circle includes representatives elected by other parts of the organization and its decisions are subject to consent. While the top circle includes the functions of the traditional board of directors, like long-range planning, it does not have autocratic control over the organization. In addition, because the organization's plans and finances are transparent, available for review by all members of the organization, the activities of the top circle are open in a way that most board decisions and actions are not.

Later, we will discuss ways to maintain transparency within the

COMPENSATION RIGHTS OF STAKEHOLDERS COMPARED

	Fixed Compensation	Variable Compensation	Compensation Policy Decisions
In Autocratic Corporations:			
Capital Providing	–	x	x
Labor Providing	x	–	–
In Sociocratic Corporations:			
Capital Providing	x	x	x
Labor Providing	x	x	x

Figure 9.5 Compensation Rights of Stakeholders Compared. The rights of stakeholders in an autocratic corporation vary according to whether a stakeholder is providing capital or labor. In a sociocratic organization, all stakeholders have equivalent access to both compensation and policy decisions about compensation.

company without leaking key information to competitors.

PLANNED PROFIT DISTRIBUTION

Another distinction between an autocratically structured and a sociocratically structured company is that in an autocratically structured company, the shareholders determine *in retrospect* how the profit is going to be shared. It may be distributed to shareholders as dividends, reinvested in one or another aspects of the organization, paid to the CEO as a bonus, put in reserves, etc. In a sociocratic organization, circles establish the distribution of profits (or losses) *in advance* so everyone knows what to expect and the distributions are more likely to be made on the basis of solid planning, rather than the whims or political pressure exerted by one group or the other.

A sociocratic organization is not an employee-owned company. Most employee-owned companies are autocratically structured. All or most of the employees are shareholders and share profits as shareholders, but they most often do not share in policy-making. A board of directors will make decisions, just as they do in non-employee-owned companies. Employees, even as shareholders, in an autocratic company do not participate in policy decisions, make the day-to-day operational decisions, determine the best way to complete their assigned tasks, or participate in an incentive plan. The only source of their control is ownership. They have no voice in how the company is run except indirectly, as owners, by voting for members of the board.

Further, because control of an employee-owned company rests with a majority of the shares, employee-owned companies are limited in their ability to attract investor capital. Sociocratic companies, however, can freely raise capital through the sale of stock without losing control of the organization, because they are controlled by all the participants—shareholders, labor, management, volunteers, etc. The double-linking of circles provides the protection of consent to all members of the organization. Figure 9.2 illustrates the compensation structure for capital and labor providing participants in both autocratic and sociocratic companies.

NO OWNERS, NO SLAVES

Traditionally, those who provide the capital own the organization and control it by virtue of that ownership. Capital may come from shareholders, a foundation that provides funding, or an individual owner. The employees as shareholders may own it. But whoever provides the funds owns the company and can sell, close, or trade it. In other words, they can do whatever they wish with the organization.

Even though people's lives and welfare are involved, owners tend to view the company as an object like a building or a horse. A fully sociocratic corporation, however, owns itself, like any free citizen. The corporation is not a possession. It arises from the people who create and re-create it each day.

The participants in the organization can agree to form alliances or to merge with other organizations, but the organization cannot be "taken over" or sold against its will. The participants as a group, including the shareholders, are the organization and no part can sell them or the organization without the consent of the other parts. As a free corporation, no longer an object, a sociocratic organization is liberated to operate like a fully living system. As with a person, emancipation has a strong beneficial impact on an organization's vitality and profitability. As a free entity, it is in the organization's best interests to foster a compatible, sustainable environment—to operate in the best interests of society.

A fully sociocratic corporation owns itself, like any free citizen. The corporation is not a possession. It arises from the people who create and re-create it each day.

PART III

Organizing Our Strengths

In 1876, in response to his observations of great disorder in debate in democratic organizations, General Henry M. Robert (1837–1923), an expert on parliamentary procedure, wrote *A Pocket Manual of Rules of Order for Deliberative Assemblies*. Now known as Robert's Rules of Order, it has become the standard reference for applying parliamentary procedure in the United States. Robert's aim was to ensure fair debate, but his work was based on the assumption that majority rule was the best decision-making method possible. Compared to autocratic decision-making, perhaps it was, but with sociocratic governance, there is an even better method available. In Part III, "Organizing Our Strengths," we will explain the "rules of order" of sociocratic organizations.

Before we go too far with that analogy, however, we must say that Endenburg didn't set out to create Endenburg's Rules of Order, nor are the principles "rules" in the same sense as Robert's rules. Sociocratic principles and practices take what is known to be true in the physical and natural sciences and apply it in the social sciences of governance and management. The principles and practices are not a set of arbitrary rules.

Robert's rules also have nothing to say about organizational structure, effectiveness, or work process. They are limited to regulating and recording debate and the functions of officers. They establish an order of debate; for example, points of information should be addressed before debate continues. They do not address leadership, measurement, feedback, or any other processes necessary to for organizations to govern themselves.

Robert's rules are valuable in large bodies, where they bring

Endenburg didn't set out to create Endenburg's Rules of Order, nor are the principles "rules" in the same sense as Robert's rules.

discipline to debate and voting, but they can be overwhelming as well. The process of following them can divert attention from the basic argument. In parliamentary law, the good decision is expected to emerge from following the proper order of debate, and the proper conduct of voting and the recording of votes. The only judge of quality is majority vote.

Sociocratic debate, in contrast, focuses on the reasoning—the argument, not the majority opinion. Arguments are stated in the context of the aim: the purpose of the organization, the department, the circle, or the specific decision. The fundamental questions are: Does this address our aim? Is this a measurable way to move toward it? Will everyone be able to work effectively?

To ensure that all members of the organization understand the aim, roles and responsibilities are defined in relationship to the aim. This is one factor that makes sociocratic organizations more satisfying for their members and more powerful in doing their work.

... sociocratic debate focuses on the reasoning, the argument, not the majority opinion.

THE HOW TO

This section provides practical advice on how to apply sociocratic concepts, and the principles and practices±, to maximize the strengths your organizations. We encourage you to read this section even if you do not have immediate plans to implement any of the principles or practices. Concepts are often clearer when explaining implementation. If you are already a member of a sociocratically governed organization, these explanations can serve as reinforcement and as a reference—a quick way to look up definitions and processes.

This information is not a substitute for the advice of a professional sociocratic consultant, who can address specific situations, but it is a foundation for understanding which professional you may need and what the professional may be advising.

Sociocratic methods will continue to develop, just as the scientific understandings from which they are derived develop. The only aim is to establish and protect the equivalence of each person and enhance their ability to live and work in harmony and prosperity. In this sense, sociocracy is often referred to as an "empty" method. It has no other political agenda.

Chapter 10, "Circles," outlines the process for implementation and structuring your organization. Chapter 11, "Consent & Rounds," outlines the process of conducting circle meetings and explains how making space for each person to speak maintains equivalence and ensures that each person can raise objections when necessary. Chapter 12, "Electing People," discusses in detail how to elect people in open discussion by consent. This decision-making process is unique to the sociocratic circle-method and essential to maintaining consent in all aspects of circle functioning. Chapter 13, "Organizing Work," outlines the process of defining an aim and the execution of the work process. Chapter 14, "Money as Measurement," explains how the short- and long-term incentive payments are calculated.

These methods are simple, but their careful application is important. In the Appendices, these methods are outlined in "Guides" for study and for use in meetings.

In our experience, implementation is easier when circles and individuals have contact with others who are learning and applying the method. In the "Afterword," we explain how to network with others who are implementing sociocracy in their businesses and organizations.

CHAPTER TEN

Circles & Implementation

Policy decisions form the foundation of governance. A policy is a decision that determines how an individual, a circle, or an organization will function in the future. Policies say who may *be* or is responsible for doing what when. They can say yes or no, or yes and no. Policy determines how operations are conducted.

In sociocracy, policies are circle decisions about future operations made within the policies of the larger organization, and with the consent of all circle members.

Implementation of sociocratic governance in either a forming or existing organization begins with:

- ❖ training in the principles and practices with the aid of a certified sociocratic consultant,
- ❖ forming an implementation circle, and
- ❖ designing the circle structure that will assume responsibility for governance.

The implementation circle members are typically a cross-section of the organization, including the:

- ❖ top managers or officers in the current structure,
- ❖ representatives from the major departments or units,
- ❖ staff members, and
- ❖ if appropriate, volunteers.

In a forming organization, the initial core members might be the members of the implementation circle.

Using the circular process of leading-doing-measuring, the implementation circle makes a plan, tries a small step, measures the results, then evaluates and adjusts the plan, repeating as necessary. While

… the implementation circle makes a plan, tries a small step, measures the results, then evaluates and adjusts the plan, repeating as necessary.

changes in operations may occur in this process, these are normally improvements of producing organization and detailing the work process reveals to be advisable, rather than changes required to accommodate the new structure. For example:

◆ In a Dutch police organization, the implementation circle drastically reduced the number of reporting levels, because its members could see that they were unnecessary and the new structure provided a better alternative.

◆ In the United States, implementation in a rapidly growing nonprofit organization with many local chapters and a very flat operations structure led to the creation of a regional structure, establishing a step in the hierarchy that did not previously exist.

In other cases, the circle structure simply reflects the existing operations structure.

Once in place, the circle structure, which sets policy guides development in the operations structure. The implementation circle may continue to work with the general circle , while merge its functions into the organization as appropriate.

While some are able to implement sociocracy after reading this book, the support of a certified sociocracy consultant can be very helpful because sociocracy introduces a number of subtle changes in our familiar patterns of behavior.

IMPLEMENTATION CIRCLE

While some are able to implement sociocracy after reading this book, the support of a certified sociocracy consultant can be very helpful because complex organizations require expertise in organizational design in order to change smoothly. Sociocracy also introduces a number of subtle changes in familiar patterns of behavior that a consultant is experienced in recognizing and correcting.

It is important that the whole implementation circle receive training, not just the leaders of the circle. From the beginning, the implementation circle should function sociocratically, using the principle of consent, thus gaining important experience that later can be shared with the rest of the organization.

The first steps of the implementation circle and of each circle as it forms are:

◆ electing circle members to roles and responsibilities,

◆ establishing logbooks,

◆ designing the work process in each area of its responsibility, and

◆ planning for the ongoing education and development of its members.

The implementation circle establishes the infrastructure for maintaining the governance structure, which include:

◆ logbook systems for record-keeping,

◆ policies on distributing minutes,

◆ regular meeting schedules,

◆ training for current members of the organization, and

◆ orientation and training of new people who join the organization.

The implementation circle should plan the order of activation of the circles. If the top circle (including the board of directors) has not been activated, it should be activated as soon as possible. Sometimes the top circle is activated before the implementation circle, meaning it has already begun to operate sociocratically and has elected the implementation circle. In other cases, the implementation circle begins functioning first. This order depends on the size, complexity, and preferences of the organization.

Once the general circle is established and fully functioning, the implementation circle becomes a helping circle reporting to the general circle. Some members of the implementation circle may continue as internal trainers for the organization. In some organizations, a current member or employee will become a certified consultant and assume responsibility for ongoing training.

TOP CIRCLE

In many kinds of organizations, a governing body specifically called "board of directors" is required by law or may already exist with that name. Boards of directors, however, are usually vested with powers by stakeholders that exceed those of a top circle. Boards typically control the organization autocratically, including veto power over financial decisions and the right to sell or merge the organization.

The top circle, in contrast, does not hold this power, although it is

In many kinds of organizations, a governing body specifically called "board of directors" is required by law or may already exist with that name. Boards of directors, however, are usually vested with powers by stakeholders that exceed those of a top circle.

responsible for the other duties of a board of directors. Understanding this distinction, however, many organization prefer to prefer to call their top circle the board of directors or, to satisfy legal requirements, define it as identical to the top circle.

The top circle includes:

◆ a chief executive officer (CEO) or general manager who is hired by the top circle and may also be elected chair of the top circle

◆ other executives of the organization, such as the chief financial officer (CFO), executive vice president, or executive secretary, as determined by the top circle

◆ representative of the shareholders or investors, if there are any

◆ representative(s) of the General Management Circle

◆ representatives of other stakeholders, such as members of the community

◆ external experts, who generally include financial, legal, and areas related to the organization's aim

While important and essential, only 5-10% of a top circle's time involves financial and fiduciary responsibilities.

After implementation, the top circle should conduct regular assessments of the new governance method and eventually amend the documents that created the organization—the bylaws or constitution—to establish consent as the basis of decision-making, circle meetings as the context for policy decisions, double-linking between circles, and the election of people to roles and responsibilities. (See Appendix E and F for examples of how these clauses might be worded.)

The duties of the top circle go beyond legal and financial oversight. According to Board Source, an organization that provides governance resources, training, and consulting for education and nonprofit boards, the top circle members should spend 65% of their time on connections to other organizations, educating themselves about new trends and developments, studying competitive forces, etc., and 30% on strategic planning.

In other words, the primary responsibility of the top circle, like the traditional role of boards, is outward-focused: building networks, bringing in ideas, making professional connections to benefit the business or organization, and planning for the future. However, while important and essential in sociocracy as well, only 5–10% of a top circle's time involves financial and fiduciary responsibilities.

The role of the top circle is, thus, focused on generativity, the creative challenging and broadening of businesses, organizations, associations, and networks. While generativity is also included in the ongoing development of each circle within its domain of responsibility, the board is responsible for the direction of the organization as a whole in relation to its environment.

The top circle elects the outside members of the top circle and the operations leader—a CEO or general manager, who manages the day-to-day operations.

GENERAL MANAGEMENT CIRCLE

The general management or coordinating circle is composed of the operations leaders and representatives of all the department circles, and is responsible for ensuring that operations are implementing the strategic plan of the top circle. Through the CEO and its representative(s) to the top circle, it participates in the planning process and ensures that it meets the needs and capabilities of the department circles. This circle is responsible for strategic planning for the operations covering the next few years, making policies that apply to all departments, and deciding issues that department circles have not been able to resolve.

The general management circle also determines when a new departmental circle is necessary. It establishes the new circle by:

- ◆ defining the aim,
- ◆ defining the domain of responsibility,
- ◆ electing the operations leader,
- ◆ establishing a budget, and
- ◆ allocating resources.

The top circle, based on feedback from all circles, determines the organization's budget. The general management circle then determines the organization's operations budget and allocates resources for each operations department.

It is generally new to departments to have a governance structure, and members at this level may be less familiar with making policy decisions.

During implementation, the management structure will be evaluated to determine whether there is a governance body that serves these functions and meets these requirements. If not, one should be formed and also receive training.

DEPARTMENT CIRCLES

When implementing sociocracy in an existing organization, departments are usually already established. The implementation circle and the general management circle will review the department structure, aims and domains of responsibility, and budget allocations to determine, if they are all optimum. They may be reorganized, but this is not the goal of implementing sociocracy. The implementation sometimes reveals a better organization structure, however, and it may be instituted now or later.

It is generally new to departments to have a governance structure, and members at this level may be less familiar with making policy decisions. Thus, departments may need more training in governance on an ongoing basis than the top circle or the coordinating circles. This is often neglected, because the norm is to train managers and expect it to "trickle down." This is not always the case. If all circle members are expected to participate as equals, they will benefit more from equivalent training.

The departmental circles will elect a representative to serve on the general management circle with the operations leader, who has been elected by the general management circle. In all circle meetings, the participants function as equals, so the representative is not subordinate to the operations leader. When the general management circle elects the operations leader of a department circle, the representative of the department circle is present and their consent to the election result is necessary. In this way, department circles consent to the election of their operations leaders.

Because department-level circles are involved in setting policy to guide daily operations rather than longer-term planning, they meet more frequently than the general management circle or the board.

When the general management circle elects the operations leader of a department circle, the representative of the department circle will be present and their consent to the election result is necessary.

policy to operations not distinct here

During implementation, with few or no policies established, they will meet much more frequently. Once established, circles meet as necessary but at least every six to eight weeks to review policies and make new ones, if necessary.

Decisions made by circles include defining roles and responsibilities of its members, including the operations manager, allocation of resources, election of officers and people to roles, and the work process.

Department circles decide whether they require unit circles. If they do, they follow the same process that the general circle follows in establishing a department circle.

FORM THE FOUNDATION OF GOVERNANCE.

There are four officers in each circle, each one elected by consent for a specific term:

- operations leader,
- circle meeting facilitator,
- secretary and logbook keeper, and
- representative(s) to the next circle.

Subject to policies set by the circle and the organization, operations leaders have authority over daily operations decisions and any task assignments not covered in role and responsibility descriptions. They may call operations meetings as needed and normally conduct the business of those meetings in the traditional autocratic manner. Circles may elect the operations leader to serve as the circle meeting facilitator or secretary and logbook keeper, but *not* to serve as a representative.

The circle meeting facilitator is responsible for leading circle meetings and is elected by the circle. The facilitator should be someone who is adept at steering discussions, moving decisions forward, and keeping everyone focused on the aim of the meeting, the aim of the circle, and the aim of the proposal or other matters being discussed.

The circle also elects a person to serve as secretary and logbook keeper. These roles may be separated or combined, depending on the size of the circle and the complexity of the circle's work. The secretary

Representatives are not mere vote carriers or delegates who function at the direction of the circle. They participate fully, with consent, in both circles, using their best judgment in making decisions.

is responsible for receiving agenda items, collaborating with the facilitator to prepare the agenda, sending out the agenda and meeting reminders, confirming attendance of key people or invited guests, preparing the meeting room, taking minutes of the meeting, and distributing the minutes and related documents.

The logbook keeper is responsible for maintaining the documents related to the work of the circle and distributing copies to circle members as appropriate, as explained later in this chapter.

REPRESENTATIVES

In addition to electing the circle meeting facilitator and secretary/logbook keeper, the circle elects one or more representatives to participate in the next-higher circle. The representative may be the same person elected to be circle facilitator or secretary/logbook keeper, but cannot be the person serving as the operations leader. As discussed in Chapter 7, "Steering & Structure," the representative carries information and power "up" the organization while the operations leader carries it "down." Like electricity, power can only go in one direction in one channel at a time. Since the double-link forms a feedback loop between two circles, it is essential that each be capable of carrying distinct information.

Representatives are not mere vote carriers or delegates who functions at the direction of the circle. They participate fully, with consent, in both circles, using their best judgment in making decisions. A representative must be able to:

- ❖ understand and communicate the lower circle's interests,
- ❖ participate in decisions at a higher level of abstraction,
- ❖ explain issues and decisions to their circle members so the members understand them,
- ❖ develop a larger perspective, and
- ❖ do longer-term planning.

By "ability," we also mean an interest. Not everyone who can fulfill the role of a representative is interested in doing so.

A circle may have more than one representative, based on the

Holding the opening round before any other activity establishes the tone of the meeting as "we the people," allowing everyone to attune to each other and to the aim of the meeting.

complexity and needs of the circle. It may also elect additional representative(s) to temporarily represent the circle in a specific decision, as in the case of the story of the worker who was elected to participate in the top circle to be able to present his idea for reassigning the shipyard workers as salespeople to solicit new business, rather than being laid off. (For the full discussion, see Chapter 4, "Cybernetics & the Principles of Sociocracy.")

CIRCLE MEETINGS

Circle meetings are usually busy, even exciting, events, since they make or delegate all the policy decisions that guide the day-to-day operations of the circle. The whole person, not limited to their role in the organization, is invited to share ideas, knowledge, and feelings with all members of the circle. The topics a circle might address in any given meeting include:

- ◆ vision, mission, and aim;
- ◆ policy and strategy plan;
- ◆ progress of the circle toward its aim;
- ◆ design of work processes;
- ◆ the circle's organizational or operations design and procedures that flow from it;
- ◆ role and responsibility descriptions of circle members;
- ◆ allocation of roles and responsibilities;
- ◆ addition or removal of someone from the circle;
- ◆ the circle's development process—plans for training, teaching, and researching—and
- ◆ personal discomfort with some aspect of ongoing operations.

As discussed in Chapter 6, "Developing Quality," a circle is a group of people with a common aim who make decisions together within an agreed upon framework. It is semi-autonomous and self-organizing. It determines its own policies and decides how it will complete its work within the limits of its aim and budget. Thus, the structure of circle meetings differs from that of operations meetings.

In a circle meeting, all members participate as peers. Sociocratic organizations continue to need operations meetings to guide day-to-day work, but they are typically shorter and more efficient because they focus on the "dials of the dashboard of daily operations" and the work process designed by the circle includes clear delegation and effective follow-up.

In Chapter 13, "Organizing Work," we present a detailed discussion of the process of "producing organization."

As described above, the secretary is responsible for meeting logistics. Several days before the meeting, the secretary confers with the facilitator and the operations leader and publishes the agenda and supporting documents to all circle members.

A circle meeting follows a predictable pattern:

1. opening round,
2. administrative concerns,
3. content, and
4. closing round.

Doing an opening round before any other activity establishes the tone of the meeting as "we the people," allowing everyone to attune to each other and to the aim of the meeting. One experienced consultant will do several rounds before attempting to have the group make a decision. "To make a group decision, you have to have a group." Rounds focus everyone on their joint task.

Administrative concerns follow the opening round. They include any information that needs to be communicated to support the meeting.

- ◆ Introduce guests, if necessary.
- ◆ Make announcements.
- ◆ Address logistics (Is the temperature of the room okay? Does anyone need a copy of the handout?)
- ◆ Solicit objections to the minutes of the previous meeting and then adjust minutes, if necessary.
- ◆ Consent to the agenda of the meeting.

The opening round and administrative details are the preparation for the meeting and should end with consent to the agenda for the

... a circle is a group of people with a common aim who make decisions together within an agreed-upon framework. It is semi-autonomous and self-organizing. It determines its own policies and decides how it will complete its work within the limits of its aim and budget.

following content of the meeting. This agenda is the contract that members make for the work that will be done in the meeting.

The content section usually has three kinds of agenda items:

◆ informational reports,
◆ policy proposals, and
◆ discussion of issues that may lead to proposals.

If an agenda item is simply an informational matter, such as a financial report, the policy decision is whether to accept the report. If it is a policy proposal, the decision will be whether to accept the proposal. The task may be to hold an elect for a role or responsibility.

Sometimes issues are explored and proposals are developed in the meeting. All these decisions require the consent of all circle members, making decisions as peers. A circle meeting will normally conduct its business in a combination of rounds, discussion, and dialogue. Rounds are very important in sociocracy because they establish equivalence between members and give each person not only an opportunity, but an invitation, to express objections. (See Chapter 11, "Consent & Rounds".)

The closing round is the measuring part of the meeting. Comments might address the questions:

◆ Did the meeting go well?
◆ What could have been improved?
◆ What was the quality of the discussion?
◆ Was the agenda completed?
◆ Should any items be revisited in the next meeting?
◆ How well was time managed?
◆ How are the members feeling?
◆ What will members need to do before the next meeting?
◆ What training or information do we need?
◆ What are members taking away from the meeting?

While these are recommended practices, the preparation and conduct of circle meetings is widely varied. Some do no preparation before a meeting, for example, and collect agenda items after the opening round. The topics may also vary widely with one meeting covering

The circle should develop its own process of ensuring that circle members have prompt access to the minutes and a chance to express any objections.

many items and another may be focused entirely on the work process and certain roles and responsibilities.

Circle meetings may also include several departmental circles or even all the circles in a full-circle meetings. Full-circle meetings might focus on very different topics and use a variety of approaches, for example:

◆ Open Space Technology (OST), which begins with identifying and clarifying issues and has been used with groups as large as more than 2,000 people;

◆ SWOT analysis or matrix for evaluating strengths, weaknesses, opportunities, and threats;

◆ Appreciative Inquiry for analysis, decision-making, and creating strategic change;

◆ Brainstorming—gathering a list of ideas spontaneously contributed by members;

◆ Kepner-Tregoe Matrix to help evaluate and mitigate the risks of decisions.

There are many others. The choice depends on the desired outcome and the nature of the organization.

THE LOGBOOK & CIRCLE MEETING MINUTES

Each circle is responsible for its own memory system, namely the logbook, which contains minutes of meetings, policy decisions, strategic plans, work process documents, etc. The administrative secretary/logbook keeper is responsible for keeping the circle's logbooks up to date. The logbook typically includes:

◆ the organization's and the circle's vision, mission, and aim statements;

◆ the organization's bylaws;

◆ the organization's strategic plan;

◆ a diagram of the organization's circle structure;

◆ the circle's policies and practices;

◆ all circle meeting records;

◆ roles and responsibilities of circle members;

Rounds are very important in sociocracy because they establish equivalence between members and give each person not only an opportunity, but an invitation, to express objections.

◆ diagrams of the circle's work process—the leading, doing, and measuring activities of the circle; and

◆ circle development plans.

Minutes of meetings should include:

◆ name of the circle,

◆ date and time of the meeting,

◆ attendees,

◆ text of decisions, and

◆ any actionable closing round comments.

Minutes should contain no more than is necessary to understand the context of decisions. Taking detailed notes prevents the secretary from participating in the meeting and can lead to spending more time on the details than is productive.

On complex and difficult decisions, a summary of the reasoning or assumptions made in reaching the decision may be requested so the rationale for the decision is clear. If the circle holds an information discussion for proposal-forming and consents to a resulting list of issues, this list of items may be included in the minutes. The minutes should record delegation of tasks, such as the writing of a proposal.

Otherwise, only a record of decisions is required, including a record of any assignment of roles or responsibilities and action items.

Recording action items from the closing round, such as "The room was too hot" or "We needed the documents earlier" may also be helpful reminders.

The circle should develop its own process of ensuring that circle members have prompt access to the minutes and a chance to express any objections. This includes members who may have been unable to attend the circle meeting. The point of objections is to ensure that everyone can work effectively if a policy is adopted and has been able to contribute information that would improve the proposal. That a person missed the meeting is not a strong argument for excluding this information, since providing it is in the best interests of the circle.

CHAPTER ELEVEN

Consent & Rounds

There are many well-known skills and techniques for facilitating successful meetings, from flip charts to eye contact, and guidelines for organization secretaries on taking notes and keeping records. Many of these are equally useful for circle meetings; we have not repeated them. We will only discuss the particular rhythm of the sociocratic circle meeting, and the use of rounds to establish and maintain equivalence in making consent decisions.

ROUNDS

The more common types of rounds are opening and closing rounds, reaction rounds, and consent rounds. Facilitators use rounds in circle meetings for many purposes, but their essential function is to create and maintain equivalence. In a round, each person in the meeting is given an equivalent opportunity to speak.

The facilitator should begin the round by asking a person to speak first. Each person will continue (or pass), moving clockwise or counterclockwise around the circle. The facilitator should sometimes choose a person across the circle and sometimes someone to the right or left. This allows the facilitator to speak in the middle of the round, instead of first or last, and a different person to start each round.

If the circle members are not sitting in a circle or around a conference table and there is confusion over who should speak next, the facilitator can indicate the next person with a nod. If the circle meeting is conducted by telephone or by video conferencing, it is helpful for the facilitator to assign circle positions to the participants using a virtual table or clock, "George is at 1 o'clock, Marsha is at 2 o'clock, etc." (See Chapter 12, "Electing People," for rounds variations.)

… a round's essential function is to create and maintain equivalence. In a round, each person in the meeting is given an opportunity to speak in turn.

It is a mistake to ask, "Who would like to start?" First, the facilitator should *lead* and the circle will be more comfortable with clear direction. Second, what if the person who volunteers to start is in a horrible mood and has a negative impact on the tone of the meeting? Or no one wants to start? Or if several people want to start? Choosing between them immediately affects one of the key purposes of the round—to establish equivalence. A random choice by the facilitator is usually the most effective.

In considering a proposal, rounds dominate, with occasional open discussion and dialogue. In open discussion, the facilitator keeps a mental queue of which person wants to speak next. If the queue becomes too long to remember, this a good indication that a round may be more useful. Discussion can have the advantage of allowing ideas to build quickly. It has the disadvantage that some personalities may dominate and others not speak at all, unbalancing the equivalence that is crucial to the self-organizing process. A round will reestablish equivalence. Dialogue between one or more people can provide information and clarify specific issues.

In a circle meeting, rounds ensure that everyone has an opportunity to speak. In addition, they make it clear that each person is expected to participate in the deliberations.

OPENING ROUNDS

The sociocratic meeting format both produces and contains the heat of chaos. The opening round creates energy in the room and is very important as the first action of a meeting, because the meeting then belongs to each person in the room. It builds energy and creates group awareness. If the facilitator begins the meeting with announcements or a discussion of the agenda, the unintended effect is to establish that the facilitator has power over the meeting and everyone should follow their lead.

This undercuts the purpose of conducting circle meetings as peer decision-making forums. And it drains energy. Any excitement in the room has to be suppressed until the facilitator stops speaking.

Discussion can have the advantage of allowing ideas to build quickly. It has the disadvantage that some personalities may dominate and others not speak at all, unbalancing the equivalence that is crucial to the self-organizing process.

The opening round establishes several things:

◆ It attunes group members to each other, creating harmony.

◆ It establishes that "we the people" are collectively in charge.

◆ It emphasizes that decisions will be made by working together.

In an opening round each person will share their uppermost concerns of the moment, particularly in respect to the aim of the circle. People change between meetings, so re-connection is important. An opening round both expands a member's zone of alignment to all the members of the circle and is critical to self-organizing behavior.

What people choose to share in an opening round may be related to the organization or to something else that is important to them at the moment. While the phrase "from the heart" may be too personal for some contexts, bringing oneself forward as a person is important in the opening round.

A member may pass, but sometimes a member will pass with an attitude that suggests significant frustration or anger. It is important that the circle respect the person's right to silence, but the facilitator should also take note. Since negative feelings affect the circle, they need to be explored, and if possible, resolved later in the meeting.

From the reaction round, the facilitator can propose referring the proposal back to the presenters or moving forward to clarifying questions.

CONSENT PROCESS

The process for reaching consent varies depending on the matter at hand. In a simple decision where objections are unlikely, the facilitator may simply propose an action and ask, "Are there any objections?" With a complex or controversial policy, the circle may delegate the proposal-writing process to a subgroup or form a helping circle that includes members of other circles and possibly outside consultants. Some decisions may require several meetings, lots of discussion, and many rounds to reach consent. Most will fall somewhere in between, being resolved in one or two circle meetings with some work outside the meeting to research alternatives. Achieving consent is likely to be aided by consultation with those directly affected by the proposal.

Many decisions will also be made with the facilitator simply asking for objections because previous discussions have clarified any questions or it is a routine decision with no new complications. Sometimes a problem or opportunity has to be discussed before a proposal can be written. It is also possible, however, to come to a meeting with an unannounced proposal or to develop a proposal with information presented in the meeting.

PRESENTING THE PROPOSAL

To reduce meeting time, a well-disciplined circle will distribute reports, policy proposals, and descriptions of issues to be discussed before the meeting. Members can read these and formulate any questions, do their own research, and speak with the proposal writer. If the proposal has been distributed before the meeting, the facilitator may simply refer to the item without requesting a presentation, and ask, "Are there any objections?" Or any necessary presentation may be a simple summary.

The circle might want to set a policy about circulating proposals at least a week before the circle meeting whenever possible. A circle may also decide to build an agenda spontaneously at the beginning of the meeting, or do a combination of both.

QUICK-REACTION ROUNDS

After a proposal is presented and clarified, the facilitator calls for quick reactions, in which members of the circle give short responses to indicate their opinions and responses to the proposal. From the reaction round, the facilitator can propose referring the proposal back to the presenters or moving forward to clarifying questions, or just move to a consent round. It is not necessary to follow all the steps if some of them serve no purpose.

ROUND TO REFER PROPOSALS BACK

If appropriate, a round may be done to clarify the reasons why circle members think a proposal needs more work. If the proposal has obvious flaws, these may be addressed more thoughtfully outside the meeting. When the proposal development process has been done well,

In an opening round, each person will share their uppermost concerns of the moment, particularly in respect to the aim of the circle.

this will rarely happen, but things can change between developing and presenting.

This round may occasionally be followed by dialogue or discussion in which those with the strongest concerns can share them with circle members as well as proposal makers.

CLARIFYING QUESTIONS

After the proposal is presented, whether before or during the meeting, the facilitator asks if anyone has clarifying questions. If there are many, they are best addressed in a round. As participants ask clarifying questions, the facilitator should ask anyone who starts to express their opinions to "hold that for the moment until we are sure everyone is clear on the proposal."

The purpose of clarifying questions is to ensure that each person has seen or heard the same words and understands what is being proposed. After the round, any changes and clarifying wording needed to address the confusions can be made, usually on the spot. For example, if the proposal is that cats and dogs be prohibited in the office, and someone asks if this includes seeing-eye dogs, the proposal can now be re-worded to "with the exception of working dogs."

When all the questions have been answered, the circle moves forward to amending the proposal and resolving objections. At any point, a proposal can be referred back for specific changes. Word-smithing and updated calculations, in particular, are best done outside a meeting.

Responses intended to resolve objections often build on each other as important new ideas bubble up in a round or in discussion.

RESOLVING OBJECTIONS & IMPROVING THE PROPOSAL

The purpose of resolving objections is to improve the proposal. This can't be stressed enough. The purpose of objections is to improve the proposal.

Objections should be clearly stated and grounded in experience or evidence. Some hypothetical examples are based on experience or evidence, or both, but if not, they usually distract from the proposal.

Objections may begin as concerns and may not be "clearly stated."

But it is important to tease these out because they may be flagging something important that should be addressed. There are many guides to critical thinking and problem-solving that can be helpful in learning to resolve objections. They can develop circle members' ability to recognize blind spots, avoid either-or thinking in favor of both-and thinking, and learn how to break proposed actions down into small steps that can be measured before implementing the next.

The process of resolving objections includes proposed changes. "This might work better if ...," "There might be a problem with ... if this changes," If we add ..., we could resolve two problems at the same time."

Responses intended to resolve objections often build on each other as important new ideas bubble up in a round or in discussion. A new round will give all circle members an opportunity to react to these new ideas. Again, a proposal can always be referred back, in this case to consider new ideas. Generally, however, the facilitator will be able to work this out and facilitators elected who have this skill.

Experienced groups can often reach consent more easily than new groups but, of course, some issues are just difficult, even for experienced groups. Multiple rounds and improvements may be needed for some proposals. Some of the more common methods facilitators and circle members might use are:

The purpose of clarifying questions is to ensure that each person has seen or heard the same words and understands what is being proposed.

- ◆ Suggest an amendment to the proposal.
- ◆ Do a round asking, "How might we resolve this?"
- ◆ Have a brief dialogue between two or three people.
- ◆ Encourage open discussion on a possible amendment.
- ◆ Propose an experiment to test the proposal.
- ◆ Refer the proposal back for reworking.
- ◆ Create a resolution task force to debate the issues.
- ◆ Refer the objection to a subgroup or a higher circle.

Repeat discussion and consent rounds several times, as necessary.

Resolving an objection is always an interesting process. Sometimes this process is challenging with heavy tension; sometimes there's lots of laughter. It is important to remember that as soon as a member of the circle makes an objection, it belongs to the whole circle, not just to the person who voiced it. An objection is saying, "We have a system for accomplishing our aim, and something isn't working or wouldn't work if we make a change."

To use a mechanical systems analogy, if a spark plug of a lawn mower is full of gunk, it will register an "objection" because gunk prevents it from making sparks. It isn't in disagreement with the rest of the lawn mower; it just can't respond to the operator's attempt to start the mower. The source of the problem is not the spark plug. Spark plugs do not produce gunk. Systems analysis is needed to find the cause of the gunk. Perhaps the underlying cause is a dirty oil filter. Or a loose crankcase. Whatever the problem, the answer is somewhere other than the spark plug.

Thus, in human systems, an objection requires thinking about the whole system. Humans, of course, are a lot more complicated than spark plugs, but we do get "gunky" and the principle is still the same—troubleshooting involves everyone in the system. Thus, in very practical terms, everyone "owns" the objection.

Taking the approach that an objection, once voiced, becomes the property of the whole circle also encourages all members of the circle to feel empathy for the objector, a condition that greatly facilitates group problem-solving.

CONSENT ROUND

Once the proposal is clear, any amendments have been made, and major objections seem to have been resolved, the facilitator announces a consent round. Even when there may be some remaining concerns or objections, the facilitator should proceed to the consent round because it will be helpful in identifying the most essential issues.

If the proposal has been amended, the facilitator asks the secretary to read the proposal and then conducts a round asking if there are any objections to the revised proposal.

In consent rounds, objections are not only welcome but sought out. They are not considered barriers to moving forward but opportunities

> A round is intended for listening; beginning a commentary in the middle of a round will divert attention away from hearing everyone before moving on.

to resolve problems before they obstruct the execution of a policy. If the circle is trying to develop a system that will effectively meet its aim, the circle needs to know if something is wrong with that proposed system. A skilled facilitator, observing a participant say "no objection" with a shrug during the consent round, might note the shrug as an objection and say, "Jerry, I'm concerned about your shrug. I'll note it as an objection and come back to you."

Consent decisions are "whole person" decisions. Objections that cause heavy feelings should be clarified and resolved, although not every concern about a proposal will warrant resolution. It is up the objector to determine whether their objection is important or has been resolved.

The facilitator should not allow any discussion of an objection or ask for any details until the consent round has been completed and all objections are noted. A round is intended for listening; beginning a commentary in the middle of a round will divert attention away from hearing everyone's input before moving on. If no one voices an objection, the facilitator says something like, "Since there are no objections, the proposal is adopted."

After a long and protracted decision-making process, the circle might want to celebrate. In general, however, circles often make many decisions in circle meetings and it is not a complicated process.

CLOSING ROUND

Circle meetings end with a closing round that may address:

♦ issues that were unresolved in the meeting,

♦ an issue a person would like to share,

♦ an evaluation of the meeting, and

♦ what a person is taking away from the meeting.

There is a tendency for people first learning the sociocratic meeting process to make general comments such as "felt nice, we did a lot, enjoyed the company, long and boring, etc." What are needed are specific comments, such as:

♦ "If we'd all read such-and-such document before the meeting,

In consent rounds, objections are not only welcome but sought out. They are not considered barriers to moving forward, but opportunities to resolve problems before they obstruct the execution of a policy.

the decision would have been a lot easier."

◆ "We all need to arrive a few minutes early so we can start on time; today we got started 15 minutes late."

◆ "So-and-so's comment about the matter was very helpful — it made the issues so much clearer and, facilitator, you picked up on the comment and led us on to a quick decision."

It is important to remember that the meeting belongs to everyone. An evaluation of the meeting is not solely an evaluation of the facilitator.

Evaluative comments will vary with the kind of group. A group focused on more personal matters will expect comments like "I feel better after this meeting, more like I belong in this group" or "This discussion of meal planning really cleared the air for me." Sometimes the comments may be more along the lines of "I don't feel comfortable when we rush through so many items in one meeting. Perhaps some of them could be handled another way so we have more time for listening to other ideas." Or someone may say, "At the next meeting, I would like to take time for simple discussion and reflection."

A facilitator preparing to lead a meeting should always look at the closing comments from previous meetings. It's very helpful for doing better on the new meeting. For example, given the comments in the previous paragraph, the facilitator might ask the note-taker, when sending out the agenda, to remind people to arrive a bit early.

CONSENT DECISION-MAKING TO THE RESCUE

By Tena Meadows O'Rear

The following story illustrates how sociocratic principles and methods can be used by an experienced facilitator even when the group has little knowledge of sociocracy and is not organized sociocratically.

Sara had worked for a few weeks as a consultant to a residential school for emotionally disturbed children, focusing on ways to help the school improve its operations related to safety. A professional facilitator and former mental health worker and administrator, Sara had had training in the sociocratic circle-organization model as part of her work in founding a model community. Sara was facilitating a tense meeting of about 20 people including staff, the school director, and other school executives, to discuss closing the crisis-stabilization unit and decentralizing the provision of crisis services. The current crisis-stabilization staff would be reassigned to other residential units to provide support in situ, and the former crisis-stabilization unit would be turned into a regular dormitory for boys. This recommendation was made by a task force consisting of staff members across the organization who had analyzed safety concerns in the crisis unit.

The general staff morale was low. Many workers felt that the administration was arbitrary and hypocritical, espousing staff inclusion in decisions but in reality ignoring staff. The director felt frustrated with the staff's constant complaining and felt that several members were only marginally competent.

Crisis in the Meeting

Many meeting participants had opinions about this decision, some on subject, and some wandering off subject and nearly disintegrating into bickering about the reasons why the unit was

169

failing. Everyone agreed that the current unit was not safe. One therapist was particularly opposed to the proposal because she thought that they needed an additional unit for girls much more than an additional unit for boys. The director of admissions was also concerned about closing the unit because it might affect the school's admissions, limiting the school to children with less acute needs.

Then, some of the participants started saying that they should defer the decision, and Sara realized she had to act. It had taken days to coordinate schedules and set up the meeting, and she needed a decision now, not four weeks from now. She hadn't planned to introduce sociocratic methods to the school, but here was a situation crying out for a consent decision.

Mini-Training on Consent

"Actually we can make a decision today," she asserted firmly. She could see several people exchanging amused, sardonic looks. They clearly expected her to fail. "I am going to give you a crash course on the decision-making methodology that we will use. The process I'll describe follows a specific procedure using 'consent.' That sounds like consensus but it's not. One consents to a decision if it is within your range of tolerance. Let me give you a very simple example of what I mean by 'range of tolerance.' When I shop for clothes, I'm likely to pick a blue or green because those colors go well with my complexion. For variety, I might pick out purple, red, or even orange. But yellow is outside my range of tolerance because I look downright sick in yellow." The room began to relax a little.

"Let me give you a more serious example," she continued. "I enjoy relaxed, informal conversation with people, but I can also tolerate formal rituals on the one hand or bawdy locker room banter on the other hand. What I object to, what I cannot tolerate is angry shouting, hitting or humiliating, prejudicial statements of disrespect." Sara could see several nods of agreement.

"What I'm going to do now is ask each of you in turn whether you can consent to the proposal to close the crisis-stabilization unit. In other words, is this proposal within your range of tolerance? The question is not whether this is your favorite direction, but whether you can live with it. If the decision is not within your range of tolerance, I will ask you to explain to us why it is not, i.e. what are your objections. So I'm not seeking your agreement, but rather seeking your objections."

First Consent Round

She picked out one of the people in the room and asked, "George, do you object to the proposal to close the crisis stabilization unit, provide decentralized crisis services, and reopen the unit as a regular residential unit for boys?" A few people in the room shifted nervously.

"No," answered George.

"Margaret, any objections?" Sara asked the young social worker sitting next to George.

"No objection," Margaret said quietly.

The next three people also consented to the proposal. Then it was the therapist's turn. "Well, I have an objection," she said with folded arms. "I'm fine with the part about closing the crisis stabilization unit; but I think it should be reopened as a regular unit for girls. We already have two girls on the waiting list, and I think we never have enough beds for all the female referrals. Besides without an additional unit for girls, I don't have many choices regarding the mix of girls who reside in each unit, while the boys' therapists have opportunities to mix and match boys already." Sara reflected the part of the proposal that the therapist found acceptable, and the objection, and wrote the objection on the flip chart. She continued around the circle. No objections were raised until the Admissions Director stated that she objected strongly because she thought that admissions would become limited to those children with less acute needs. She suggested that if there were no in-house crisis unit, more hospitalizations would result. Furthermore, she stated that the guidelines for hospitalization were already fuzzy from her perspective.

"Now hold up," the director erupted, "That's not true. The state has clear guidelines about...."

"John," Sara said interrupting the director, "under the process I'm following we don't discuss the objections until we've heard from everyone." He acquiesced and she breathed an inward sigh of relief. It was a gamble to try this process without first training the participants. She turned and noted the objections on the flip chart.

Continuing around the room, she said to the next person, "Barbara, do you have any objections to the proposal?" Everyone else consented to the proposal, with several people throwing in statements of strong support because a regular boys unit represented greater overall safety.

Creative Thinking about the Girls' Needs

Sara said to the group, "Good. We've completed a first round. It's very important to know that two of us would find the proposal intolerable. Returning to the therapist's objection, she asked for more information. The therapist gave an example of a situation where two girls on the same dorm had a hostile relationship that had erupted in a fight. She had no other dorm to use to separate the girls, so she had moved the most volatile girl to the crisis unit. "Without that option, I would have been stuck with no other way to separate them until we could work it out." Two other people in the group chimed in with plausible alternate solutions, including bringing crisis intervention services to the girls' dorm to mediate the conflict on the spot. A second suggestion was to use a vacant extra bed, reserved for guests and rarely used, to serve as a 'cooling off' area for the girls. Mulling over these ideas, the therapist became somewhat enthused about the more flexible approach to crisis intervention, and stated that if those supports were in place, she would not have an objection to the proposal. She ended by emphasizing that she would still rather have another girls dorm, but that she could live with the proposal.

Creative Thinking about the State Guidelines

"Now let's focus on the hospitalization concerns," said Sara. Turning to the director she said, "John, would you share your thoughts about these?"

The director talked for a few moments about the existence of state guidelines for referring the children for psychiatric care. He declared that he couldn't understand why any concern about guidelines should hold up the decision to close down the crisis-stabilization unit.

Sara then asked the Admissions Director who explained that referrals to the crisis unit had been informal because the unit was under school control and located on the school's grounds, and didn't represent a discharge from the school. Yes, there are state guidelines, but they didn't address the specifics of the school's situation: insurance criteria, transportation arrangements, liability and so forth. The finance manager said she was particularly concerned about the lack of clear internal criteria for making the judgment calls necessary to initiate hospitalization.

Sara then asked, "would you be able to live with this proposal if it were modified to include an ad hoc committee consisting of you, the Medical Director, and Director of Clinical Services to produce initial guidelines by Thursday two weeks from today?"

"In that case, I could live with it," responded the Admissions Director. Sara then outlined a process for publishing draft guidelines, soliciting comments from other staff and finalizing the guidelines based on comments. Then she restated the modified proposal with the addition of the guideline work.

Second Consent Round: Decision Made

Sara conducted a second round. The round moved quickly, with each person indicating no objections. After the last person had shaken his head to indicate no objection, Sara said cheerfully, "Good work, everyone! We've all just made an important decision."

There were pleasant looks on many faces. John, the director, spontaneously said, "This is great!" After a minute or two of detailing the process on guideline consideration, the librarian raised her hand. With a puzzled look on her face, she asked, "So, when will the decision be final? In the past we've had meetings like this and thought we made decisions, then the Executive Committee changes them."

Sara explained, "The decision is final. The Executive Committee was here, and they all consented. That's it." The Executive Committee members nodded their concurrence.

Another person said, "I hope you'll tell us more about your process. We have never come to decisions this crisply."

CHAPTER TWELVE

Electing People

The principle of electing people to roles and responsibilities is a logical extension of making policy decisions by consent. The allocation of resources is a policy decision that includes human resources—who does what, how many people are assigned, etc. This practice is both unique and essential to sociocratic functioning. Consent by circle members on who is best suited ensures that people who assume jobs know they have the support of their peers. This builds a strong sense of trust and reduces the friction that results from both autocratic appointments and majority voting processes.

Sociocratic elections are usually fun and there is often a feeling of quiet satisfaction after the decision. This feeling is in contrast to majority vote elections, in which the majority is celebrating while the minority may be grieving or fuming, and to autocratic choices, in which the boss makes an announcement that may induce feelings of resentment, alienation, jealousy—or even incredulity.

Since the sociocratic process includes open nominations and discussion, all members of the circle will have a clear understanding of why each person was chosen and what will be expected of them.

> The allocation of resources is a policy decision that includes human resources—who does what, how many people are assigned, etc.

THE ELECTION PROCESS

Every one or two years, usually as part of the implementation of the strategic plan, or as otherwise necessary, the circle will meet to elect its members to circle governance offices and to operations roles and responsibilities. This may be done in a regular meeting if only one or two people are to be elected, or in a meeting devoted to elections if there are a number of positions to be filled or reconfirmed. Each election process is the same:

1. Consent to a description of the role and/or responsibility.
2. Make nominations.
3. Give reasons for nominations.
4. Change nominations based on this reasoning.
5. If a choice seems clear, the facilitator can suggest a candidate and give reasons why; otherwise, conduct discussion and rounds.
6. Confirm the decision with a consent round.

DESCRIPTION OF ROLES & RESPONSIBILITIES

The election process begins with defining and reading the description of the roles and responsibilities to be performed—the job. The description should include the duties, skills, and knowledge required; how performance will be reviewed; and the length of service. Just as no policy should be adopted for an unlimited period of time, neither should assignments of people.

The job can relate to any "doing" role or responsibility within a circle's domain. Sometimes describing the job is easy. If the task to be assigned is to "research the city laws concerning waste disposal and report back in a month," that may be a sufficient description. The term of service, in this case, is obviously one month, and one criterion for success is obvious: Was the report received in one month?

Sometimes a complex description may be needed. When a growing software company's general circle needed a full-time quality control manager, for example, they began their description by using Carnegie Mellon University's Configuration Maturity Model before they detailed the roles and responsibilities related to the job. Since they were not sure how long this job would be useful or whether they had captured everything in their description, they decided to make the term only one year with continuation contingent on evaluation and redefinition.

Complex descriptions should follow the same process as developing and consenting to any policy. (See Chapter Eleven, "Consent & Rounds," and Appendix G, "Guide for Circle Meetings.")

Defining roles and responsibilities is important not only to ensure completion, but so its benefits can be measured and evaluated properly. The description is also a basis for planning ongoing professional development programs, ensuring that each member of the circle has the necessary skills, now and in the future.

NOMINATIONS AND "WHY?"

Once the job description is completed and read, the secretary hands out small pieces of paper to be used as nomination forms. Pages from small memo pads or index cards work well for this. Nominations for positions are normally done one at a time, in an agreed-upon order.

Each circle member, including the facilitator, may nominate themselves, nominate someone else, write "no nomination," or say "hire from outside." A typical completed nomination form will simply say, for example, "Marc nominates Nancy."

The participants then pass the forms to the facilitator. The facilitator stacks the nominations in as-received order, reads the first form out loud, and asks the nominator to explain why they nominated their candidate. "Marc, you nominated Nancy because ...?" Many people are surprised to be nominated and are usually pleased by what people say about their skills. This is a particularly enjoyable part of the process.

The number of nominations received does not determine the election results. The election is determined by the arguments given for each nomination. The purpose of the nominations round is to present why the nominator believes the person they nominated might be a good person for the job. The emphasis is on what people are capable of, not what they aren't.

CHANGES OR AMENDMENTS

After all circle members have explained their nominations, it may be clear who the best nominee is. The facilitator can propose that the person be elected and give reasons. If no person is an obvious choice, the facilitator starts a change round by asking, "Would anyone like to change their nomination based on the reasoning we've heard? Linda, let's begin with you."

It is helpful to start the round with the person sitting next to the person nominated so the person nominated speaks last. The facilitator asks the nominee for his or her objection last so they have full information about the views of the rest of the circle before they respond.

Some may change their nominations to support another nominee, or may want to add more information in support of their nominees. Someone who originally did not make a nomination may now like to add one. In each case, the facilitator requests a rationale, a "because ..." In this process, participants occasionally ask questions of potential candidates who may provide clarifying information about themselves. They should not indicate whether they will serve. That would short-circuit the process.

CONSENT

Once the nominations have been explained and some, perhaps, changed, the facilitator proposes the person receiving the strongest reasons for being capable of filling the position and gives reasons for doing so: "I propose Charles for this position. The reasoning that Robert and Linda made concerning the recent training he's taken, plus his skill with numbers, make him particularly well-suited. Are there any objections to Charles for this position?"

The emphasis is on what people are capable of, not what they aren't.

The facilitator then begins a consent round, designating a person to start. It is helpful to start the round with the person sitting next to the person nominated so the person nominated speaks last. The facilitator asks the nominee for his or her objection last, so the nominee has full information about the views of the rest of the circle before responding.

There is no discussion before the consent round is completed. If there are objections but the rationale is not given, the facilitator may ask, "Because ..?" (Objections are resolved using the process explained in Chapter 11, "Consent & Rounds.")

One choice for resolving an objection is to nominate another person. Another choice is to change the description to meet the proposed candidate's objections. For example, "Can we make this a three-month position instead of a six-month?" or "I'd feel much better if the description doesn't specifically require me to consult all members of the circle unless I think it is necessary. That isn't always productive." Another is to modify the beginning dates or ending dates to fit a person's schedule of leaves or other responsibilities.

If no one can fill the position, the facilitator declares a vacancy and asks the operations leader to take the initiative to fill it from outside the circle in accordance with the circle's hiring policy. This may require budget approval from a higher circle.

When objections seem to have been resolved, possibly resulting in an amended job description or a decision to conduct an outside search, the facilitator does a final consent round to confirm the decision.

PRECAUTIONS

It is important to *avoid* asking "Who is interested?" in the position before the process begins. The election process belongs to the circle, not to individual members. In many cases, once the circle has presented its reasons for choosing a specific person, that person is more likely to accept the role. If the proposed person finds it impossible to accept, how the task description could be amended or what other qualifications are needed may be more clear.

A second reason to avoid asking who is willing to serve is that the person who volunteers for a position may not be suitable. Once someone volunteers, it is hard to reverse the process and ask for nominations. When the process begins with nominations and everyone hears the arguments for them, who is most qualified for the position becomes more obvious and unqualified people will not be put forward, by themselves or others.

As in any other round, there should be no discussion during the nominations round. It is important that the round be completed and all views shared, so everyone has a complete picture.

Objecting to a proposed person should never provide an excuse for an attack. The facilitator should stop any attempt to label, characterize, or negatively portray someone. Instead, the facilitator should help the objector formulate their objection in a productive manner— perhaps one that addresses the requirements of the position rather than makes judgments, or in terms of what the objector needs to complete their own roles and responsibilities that might not be met if the proposed person were elected.

It is important to follow this process precisely because "the elements of a system must be equivalent if they are to self-organize."

This approach makes it possible to keep the focus of the election on the aim of the circle and the aim of the job, not the personalities of circle members. No candidate is perfect; it is always more or less.

Finally, don't neglect to read the job description, no matter how trivial or familiar. Again, this focuses attention on the role or responsibility rather than on personalities. And be sure to specify a length of term. Doing so makes it much easier to evaluate and change the incumbent if necessary.

LET THE PROCESS WORK

It is important to follow this process precisely because "the elements of a system must be equivalent if they are to self-organize." Self-organizing requires freedom to make independent decisions about one's "self," to take charge, and determine a direction.

In other words, the process is designed to give each person a space and time to think about their own nominations, give their own reasons, and consider their possible objections and reasons for consenting. This brings out each person's unique ideas in each instance about who or what might be the best alternative. Having each person write their opinion separately on a nomination form creates a situation in which many possibilities are present, and in which no one's opinion is influencing others. The change round creates an additional opportunity for self-organization.

When first encountering the election process, some express concern about the power of the facilitator. The facilitator, for example, is free to propose someone with fewer nominations than another person. But in sociocracy, plurality is not a decisive factor; it is only one of the reasons to consider. The facilitator is elected, in part, for the ability to listen and to make sound judgments. The facilitator of the election process may not be the regular facilitator of the circle. It can be a member who is chosen for this particular election.

If a member of the circle objects to the facilitator's proposal, they may object and present their reasons during the consent round. Allowing the facilitator to propose what appears to be the most

It is important to avoid asking "Who is interested?" in the position before the process begins. The election process belongs to the circle, not to individual members.

workable choice moves the circle forward, and the consent round ensures that the choice is within the circle's range of tolerance.

The practice of encouraging leadership by the facilitator and requiring consent to the facilitator's actions is characteristic of both the election process and facilitation in general. It encourages strong leadership and provides a process for correcting any errors in judgment.

FOR OTHER DECISIONS

The process for elections can also be used to make any decision in which there are a discrete number of choices—the date of a holiday party, for example, or the location of the next conference.

CHAPTER THIRTEEN

Organizing Work

BY PRODUCING ORGANIZATION

We easily recognize the phrase "organizing production," meaning to design a process for producing a product or providing a service to a customer. The reverse is not so familiar, "producing organization."

Producing organization is a very important concept in sociocratic organizations. It involves planning all the processes that will form and guide the "doing" in the circular process, the doing of the work. A poor doing process will have a negative effect regardless of how skillful the leader is or how much money is spent implementing it. As noted earlier, a four-wheel car with one wheel missing will be difficult to drive despite the capabilities of the driver or the quality of the other three wheels.

In addition to designing organizations that "have all their wheels," sociocratic methods focus on designing organizations that thrive in changing environments. To use the car analogy again, shock absorbers are necessary not just to keep the passengers comfortable but to protect the engine and all its parts from vibrations and jolts. To operate in changing temperatures, cars need fluids that flow when cold and do not combust or evaporate when hot. Similarly, organizations need mechanisms that allow them to adjust when necessary.

Like automobiles, organizations are designed to function in changing conditions. Unlike automobiles, however, organizations must be designed to adjust to *unforeseen* changing conditions such as economic swings, government regulations, social trends, and technological developments. Like deer avoiding a predator or discovering a new pasture, organizations need to be able to sense changes in the environment and adapt quickly. An organization has to be designed *and*

A poor doing process will have a negative effect regardless of how skillful the leader is or how much money is spent implementing it.

redesigned—and it has to keep functioning while being redesigned. Very rarely can a whole plant be shut down, nor can a university send the students and faculty home for months in order to reorganize. Organizations must be able to function and adapt at the same time.

Producing organization is one of the chief activities of a circle. Just as everyone in most offices now has basic computer skills, everyone in sociocratic offices needs organization-engineering skills. Once limited to industrial engineers and management consultants, today these skills are the responsibility of leadership. In a sociocratic organization, *everyone* is responsible for leadership.

In Chapter Six, "Ensuring Quality," we presented the basic steps in producing organization. We also discussed vision and mission in some detail. While remembering that an aim exists in the context of the vision and mission, we will focus here on the aim and the "doing," the accomplishing of the aim. These steps are illustrated in Figure 13.1, "Producing Organization."

DEFINING AN AIM: "A NAMED PRODUCT OR SERVICE"

The three elements of a good aim statement are:

1. A named product or service
2. Differentiated from other aims
3. Described in terms the customer or client understands.

A well-defined aim attracts clients, focuses the production process, and prevents working at cross-purposes. To be effective, you have to know where you are going, which is determined by your aim, and to be able to steer yourself there, in order to accomplish your aim.

To test the clarity of your aim, ask yourself, "Could I buy one? Or hire it? Use it? Enjoy it? Point to it?" If someone said, "My aim is to change the world," you could test the clarity of their aim by asking, "Can I buy three changed worlds? Can you deliver them tomorrow!" Obviously, a changed world is not a product or service. A changed world may be your vision, but you couldn't hand it to me or do it for me if I gave you a check. An aim is something you will be able to produce and give to others. A manicure, for example, is an aim.

An organization needs to be designed and redesigned—and it has to keep functioning while being redesigned. Very rarely can a whole plant be shut down and a university can't send the students and faculty home for months in order to reorganize. Organizations must be able to function and adapt at the same time.

An aim is also something that can be *exchanged*. Something you can trade for something else. You give and receive in relation to an aim, including giving and receiving appreciation.

We make many exchanges every day. We give the grocer money and the grocer gives us vegetables. We walk the neighbors' dog when they are away and they feed our cats when we are away. We work in exchange for a salary. We also do many things for others for which we do not expect anything from them because we receive something from ourselves—self-respect, or pride in our work, or the joy of making a contribution. This is also an exchange.

The objective of an aim statement is to define a product or service that can be traded or exchanged, that will have *exchange value.* Creating exchange value means both making and then keeping an agreement with yourself, your family, your community, a client, a customer—whoever is your exchange partner.

In writing an aim, listen to your customers or clients and, if possible, your *potential* customers or clients. What do they say about their needs in relationship to your area of expertise? What product

---

Producing Organization

Define an Aim

  1. Design a Production Process

    2. Design a Steering Process

      3. Determine Task Division and Delegation

        4. Design a Program of Ongoing Development

Figure 13.1. Producing Organization. The steps begin with defining the aim.

would fulfill those needs? Does it exist already? Can you improve it or replace it?

The old adage "Before you build a better mouse trap, find out if there are any mice" is a good one to judge whether there is an opportunity for an exchange—whether people want or need it.

Once you determine that there is an opportunity for an exchange, that a product or service is needed and that you can provide it, the next step is to write your aim statement. Be as objective and factual as possible so clients can easily understand whether your product or service meets their needs. Saying "Our aim is to make exciting new ergonomic chairs that will ease many people's back pains" is to state an aim with a story added. If you say, "Our aim is to make comfortable chairs you can sit in for hours," you are addressing the benefits you offer to clients in terms they will understand.

"DIFFERENTIATED FROM OTHER AIMS"

How does your comfortable chair differ from other chairs, particularly other comfortable chairs. What is your market niche? Your aim will be even more focused and distinguishable from those of other companies if you say "Our aim is comfortable, light-weight plastic chairs for use in assisted living facilities." This definition focuses the steering of your organization toward exchanges with assisted living facilities.

Aims rarely exist in isolation. They are often sub-aims of a larger aim:

> **Aims rarely exist in isolation. They are often sub-aims of a larger aim.**

- One section of a department store might have the aim "to provide children's clothing," but it would be defined in the context of the clothing department's overall aim "to provide affordable clothing."

- A community development organization might have an aim that is not just "to create community" but to "develop community relationships and services in condominiums of under 400 units." Or to develop community by "providing a special online community management software." This might determine whether the organization will be working nation- or worldwide or in a specific geographic area.

- A rubber producer might have an aim not just to produce rubber but to produce rubber for a specific industry. This aim would determine, for example, whether the rubber producer would make its product in huge quantities or in smaller quantities.

- Plays might be produced under a theater's aim to improve arts education in urban neighborhoods or within a theater's aim to produce plays that compete for national awards. In this case, the

VISION, MISSION, AND AIM EXAMPLES

Organic Gardener

Vision: Inexpensive organic vegetables on the family table all year

Mission: Plant a garden large enough to provide vegetables all year

Aim: Fresh vegetables in summer; canned and frozen in winter

Technical Support for a Large Company

Vision: Access for all employees to the information they need 24 hours a day, 7 days a week, anywhere in North America

Mission: To provide secure remote access to all company data

Aim: A portal screen linked to satellite internet services and a secure laptop connection

City Fire Department

Vision: No deaths by fire and lowest annual per incident losses in the nation

Mission: Develop an outstanding fire safety infrastructure and education program

Aim: Fire stations within 10 minutes of all houses. Comprehensive fire safety program including all schools and businesses. Required building inspections.

Spring Manufacturer

Vision: Cars moving safely and people riding comfortably

Mission: Provide car manufacturers with high-quality springs for shock absorbers

Aim: Springs of gauges x, y, and z with a full range of tensile strengths.

Hospital Emergency Room

Vision: Immediate access to high quality emergency health care for everyone

Mission: Provide effective and supportive emergency care with effective and adequate equipment and a highly trained staff in a caring environment

Aim: Emergency services for acute trauma or illness; in-patient services that allow family visits 20 hours per day; and in-person on-site access to trained spiritual advisors and counselors 24 hours a day, 7 days a week, for all patients and family members.

Figure 13.2 Vision, Mission, Aim. Sometimes it is easier to begin with the aim.

aim of producing plays would be affected by the larger aims and require different work processes and measurement criteria.

"TERMS YOUR CLIENT UNDERSTANDS"

The aim should use language that your customer or client understands and finds attractive. If a software company has developed a new game that introduces five-year-old children to mathematics, it would not use highly technical computer programming language on the package to describe the product. The description of the product will be affected according to whether the aim is software that will be attractive and useful to parents shopping in toy departments or to education technology experts making choices at conferences or from specialized websites.

DESIGNING THE PRODUCTION PROCESS

After designing the aim, the next step is to determine how you will fulfill your aim. In Figure 13.1, "Producing Organization", step 1 "Design a Production Process" means design the planning. How will you market, produce, and deliver your product? This requires laying out all the steps necessary to produce the product or service described in your aim. The aim that you worked so hard to focus on and simplify will now typically expand into a complex but orderly process. The clarity of this process will be enhanced by the clarity of the aim. In designing a work process, define how you will:

Analyzing, planning, and describing each step of this process in detail produces a strong organization.

- ◆ Find and negotiate an exchange with your client,
- ◆ Create the product or service by transforming assets (money, skills, materials, etc.) into something new, and
- ◆ Deliver the product or service to your client to complete the exchange: something of value to your client in exchange for something of value to yourself. The success of this exchange is a measurement of the quality of your aim and production process.

These three steps are not arbitrary. They reflect the systems engineering concept that processes have three components: *input*, *transformation*, and *output*. For example, input is the process of reaching an agreement with your customer or client. You then transform materials, skills, and other assets into a product or service, and finally output them to your customer or client. Output includes receiving monetary or non-monetary compensation, such as personal satisfaction, and completes the exchange process.

Each of those components also has its own process. The larger component of input, for example, consists of input: marketing to find a potential customer; transformation: negotiating with the customer; and output: making a contract with the customer. Defining each component in three steps, and each of those steps in three steps produces a 27-block chart. Most of us could execute each step in producing a family dinner without designing a production process. If the family dinner is for an extended family of 67 people, however, the process will involve many tasks and people that will have to be coordinated. If it is in honor of a 50th wedding anniversary, and includes press coverage, planning will benefit from pulling out the 27-block chart.

In manufacturing, planning work processes can be very complex and if not done well can cause expensive failures. Figure 13.3 is an example of a 27-block chart for a company that produces medical digital cameras. Breaking the process down into smaller and smaller steps creates a block for all the roles, responsibilities, and task descriptions necessary in organizing a work process from beginning to end.

Too often, organizations focus on the transforming step and neglect to organize the input step—getting the agreement, and the output step—delivery and payment. For example, we are aware of a software development company certified at a high level in the Capability Maturity Model (CMM), a measurement to determine the degree of optimization of processes in software development, but that has no unified database of contacts for its sales force. They forgot to organize their input; their sales and contracting process.

It won't matter that their software is of the highest quality. They won't be able to support their software development financially by finding customers efficiently. Careful attention to the production process of input-transformation-output will produce a healthy organization.

Work processes are policy decisions. Any decision that controls future behavior is a policy and subject to the same consent process as budgets, assignment of roles and responsibilities, etc.

190

A 27-BLOCK CHART FOR PLANNING

AIM Producing Medical Digital Cameras	INPUT (I) Establish Exchange Relationship			Generate
	(I) Marketing	(T) Negotiating Enrollment	(O) Contract, Registration	(I) Prep & Work Order
LEADING ACTIVITIES	OEM engagement plan, email, website, exhibition, sales strategies	Data sheet for technical negotiations, follow up procedures	Standard documents & contracting checklist	Dispatch checklist, BOM format, purchase SOP, personnel
Who does it?	Marketing & Sales	Sales & Managing Director	Sales, Attorney	Purchasing, Sales, Administration
DOING ACTIVITIES	Make contacts with OEM, attend exhibitions, research & make sales calls	Discuss customer technical requirements, send quote, follow up, log	Send order acceptance email & letter	Issue work order, drawings to production and QC. Issue BOM, order shortages
Who does it?	Marketing & Sales	Sales	Sales	Sales, Design, & Purchase
MEASURING ACTIVITIES	Number of inquiries & invites to bid that came via email, website, exhibitions, cold calls	Pending quotations & customer tech doubts? Errors in quotations? Errors caught by customer?	Did customer respond in "HAPPY MODE" after sending order acceptance?	Material & personnel shortages, drawing errors?
Who does it?	Office Assistant	Sales	Sales	Production

Figure 13.3 The 27-Block Chart for Planning and Organizing the Production Process. The chart shows the intersections between the input-transformation-output process and the circular process of leading-doing-measuring. The blocks are used to itemize each step in planning any work process, whether it is an event, a product, or a service. The chart was designed by Umesh Mangroliya, Ahmedabad, India.

AND ORGANIZING OF A PRODUCTION PROCESS

TRANSFORMATION (T) Exchange Objects or Services			OUTPUT (O) Conduct the Exchange	
(T) Doing Job	**(O) Testing / Checking**	**(I) Preparation to deliver**	**(T) Delivery**	**(O) Payment/ Acceptance**
Drawings for machining & QC, department head plans, SOPs for production, QC, subassembly	Testing equipment setup, SOP for testing & reporting	Transport and packing procedures, predispatch inspection procedures	SOP for dispatch, tracking procedures	Payment tracking & overdue follow-up procedures, customer survey methods
Design, Production & QC	QC	Accounting & Dispatch	Accounting & Dispatch	Accounting & Sales
Machining, QC, parts & components, prepare & complete subassembly & assembly	Check performance parameters of cameras per customer order	Package cameras, Prepare dispatch documents, coordinate with transporter	Send material to transporter	Call for payment release, customer satisfaction verification
Machine Shop, QC, Assembly Worker	QC	Production, Accounting, Dispatch	Dispatch	Accounting, Sales
Defects, rework and scrap rates	Customer complaints about performance	Damage complaints? Missing documents? Predispatch inspection reports?	Timely delivery? Dispute or confusion with transporter?	Customer satisfied? Payment received per payment terms & conditions?
Production & QC	Sales	Accounting, Dispatch, Sales,	Accounting & Dispatch	Accounting & Sales

THE STEERING WHEEL: LEADING AND MEASURING

Step 2 in the process of producing organization shown in Figure 12.0 is "Design a Steering Process." Figure 12.2 combines the circular steering process of leading-doing-measuring discussed in Chapter Six, "Ensuring Quality" with the linear process of input-transformation-output. Figure 12.2 illustrates this combination of linear process and the circular steering process for a company that manufactures cameras. Since the chart is nine linear steps shown in columns and three steering steps shown in rows, it is a 27-block chart.

In Figure 12.2 you will see that each of the nine linear steps has its own circular steering process of leading-doing-measuring—a feedback loop. The items in the horizontal "Leading" row guide how the "Doing" activities will occur. The items in the "Measuring" line indicate the information that feeds back to the Leading step. This feedback indicates the degree to which "Leading" is functioning. For example, in the "Marketing" column, if the number of inquiries and invitations to bid resulting from the email contacts is low or falling, the Marketing and Sales departments might decide to change the email formats, or even drop them altogether.

The 27-block chart is useful for planning each step of the input-transformation-output process in relation to the circular process of leading-doing-measuring. It is also a very useful aid for pinpointing and troubleshooting problems when they arise.

WORK PROCESS POLICIES

Work processes are policy decisions. Any decision that controls future behavior is a policy and subject to the same consent process as budgets, assignment of roles and responsibilities, etc.

The guide for developing policies, presented in Appendix G, "Guides," illustrates how policy development also follows the process of producing organization. The information gathering process, or "picture forming," is the input; proposal development is the transformation; and consent to a final version, including amendments and changes, is the output.

> Almost any process can designed and improved using the input-transformation-output paradigm in relation to the circular process of leading-doing-measuring.

Almost any process can designed and improved using the input-transformation-output production process in relation to the circular process of leading-doing-measuring.

In designing a work process, as discussed in Chapter Six, "Ensuring Quality," it is generally easiest to begin with the aim, or the doing. Then lay out the nine steps of input-transformation-output. Once these steps are defined, add the leading and measuring processes to each step. The circular process of leading-doing-measuring is discussed more fully in Chapter Seven, "Steering & Structure."

LEADING

Unpredictable events will always occur as we pursue our aims. The purpose of leadership is to steer us through or around them. Without disturbances, we could organize our work processes just once and function robotically without leadership. Everyone would show up for work on time and never take more than the allotted time for lunch. This is what strict, static, autocratic organizations attempt to enforce.

In most work environments, of course, life is not so predictable. It is the task of the operations leader to make the moment-to-moment decisions that are necessary to move forward when things do not go as planned. Thus, every step in the producing organization process includes a leading function.

Similarly, in all work processes leading requires information about the results of doing. Each step must have a measuring function.

Like recognized quality control methods such as ISO 9000, the sociocratic process encourages documentation of every step so everyone knows, as specifically and reliably as possible what to do. As we discussed earlier, this also makes ISO certification much simpler.

One measure of the quality of the leading function is learning from problems. When breakdowns, errors, bickering between coworkers, or other trouble situations occur, an effective leader will solve the immediate problem and then ask, "In what way did the structure and policies I have established contribute to that problem?" The authors' own experience indicates that troubles on the floor always have some corresponding error or omission in the supervisor's office. The leader must re-examine policies when an anticipated success does not occur.

MEASURING

In addition to leading, an essential part of the steering process is measuring. Riding a bike, for example, requires measuring, as well as leading and doing. A cyclist's eyes measure the changing environment and the road ahead. The nervous system and inner ears measure balance. Without these measurements, pushing the pedals wouldn't accomplish the aim. In all work processes, planning and leading require information and measurements about the results of doing.

Measurement is just as challenging as leading. A clumsy measurement process chews up time better spent on other matters. Anyone who has ever completed an order or a sale by filling out voluminous accounting forms knows too well about the potential frustrations of a measurement burden.

To check the quality of your measurement process, ask yourself how well the measurement reflects the processes it is measuring. If you are the captain of a large ship, you want to know how your engine is functioning. You must stay on the bridge and cannot go personally to see the engine; you rely on instruments. One dial shows the pressure in the boiler. Another shows the amount of fuel remaining. Yet another shows the revolutions per minute, and so forth. These dials are quite different physically from the dramatic reality of a loud, hot engine churning. Abstract representation of results is the essence of measuring. Numbers can be analyzed and compared in ways that other information cannot.

Inventing a useful and relevant measurement tool can mean success or failure of a project. The Wright Brothers, for example, managed to invent the airplane before their competitors, in part, because they invented measurement tools—wind tunnels and other devices that measured lift and steering abilities.

ALLOCATION OF TASKS

Step 3 in the process of producing organization shown in Figure 12.0 is "Determine Task Division and Delegation." People have to be assigned not only to the doing tasks but to the leading and measurement tasks

Like recognized quality control methods such as ISO 9000, the sociocratic process encourages documentation of every step so that everyone knows as specifically and reliably as possible what to do.

as well. In Figure 12.2, this step is labeled "Who Does." Typically a person will have a doing function as well as a measurement function or a leading function for other steps. In a sociocratically organized Dutch hairdressing salon, for example, clients are received by the receptionist and then handed off to someone who washes their hair in preparation for the hair dressing process. The hair washer washes hair and is also responsible for measuring the receptionist by asking the client, "Did you get a cup of coffee while you were waiting?" Or, "What do you think of the new décor in the waiting area?"

After the client moves on, the hair washer takes a moment to jot down feedback from the client on a card. Later in the day, she gives all the cards she has filled out to the person responsibility for determining if any changes are required in how clients will be received or how the reception area appears to them.

Circles can assign roles and responsibilities using the election process or delegate it to the operations leader to be done in the traditional way. A fully functioning sociocratic organization will usually review and revise, as necessary, at least every two years, based on the new aim statements of the larger organization, new assigned domains. As part of this review, the circle may re-elect its members to new roles and responsibilities.

> A fully functioning sociocratic organization will usually revise its aim at least every two years, redesign the organization based on the new aim statements, and elect everyone to new roles and responsibilities.

5% FOR DEVELOPMENT

Step 4 in the process of producing organization shown in Figure 12.0 is "Design a Program of Ongoing Development." Development is a circle responsibility and involves research, learning, and teaching as appropriate for the aim of the circle. Endenburg recommends that 5% of an organization's resources, both time and money, be reserved for development.

On the loading dock for example, the workers would keep up to date on technology, new developments in packaging and trucking, practices of other loading docks, best practices for physical health, etc. Each circle member keeps their own development plan and the larger circle plans in their personal logbooks, with the circle's development plan.

During a recession when many small business close, workers who have continued to develop their skills will be better able to improve processes and develop new products in order to stay in business. During the Great Recession in 2008, a sociocratic ally organized plastics manufacturer in Virginia survived by economizing, redesigning itself, and finding new markets.

WHY DESIGN THE WORK PROCESSES?

The sociocratic circle-organization model is similar to best practices in other organizations, particularly engineering and manufacturing, but is not normally extended to the level where the workers or members design the process, nor are they usually as explicit in defining the steps of production. The detail in this process has a number of advantages:

- Complex processes remain steerable.
- Processes do not become isolated from their environment.
- Circle members can understand their domain more clearly
- Circle members become responsible for the results of their circle. "*They* ought to ..." becomes "*We* ought to ..."
- Because each process, on every level of the organization, follows the same conceptual model, troubleshooting organizational problems becomes much easier.
- No gaps will occur between processes. Tasks are less likely to fall through the cracks.
- The management and information systems are an integral part of the primary production process.
- Orientation towards the client is included as a crucial step.
- Coordination problems between people, which are often due to errors in defining processes, are lessened.
- Exchange relationships remain satisfactory to all parties.

Development is the responsibility of each circle and involves research, study, and teaching as appropriate for the needs of the circle. Endenburg recommends that 5% of an organization's resources, both time and money, be reserved for development.

CHAPTER FOURTEEN

Money as Measurement

Calculations and tables in this chapter can be skipped without impairing your ability to understand the concepts. They are included for those who want to know how variable compensation is calculated.

Sociocratic organizations use many kinds of measurement to determine whether they are achieving their aims. As we discussed in Chapter Six, "Ensuring Quality," measuring is the third step in the circular process of leading-doing-measuring. While we normally recognize the need to lead and do, we often give little attention to measuring, but measuring, as we have seen, is essential for a self-organizing system to steer itself. For people to participate fully and share the risks and rewards as entrepreneurs, they need to be part of the measuring just as they are part of the leading and doing. They need this feedback, negative or positive, to know whether their actions have been effective.

Measuring consists of collecting and reporting data. Data are rarely reported in their original bits. They are "compressed," which means they are reported after being analyzed, using various statistical methods.

Money is a very useful indicator of overall performance, but it is also highly compressed. An annual profit or loss statement, for example, compresses highly complex physical assets and the activities of thousands of people into one number—the net profit or loss.

MONEY, MOTIVATION, & MEASUREMENT

Compression of data can easily confuse information. For example, there is little clear relationship between money and motivation, even though common sense would say they are closely correlated.

While we normally recognize the need to lead and do, we often give little attention to measuring. But measuring, as we have seen, is essential for a self-organizing system to steer itself.

American psychologist Abraham Maslow (1908-1970) recognized that some factors in motivation are dissatisfiers and some are satisfiers." Safety, for example, is not a motivator; it is a dissatisfier. It motivates if absent and does not motivate if present.

American motivational psychologist Daniel Pink (1964–) reports research findings that money can be a motivator for repetitious jobs that require skill but no creative thinking. Money can demotivate if it is used to reward work that requires originality and problem-solving. Self-actualization—the opportunity to accomplish a desired task— is a powerful motivator. For some, accumulating money represents self-actualization. For them, money—and the power that often comes with it—becomes a very strong motivator.

The complex relationship between money and motivation affects our ability to gain and exercise power; the power to accomplish our aims and achieve our vision. One function of measurement is that it provides a basis for understanding the appropriate roles of money and motivation: what it can do and what it can't.

EVERYONE STEERS THE ORGANIZATION

Sociocracy provides a structure that gives everyone a role in the management of the organization. This is one consequence of considering everyone equivalent. As managers of their own work and that of others when they plan the work process, everyone is involved in steering. Since steering is dependent on feedback, everyone must understand how money reflects the effects of their decisions, how well or poorly they are accomplishing their aims.

In businesses and the business side of nonprofits and associations, money is intrinsic to the success of the organization. It isn't the only measurement of success, but it is an essential measurement. Money provides the power the organization needs to accomplish its aims. As Maslow said, it is unimportant until it is important.

Involving everyone in measuring provides feedback about their individual and collective performance. In Chapter Nine, "Fair Compensation & Free Organizations," we presented the concepts of profit as measurement and the division of compensation into the fixed Guaranteed Base Wage (GBW) based on the labor market and the variable Short-Term Measurement (STM) and Long-Term Measurement (LTM) based on performance. In this chapter, we will explain how to calculate these measurements based on profits so each participant in an organization experiences the results of performance directly, whether favorable or unfavorable.

Too much money can be as damaging as too little. High profits and monopolies reduce the value of money as a measurement of whether the organization is serving its clients or customers well. In the absence of competition and choice, money reflects dominance, not performance. Socioeconomically, high flyers (boom) are too often tomorrow's problems (bust). An organization that makes windfall profits might do well to cut its prices, reduce its inventory, and increase research and education budgets so it remains sensitive to change.

Money has the ability to motivate and produce power, but our concern here is the ability of money to measure how well the organization is interacting and exchanging benefits with its environment.

SOCIOCRACTIC COMPENSATION STRUCTURE

The following compensation structure is based on the system developed at Endenburg Electric during the development of the Sociocratic Circle-Organization Method (SCM). Each organization that chooses to organize sociocratically adapts these methods to its own circumstances, accounting requirements, limitations, etc.

At the beginning of the budget cycle, in planning for the next fiscal year, the top circle reviews and approves the budget proposal created by the general circle based on budgets proposed by operations circles. The top circle decides how much it wants to add to the company's reserves (savings for designated expenses) in the coming year. In doing so, it considers factors such as the organization's current level of reserves, anticipated economic conditions, any anticipated cash flow constraints, planned capital improvements, etc.

Then the top circle sets an expected percentage of profit for the

... money can be a motivator for repetitious jobs that require skill but no creative thinking. Money can demotivate if it is used to reward work that requires originality and problem-solving.

coming year. Profits are the difference between the costs and income related to goods and services, funds available for paying taxes, interest on debt, expansion of operations; etc. As with reserves, many considerations will affect the projection of profit, including previous years' experience, emergence of new competition, prevailing lending rate, anticipated improvements in productivity, etc. For a nonprofit organization or a membership association, these considerations would include new grants for programs, government subsidies for services provided, donations, membership fees, changing population needs, expansion of services, etc.

After setting an overall profit target, the top circle gives guidelines to the general circle for adjusting the expected target for each department. For example, the top circle may decide to carry a department at a loss or reduced profit to reflect the startup of a new product line or a marketing strategy to fend off competition. If the decision is to reduce the target for one department, the other departments will have to make up the difference with higher targets.

Figure 13.1, for example, shows three departments of a company that provide various products and services. The top circle set a profit target of 10% for the new fiscal year for the whole company (($8M −$7.2M)/8.00=10%). Because Department A is selling a new product line in a competitive market, that department's expected profit for the year is only 5%. The services provided by Department B are suddenly in high demand, and the top circle and the department believe that a 12% profit is feasible. This higher rate of profit offsets the company's investment in Department A. Department C provides the company's established product line and is expected to have stable profits.

COMPANY-WIDE WEIGHTING FACTORS

The next step is to calculate company-wide weighting factors, including company reserves, investors, and staff on general overhead, for use in profit distribution. Investment capital is the result of past labor and can be considered "condensed" or "compressed" labor. Labor was exchanged for money that was invested as capital for the growth or

> In the absence of competition and choice, money reflects dominance, not performance.

development of a business. This means that current labor and investment capital are fundamentally similar. Therefore, both can be used in calculating percentages in profit sharing. In other words, $100 in investment capital has the same relative value as $100 of active labor.

It can be argued that investment capital should be weighted somewhat higher than active labor because investment capital represents the residue of active labor after taxes. The organization can make such adjustments as long as capital investment and labor are treated as fundamentally similar.

With that concept understood, we can calculate weighting factors and use them to calculate short- and long-term measurements.

For the company reserve, the investors, and employees on general overhead, we calculate weighting factors by dividing the reserve requirement and investor or employee contribution by the last year's gross revenue. For example, the value of the investor's shares at the end of the fiscal year was $1M. The indirect employees' labor contribution was $1.2 million. Assuming that last year's gross revenue was $8M, we calculate the weighting factors shown in Figure 14.2 for use in profit distribution for reserve, investor, and indirect (overhead) staff.

Figure 14.1 Projected Next Year's Profit

DEPARTMENT	(A) PROJECTED EXPENSES	(B) PROJECTED GROSS REVENUE	(C) PROJECTED % PROFIT ((B - A)/B)
A	$ .95M	$1M	5%
B	$2.65M	$3M	12%
C	$3.60M	$4M	10%
TOTALS	$7.20M	$8M	10%

We must divide among the company reserves, investors, and everyone who directly or indirectly contributed labor to the work.

CALCULATING SHORT-TERM MEASUREMENT

Figure 14.3 shows an example of calculating Short-Term Measurement. Assume that Department A got a fixed-price contract for $50,000. The projected profit from Figure 14.1, calculated into the contract bid, was 5% or $2,500. The work, however, went better than expected; material costs were $22,500, exactly as predicted, but labor costs were only

Figure 14.2 Company-Wide Weighting Factors

PARTICIPANT	(A) VALUE OF REQUIRED CONTRIBUTION	(B) LAST YEAR GROSS REVENUE	(C) WEIGHTING FACTOR (A/B)
Company Reserve Requirement Amount set by top circle	$0.5M	$8M	0.06
Investors' market value of shares at end of fiscal year, professional estimate, or book value of company	$1M	$8M	0.13
Staff: indirect staff base salaries last fiscal year	$1.2	$8M	0.15

$20,000 rather than $25,000. This savings was achieved, in part, by new work methods developed by workers Jones, Smith, and Green. The question is how to share the profits of this near-term success with everyone who contributed to it. The actual profit was 15% ($50,000 minus $42,500).

We must divide profits among the company reserves, investors, and everyone who directly or indirectly contributed labor to the work. The indirect participants were the company general manager, administrative department (general overhead), and manager of Department A. Because Department A's manager handles several contracts and does not report time by each contract, her contribution is calculated as indirect for purposes of this example.

We calculate the weighting factors for those who contributed direct labor as the ratio of their projected wages to the value of the contract. The wages were originally estimated at $25,000; thus, the direct labor weighting factor is $25,000/$50,000 = 0.5. We will use this factor along with the factors calculated in Figure 14.2 to calculate the STM for each contributor.

To calculate the weighting factors for the individual workers, we subdivide the 0.5 direct labor weighting factor as shown in Figure 14.4. Finally, we calculate each contributor's share of the $5,000 STM as shown in Figure 14.5. Each contributor's STM factor is calculated by dividing the individual weighting factor (A) by the sum of all the weighting factors (Sum A). The dollar amount is derived by multiplying this ratio by $5,000 (Column C).

CALCULATING LONG-TERM MEASUREMENT (LTM)

The $2,500 that represents the earnings from the anticipated 5% profit is divided among the participants using parallel formulas once every six months or a year. Staff should be able to choose to invest some of their savings in the company—essentially like stockholders. In this way, they increase the amount they earn in both the short- and long-term measurement payments because they are compensated for their investment of both labor and capital.

Compensating the administrative staff promotes great efficiency instead of their typical attitude of disinterest in operations.

SOME EFFECTS OF THE SYSTEM

Because a company's books are open to all employees, with appropriate safeguards to preserve competitive secrets, this measurement

Figure 14.3 Amount of STM to Be Divided

Amount of Order (Revenue)		$50,000
Cost to fill order:		
Materials	$22,500	
Labor	$20,000	
Total Cost		$42,500
Net profit (Revenue - Cost)		$ 7,500
Less expected profit (5%)		$ 2,500
Amount of STM to be divided		$ 5,000

Figure 14.4 Determining Direct Labor Weighting Factors by Individual

WORKER	(A) ORIGINALLY ESTIMATED HOURS	(B) BASE WAGE RATE	(C) ORIGINALLY ESTIMATED BASE LABOR COST (A*B)	(D) ORIGINALLY ESTIMATED TOTAL CONTRACT VALUE	(E) WEIGHTING FACTOR (C/D)
Jones	200	$40/hr	$8,000	$50,000	0.16
Smith	200	$35/hr	$7,000	$50,000	0.14
Green	500	$20/hr	$10,000	$50,000	0.20

system is resistant to tricks and manipulations. The measurement reflects group performance, promoting cooperation while recognizing individual performance. Compensating the administrative staff promotes great efficiency instead of their typical attitude of disinterest in operations. For example, the accounting departments will be rather assertive in collecting on outstanding accounts since neither they nor anyone else receives their STM payment until the money is collected. The sales department has an incentive to communicate with operations to coordinate their work.

Unlike the typical arrangement in which the salespeople receive a percentage of the initial contract value, in a sociocratic organization, their percentage is based on the successful completion of the contract, not the initial sale.

As production increases, driven by both individual and group performance, the money available for STM payments increases. A worker who finishes a job in fewer hours than expected is able to go on to other work. Thus, the most-efficient workers can significantly increase their income through STM payments. Over time, their base salaries may be increased. Thus, it is possible for workers to accelerate increases in

Figure 14.5. Calculation of STM in Dollars Using Weighting Factors in Figures 14.2 and 14.4

PARTY	(A) WEIGHTING FACTOR	(B) STM CALCULATION FACTOR (A/SUM A)	(C) DOLLAR SHARE OF STM (B*5,000)
Reserve	0.06	0.071	$357.14
Investors	0.13	0.155	$773.81
Indirect Staff	0.15	0.179	$892.86
Jones	0.16	0.190	$952.38
Smith	0.14	0.167	$833.33
Green	0.20	0.238	$1,190.48
SUM	0.84	1.000	$5,000.00

their income based on objectively measured performance.

If the profit in our example had been only 4%, 1% below the expected 5%, it would create a deficit that would have to be corrected before further STM payments could be made. Everyone would feel the effects of less-than-expected performance. But perhaps even more important, workers themselves would be able to correct the deficiency rather than shut down a unit and fire workers.

When everyone is a partner and assumes equivalent risks and rewards, everyone is motivated to help maintain fiscal health.

SPECIAL OPTIONS FOR NONPROFITS

The measurement system outlined can be applied to nonprofit organizations as well, but the category for investors is not applicable, just as it may not be applicable for small, unincorporated businesses.

If the nature of an organization's contracts is not fixed fee, provision should still be made for STM/LTM payments. For example, if a contract is cost plus fixed fee, part of the fixed fee can be set aside for the short-term measurement. If the contract is purely time and materials, then part of the profit calculation embedded in labor rates should be set aside for STM/LTM payments.

Finally, how can a company use this system in a transparent way without increasing the risk that key financial information will leak to competitors? That is, how can an organization both be transparent and have a black box? Under normal circumstances, circles simply accept that sensitive figures such as overhead rates are correctly reflected in calculations of short- and long term measurements. If a circle suspects "something funny" in those calculations, however, it can elect a member of its circle to review the accounting books. That member can then report back to the circle that "everything is okay."

There undoubtedly are many other possible solutions. This "special eyes" strategy has been used successfully for many years at Endenburg Electric.

When everyone is a partner and assumes equivalent risks and rewards, everyone is motivated to help maintain fiscal health.

AFTERWORD

Invitation to Share

We hope the sociocratic principles and practices we have presented will help build the businesses, neighborhoods, communities, and cities we most want, in which we can live more freely and richly with less strife and waste. Sociocracy is, above all, about engaging with one another to achieve our common aims.

In closing, we would like to share some ideas that are still fragmentary and some experiences from recent training. A mother preparing her family for a holiday celebration reported one such experience:

> We had a sociocratic family meeting last week in which we wanted to plan the activities of our Christmas holidays. Because many questions came up in the previous meeting, my family members had requested an introduction to sociocracy. I was facilitating. I did a short presentation, and then we went on with the agenda. Because we were short on time, I made a proposal to form sub-groups for special preparations, for example, one to plan for meals, one to plan for games, etc. In the whole family group, we created a timeframe and fixed dates for the small groups to complete their work. The next day, we met in a small group for preparation of meals. Elisabeth, age 10, facilitated in the way she had seen me do. She also took notes. You cannot imagine how quickly children absorb. After this small group, the children met in their sub-group with the intention to prepare games. This time Leonard, age 13, facilitated. I was not a member. That evening, we gathered, and Elisabeth and Leonard presented the decisions of the small groups. It was amazing to see this happen.

Sociocracy is, above all, about engaging with one another to achieve our common aims.

This is one small example of how sociocratic methods work to help us organize our lives harmoniously. The principles and methods are simple and straightforward enough to be understood by children with little training, but the effect is very powerful.

What would it be like to have sociocratic institutions everywhere: the government, schools, theaters, banks, businesses—all coordinated sociocratically? We don't know, but work is going forward. For example, in the city of Woerden, the Netherlands, many neighborhoods and neighborhood centers are organized sociocratically. In Enschede, the Netherlands, all 30 schools in the public school system function sociocratically.

As more organizations adopt sociocracy, people will become more connected in more-supportive ways. In the Netherlands, there are circles composed of the general managers from a wide variety of sociocracy organizations in which the managers meet to support each other and share ideas about the application of sociocratic methods. In India, a network of 100 neighborhood circles meets to make decisions that govern their neighborhoods.

This kind of organizing can lead to the election of representatives to citywide general circles. This is the kind of adventure that could inspire you as you develop your own sociocratic organizations.

Sociocratic thought continues to develop and to spread around the world. This book has focused on the basic theory and its application in the management of organizations, but the other dimension of sociocracy is its vision for society.

For example, if a modern police department succeeds in reducing crime or auto accidents, who profits? Not the police department; rather, the insurance companies. Ironically, it is not in the best interests of the police department to eliminate crime completely. If crime disappeared, so would the budget for the police department, because the police depend on criminals for their jobs.

Thinking sociocratically, is there another way to pay the police department? For example, could tax money be treated like an insurance payment in which the police, rather than the insurance company, would pay you if your house was robbed? This would make the aim of the police department truly to stop crime because they would profit from less crime, not from more. This is the kind of creative thinking that sociocracy encourages.

Consider health care, for example: a system whose costs are accelerating faster than costs in other parts of society. Under the current medical care system, where people pay to be restored to health, is it in a doctor's best interest to have no sick patients? If a doctor has very healthy patients, the insurance company profits, not the doctor. In traditional China, people paid acupuncturists to keep their familieshealthy. If someone got sick, the acupuncturist would charge nothing. This is truly health care. The aim is to maintain health and to profit from doing so, not to profit from illness.

But health care is intricately intertwined with other parts of society. For example, on-the-job stresses seem to contribute to medical problems. People probably would be healthier if those stresses could be controlled. Looking at problems this way makes us realize how complex society is and how fragmented our means of not only resolving problems, but even sharing information about them, is. Sociocracy provides a structure for linking organizations in a meaningful way with the potential of addressing such complex and interrelated problems in an integrated way.

If you were trying to apply sociocratic principles in your city or town, how would you go about creating a circle structure? How might a circle structure for an entire region accelerate the development of better ways to organize society? These are still open design questions, and we invite your thoughts.

We are interested in knowing about your personal story in relation to sociocracy, and your responses as you read the book. What caused you to push through to this point? Perhaps you are a business leader looking for ways to make your company more profitable; perhaps a member of a social change organization searching for a way to make your group more effective in harmony with your values; or perhaps you are an law enforcement officer wondering how to organize your department to reduce job stress.

Whatever your perspective, we encourage you to share it with others. Active training programs and discussion groups are accessible from all parts of the world.

Contact John Buck at the Sociocratic Consulting Group:

Telephone: (240) 468-7102
E-mail: contact@sociocracyconsulting.com
Website: sociocracyconsulting.com

Contact Sharon Villines at the Sociocracy.info website:

E-mail: sharon@sociocracy.info
Website: sociocracy.info

At Sociocracy.info, Sharon writes a blog and maintains information about sociocracy. She also moderates an international e-mail discussion list. Discussions vary from beginner questions to related topics in history, philosophy, systems, and other concerns of members.

To subscribe to the discussion list, send a blank message from the e-mail address you want to use to:

sociocracy@groups.io

We look forward to a more interactive connection as we explore new ways to make our cultures and society as much fun as possible.

Sociocratic Centers & Resources

As we discussed in the "About this Book" chapter, sociocracy is actively practiced and taught in all the Americas, Africa, Asia, Australia, Europe, and Oceania. Sociocratic centers and programs are growing and changing rapidly. Since this is a book and can't be updated regularly we think it is best to s to refer you to a central source where you can find a local contact.

The global organization is the Sociocracy Group, which maintains a comprehensive website with contact information for all its centers and affiliates. You will find information on training workshops, webinars, certification programs, and consultants around the world.

> The Sociocracy Group
> Annewiek Reijmer, Director
> E-mail: jreijmer@sociocratie.nl,
> Telephone: +31 (0)6-22 24 60 89
> Website: thesociocracygroup.com

Training is already being conducted in many languages, including Dutch, English, Flemish, French, German, Hindi, Indonesian, Korean, Portuguese, Russian, Spanish, and Swedish. The number of available workshops in other languages is increasing rapidly.

One way to find a local resource—a workshop or a consultant—is to do an internet search on "sociocracy" and a specific language or country. In the United States, you might also search on "dynamic governance."

Additional Resources

In the Appendices, you will find additional materials for reference and for use as reminders. Three original texts from Ward, Boeke, and Endenburg; two examples of bylaws; and a number of guides for circle meetings. Also included is Sociocracy for One, a list of things that can be implemented in any meeting to introduce sociocratic principles and practices of inclusiveness and equivalence without mentioning sociocracy.

Sociocracy

LESTER FRANK WARD (1841-1913)

Frank Ward worked as a clerk while studying evenings to obtain college degrees in botany and law. He then worked as a paleontologist and archeologist for the federal government. At the age of 65, he accepted a professorship at Brown University. He was elected the first president of the International Institute of Sociology in 1903 and the first president of the American Sociological Society in 1906. He is often regarded as the Father of American Sociology and America's Aristotle. This selection is from The Psychic Factors of Civilization, *published in 1893.*

The world, having passed through the stages of autocracy and aristocracy into the stage of democracy, has, by a natural selection against personal power, so far minimized the governmental influence that the same spirit which formerly used the government to advance itself is now ushering in a fifth stage, that of plutocracy, which thrives well in connection with a weak democracy, and aims to supersede it entirely. Its strongest hold is the widespread distrust of all government, and it leaves no stone unturned to fan the flame of misarchy. Instead of demanding more and stronger government, it demands less and feebler. Shrewdly clamouring for individual liberty, it perpetually holds up the outrages committed by governments in their autocratic and aristocratic stages, and falsely insists that there is imminent danger of their reënactment. *Laissez-faire* and the most extreme individualism, bordering on practical anarchy in all except the enforcement of existing proprietary rights, are loudly advocated, and the public mind is thus blinded to the real condition of things.

INTELLECTUAL & LEGAL INJUSTICE

The great evils under which society now labors have grown up during the progress of intellectual supremacy. They have crept in stealthily during the gradual encroachment of organized cunning upon the domain of brute force. Over that vanishing domain, government retains its power, but it is still powerless in the expanding and now all-embracing field of psychic influence. No one ever claimed that in the trial of physical strength, the booty should fall to the strongest. In all such cases, the arm of the government is stretched out and justice is reinforced. But in those manifold, and far more unequal struggles now going on between mind and mind, or rather between the individual and an organized system, the product of ages of thought, it is customary to say that such matters must be left to regulate themselves, and that the fittest must be allowed to survive. Yet, to anyone who will candidly consider the matter, it must be clear that the first and principal acts of government openly and avowedly prevented, through forcible interference, the natural results of all trials of physical strength. These much-talked-of laws of nature are violated every time the highway robber is arrested and sent to jail.

It is utterly illogical to say that aggrandizement by physical force should be forbidden while aggrandizement by mental force or legal fiction should be permitted. It is absurd to claim that injustice committed by muscle should be regulated, while that committed by brain be unrestrained.

Primitive government, when only brute force was employed, was strong enough to secure the just and equitable distribution of wealth. Today, when mental force is everything, and physical force is nothing, it is powerless to accomplish this. This alone proves that government needs to be strengthened in its primary quality—the protection of society. There is no reasoning that applies to one kind of protection that does not apply equally to the other.

AGAINST PLUTOCRACY, RULE BY THE WEALTHY

While the modern plutocracy is not a form of government in the same sense that the other forms mentioned are, it is, nevertheless, easy to see that its power is as great as any government has ever wielded. The test of governmental power is usually the manner in which it taxes the people, and the strongest indictments ever drawn up against the worst forms of tyranny have been those which recited their oppressive methods of extorting tribute. But tithes are regarded as oppressive, and a fourth of the yield of any industry would justify a revolt. Yet today there are many commodities for which the people pay two and three times as much as would cover the cost of production, transportation, and exchange at fair wages and fair profits. The monopolies in many lines actually tax the consumer from 25 to 75 percent of the real value of the goods. Imagine an excise tax that should approach these figures! Under the operation of either monopoly or aggressive competition, the price of everything is pushed up to the maximum limit that will be paid for the commodity in profitable quantities, and this wholly irrespective of the cost of production. No government in the world has now, or ever had, the power to enforce such an extortion as this. It is a governing power in the interest of favored individuals, which exceeds that of the most powerful monarch or despot that ever wielded a scepter.

There is one form of government that is stronger than autocracy or aristocracy or democracy, or even plutocracy, and that is sociocracy.

What then is the remedy? How can society escape this last conquest of power by the egoistic intellect? It has overthrown the rule of brute force by the establishment of government. It has supplanted autocracy by aristocracy and this by democracy, and now it finds itself in the coils of plutocracy. Can it escape? Must it go back to autocracy for a power sufficient to cope with plutocracy? No autocrat ever had a tithe of that power. Shall it then let itself be crushed? It need not. There is one form of government that is stronger than autocracy or aristocracy or democracy, or even plutocracy, and that is *sociocracy*.

SOCIOCRACY, RULE BY SOCIETY

The individual has reigned long enough. The day has come for society to take its affairs into its own hands and shape its own destinies. The individual has acted as best he could. He has acted in the only way he could. With a consciousness, will, and intellect of his own he could do nothing else than pursue his natural ends. He should not be denounced nor called any names. He should not even be blamed. Nay, he should be praised, and even *imitated*. Society should learn its great lesson from him, should follow the path he has so clearly laid out that leads to success. It should imagine itself an individual, with all the interests of an individual, and becoming fully *conscious* of these interests it should pursue them with the same indomitable *will* with which the individual pursues his interests. Not only this, it must be guided, as he is guided, by the social *intellect*, armed with all the knowledge that all individuals combined, with so great labor, zeal, and talent have placed in its possession, constituting the social intelligence.

Sociocracy will differ from all other forms of government that have been devised, and yet that difference will not be so radical as to require a revolution.

Sociocracy will differ from all other forms of government that have been devised, and yet that difference will not be so radical as to require a revolution. Just as absolute monarchy passed imperceptibly into limited monarchy, with this, in many states without even a change of name has passed into more or less pure democracy, which is now known. For, through paradoxical democracy, which is now the weakest of all forms of government, at least in the control of its own internal elements, is capable of becoming the strongest. Indeed, none of the other forms of government would be capable of passing directly into a government by society. Democracy is a phase through which they must first pass on any route that leads to the ultimate social stage which all governments must eventually attain if they persist.

DEMOCRACY, RULE BY THE MAJORITY

How then, it may be asked, do democracy and sociocracy differ? How does society differ from the people? If the phrase "the people" really meant the people, the difference would be less. But the shibboleth of democratic states, where it means anything at all that can be described or defined, stands simply for the majority of qualified electors, no matter how small that majority may be. There is a sense in which the action of a majority may be looked upon as the action of society. At least, there is no denying the right of the majority to act for society, for to do this would involve either the denial of the right of government to act at all, or the admission of the right of a minority to act for society. But a majority acting for a society is a different thing from society acting for itself, even though, as must always be the case, it acts through an agency chosen by its members. All democratic governments are largely party governments. The electors range themselves on one side or the other of some party line, the winning side considers itself the state as much as Louis the XIV did. The losing party usually then regards the government as something alien to it and hostile, like an invader, and thinks of nothing but to gain strength enough to overthrow it at the next opportunity. While various issues are always brought forward and defended or attacked, it is obvious to the looker-on that the contestants care nothing for these, and merely use them to gain an advantage and win an election.

From the standpoint of society, this is child's play. A very slight awakening of the social consciousness will banish it and substitute something more business-like. Once get rid of this puerile gaming spirit and have attention drawn to the real interests of society, and it will be seen that upon nearly all important questions all parties and all citizens are agreed, and that there is no need of this partisan strain upon the public energies. This is clearly shown at every change in the party complexion of the government. The victorious party [that] has been denouncing the government merely because it was in the hands of its political opponents boasts that it is going to revolutionize the country in the interest of good government, but the moment it comes into power and feels the weight of national responsibility, it finds that it has little to do but carry out the laws in the same way that its predecessors had been doing.

THE BEST INTERESTS OF SOCIETY

There is a vast difference between all this outward show of partisanship and advocacy of so-called principles, and attention to the real interests and necessary business of the nation, which latter is what the government must do. It is a social duty. The pressure which is brought to enforce it is the power of the social will. But in the factitious excitement of partisan struggles where professional politicians and demagogues on the one hand, and the agents of plutocracy on the other, are shouting discordantly in the ears of people, the real interests of society are, temporarily at least, lost sight of, clouded and obscured, and men lose their grasp on the real issues, forget even their own best interest, which, however selfish, would be a far safer guide, and the general result usually is that these are neglected and nations continue in the hands of mere politicians who are easily managed by the shrewd representatives of wealth.

The investigation should be a disinterested and strictly scientific one, and should actually settle the question in one way or the other.

Sociocracy will change all this. Irrelevant issues will be laid aside. The important objects upon which all but an interested few are agreed will receive their proper degree of attention, and measures will be considered in a non-partisan spirit with the sole purpose of securing these objects. Take as an illustration the postal telegraph question. No one not a stockholder in an existing telegraph company would prefer to pay 25 cents for a message if he could sent it for 10 cents. Where is the room for discussing a question of this nature? What society wants is the cheapest possible system. It wants to know with certainty whether a national postal telegraph system would secure this universally desired object. It is to be expected that the agents of the present telegraph companies would try to show that it would not succeed. But why be influenced by the interests of such a small number of persons, however worthy, when all the rest of mankind are interested in the opposite solution? The investigation should be a disinterested and strictly scientific one, and should actually settle the question in one way or the other. If it was found to be a real benefit, the system should be adopted. There are today a great number of these strictly social questions before the American people, questions [that] concern every citizen in the country, and whose solution would doubtless profoundly affect the state of civilization attainable on this continent. Not only is it impossible to secure this, but it is impossible to secure an investigation of them on their real merits. The same is true of other countries, and in general the prevailing democracies of the world are incompetent to deal with problems of social welfare.

SOCIETY ACTING AS AN INTELLIGENT INDIVIDUAL

The prices of most of the staple commodities consumed by mankind have no necessary relation to the cost of producing them and placing them in the hands of the consumer. It is always the highest price that the consumer will pay rather than do without. Let us suppose that price to be on an average double what it would cost to produce, transport, exchange, and deliver the goods, allowing in each of these transactions a fair compensation for all services rendered. Is there any member of society who would prefer to pay two dollars for what is fairly worth only one? Is there any sane ground for arguing such a question? Certainly not. The individual cannot correct this state of things. No democracy can correct it. But a government that really represented the interests of society would no more tolerate it than an individual would tolerate a continual extortion of money on the part of another without an equivalent.

And so it would be throughout. Society would inquire in a business way without fear, favor, or bias, into everything that concerned its welfare, and if it found obstacles it would remove them, and if it found opportunities it would improve them. In a word, society would do under the same circumstances just what an intelligent individual would do. It would further, in all possible ways, its own interests.

AN IMPOSSIBLE IDEAL?

I anticipate the objection that this is an ideal state of things, and that it has never been attained by any people, and to all appearances never can be. No fair-minded critic will, however, add the customary objection that is raised, not wholly without truth, to all socialistic schemes, that they presuppose a change in "human nature." Because in the transformation here foreshadowed the permanence of all the mental attributes is postulated, and I have not only refrained from dwelling upon the moral progress of the world, but have not even enumerated among the social forces the power of sympathy as a factor in civilization. I recognize this factor as one of the derivative ones, destined to perform an important part, but I have preferred to rest the case upon the primary and original egoistic influences, believing that neither meliorism nor sociocracy is dependent upon any sentiment, or upon altruistic props for support. At least the proofs will be stronger if none of these aids are called in, and if they can be shown to have a legitimate influence, this is only so much added to the weight of evidence.

To the other charge the answer is that ideals are necessary, and also that no ideal is ever fully realized. If it can be shown that society is actually moving toward any ideal, the ultimate substantial realization of that ideal is as good as proved. The proofs of such a movement in society today are abundant. In many countries, the encroachments of egoistic individualism have been checked at a number of important points. In this country, alarm has been taken in good earnest at the march of plutocracy under the protection of democracy. Party lines are giving way and there are unmistakable indications that a large proportion of the people are becoming seriously interested in social progress of the country. For the first time in the history of political parties, there has been formed a distinctively industrial party [that] possesses all the elements of permanence and may soon be a controlling factor in American politics. Though this may not as yet presage a great social revolution, still it is precisely the way in which a reform in the direction indicated should be expected to originate. But whether the present movement prove enduring or ephemeral, the seeds of reform have been sown broadcast throughout the land, and sooner or later they must spring up, grow, and bear their fruit.

SOCIAL ACTION & ADVANCEMENT

For a long time to come, social action must be chiefly negative and be confined to the removal of evils that exist, but a positive stage will ultimately be reached in which society will consider and adopt measures for its own advancement. The question of the respective provinces of social action and individual action cannot be entered into here at length, but it is certain that the former will continue to encroach upon the latter so long as such encroachment is a public benefit. There is one large field in which there is no question on this point, viz., the field covered by what, in modern economic parlance, is called "natural monopoly." The arguments are too familiar to demand restatement here, and the movement is already so well under way that there is little need of further argument. As to what lies beyond this, however, there is room for much discussion and honest difference of opinion. This is because there has been so little induction. It is the special characteristic of the form of government that I have called sociocracy, resting as it does directly upon the science of sociology, to investigate the facts bearing on every subject, not for the purpose of depriving any class of citizens of the opportunity to benefit themselves, but purely and solely for the purpose of ascertaining what is for the best interests of society at large.

... sociocracy, resting as it does directly upon the science of sociology, to investigate the facts bearing on every subject, not for the purpose of depriving any class of citizens of the opportunity to benefit themselves, but purely and solely for the purpose of ascertaining what is for the best interests of society at large.

The socialistic arguments in favor of society taking upon itself the entire industrial operations of the world have never seemed to me conclusive, chiefly because they have consisted so largely of pure theory and *a priori* deductions. Anyone who has become imbued by the pursuit of some special branch of science with the nature of scientific evidence requires the presentation of such evidence before he can accept conclusions in any other department. And this should be the attitude of all in relation to these broader questions of social phenomena. The true economist can scarcely go farther than to say that a given question is an open one, and that he will be ready to accept the logic of facts when these are brought forward. I do not mean that we must not go into the water until we have learned to swim. This, however, suggests the true method of solving such questions. One learns to swim by a series of trials, and society can well afford to try experiments in certain directions and note the results. There are, however, other methods, such as careful estimates of the costs and accurate calculations of the effect based on the uniform laws of social phenomena. Trial is the ultimate test of scientific theory thus formed, and may, in social as in physical science, either establish or overthrow hypotheses. But in social science, no less than in other branches of science, the working hypothesis must always be the chief instrument of successful research.

Until the scientific stage is reached, and as a necessary introduction to it, social problems may properly be clearly stated and such general considerations brought forward as have a direct bearing upon them. I know of no attempts of this nature which I can more warmly recommend than those made by John Stuart Mill in his little work *On Liberty*, and in his *Chapters on Socialism*, of which the latter appeared posthumously. They are in marked contrast, by their all-sided wisdom, with the intensely one-sided writings of Herbert Spencer on substantially the same subject; and yet the two authors are obviously at one on the main points discussed. This candid statement of the true claims of the *laissez-faire* school is perfectly legitimate. Equally so are like candid presentations of the opposite side of the question. The more light that can be shed on all sides the better, but in order really to elucidate social problems it must be the dry light of science, as little influenced by feeling as though it were the inhabitants of Jupiter's moons, instead of those of this planet, that were under the field of the intellectual telescope.

Sociocracy
Democracy as It Might Be

KEES BOEKE (1884-1966)

Kees Boeke was an internationally known peace activist and educator. During WW II, when he was arrested for harboring Jews, in his pocket was found a declaration entitled "No Dictatorship" that nearly cost him his life. This manuscript was an early draft of a plan for a truly democratic society that was first published in May of 1945 under that title. The following article is from a subsequent version edited by his wife Beatrice Cadbury Boeke and provided here with the permission of his daughter Candia Boeke.

We are so accustomed to majority rule as a necessary part of democracy that it is difficult to imagine any democratic system working without it. It is true that it is better to count heads than to break them, and democracy, even as it is today, has much to recommend it as compared with former practices. But the party system has proved very far from providing the ideal democracy of people's dreams. Its weaknesses have become clear enough: endless debates in Parliament, mass meetings in which the most primitive passions are aroused, the overruling by the majority of all independent views, capricious and unreliable election results, government action rendered inefficient by the minority's persistent opposition. Strange abuses also creep in. Not only can a party obtain votes by deplorably underhanded methods, but, as we all know, a dictator can win an election with an "astonishing" majority by intimidation.

The fact is that we have taken the present system for granted for so long that many people do not realize that the party system and majority rule are not an essential part of democracy. If we really wish to see the whole population united, like a big family, in which the members care for each other's welfare as much as for their own, we must set aside the quantitative principle of the right of the greatest number and find another way of organizing ourselves. This solution must be really democratic in the sense that it must enable each one of us to share in organizing the community. But this kind of democracy will not depend on power, not even the power of the majority. It will have to be a real community-democracy, an organization of the community by the community itself.

For this concept I shall use the word "sociocracy." Such a concept would be of little value if it had never been tried out in practice. But its validity has been successfully demonstrated over the years. Anyone who knows England or America will have heard of the Quakers, the Society of Friends. They have had much influence in these countries and are well known for their practical social work. For more than three hundred years the Quakers have used a method of self-government that rejects majority voting, group action being possible only when unanimity has been reached. I too have found by trying out this method in my school that it really does work, provided there is recognition that the interests of others are as real and as important as one's own. If we start with this fundamental idea, a spirit of goodwill is engendered [that] can bind together people from all levels of society and with the most varied points of view. This, my school, with its [300 to 400] members, has clearly shown.

As a result of these two experiences, I have come to believe that it should be possible some day for people to govern themselves in this way in a much wider field. Many will be highly skeptical about this possibility. They are so accustomed to a social order in which decisions are made by the majority or by a single person, that they do not realize that, if a group provides its own leadership and everyone knows that only when common agreement is reached can any action be taken, quite a different atmosphere is created from that arising from majority rule. These are two examples of sociocracy in practice; let us hope that its principles may be applied on a national, and finally an international scale.

Before describing how the system could be made to work, we must first see what the problem really is. We want a group of [people] to establish a common arrangement of their affairs [that] all will respect and obey. There will be no executive committee chosen by the majority, having the power to command the individual. The group itself must reach a decision and enter into an agreement on the understanding that every individual in the group will act on this decision and honor this agreement. I have called this the self-discipline of the group. It can be compared to the self-discipline of the individual who has learned to set certain demands for himself that he obeys.

THREE FUNDAMENTAL RULES

There are three fundamental rules underlying the system. The first is that the interests of all members must be considered, the individual bowing to the interests of the whole. Secondly, solutions must be sought [that] everyone can accept: otherwise no action can be taken. Thirdly, all members must be ready to act according to these decisions when unanimously made.

The spirit that underlies the first rule is really nothing else but concern for one's neighbor, and where this exists, where there is sympathy for other people's interests, where love is, there will be a spirit in which real harmony is possible.

The second point must be considered in more detail. If a group in any particular instance is unable to decide upon a plan of action acceptable to every member, it is condemned to inactivity; it can do nothing. This may happen even today where the majority is so small that efficient action is not possible. But in the case of sociocracy, there is a way out, since such a situation stimulates its members to seek for a solution, that everyone can accept, perhaps ending in a new proposal, which had not occurred to anyone before. While under the party system, disagreement accentuates the differences and the division becomes sharper than ever, under a sociocratic system, [as] long as it is realized that agreement must be reached, it activates a common search that brings the whole group [closer] together.

Something must be added here. If no agreement is possible, this usually means that the present situation must continue for the time being. It might seem that in this way, conservatism and reaction would reign, and no progress would be possible. But experience has shown that the contrary is true. The mutual trust that is accepted as the basis of a sociocratic society leads inevitably to progress, and this is noticeably greater when all go forward together with something everyone has agreed to. Again it is clear that there will have to be "higher-level" meetings of chosen representatives, and if a group is to be represented in such a meeting, it will have to be by someone in whom everyone has confidence. If this does not prove possible, then the group will not be represented at all in the higher-level meeting, and its interests will have to be cared for by the representatives of other groups. But experience has shown that where representation is not a question of power but of trust, the choice of a suitable person can be made fairly easily and without unpleasantness.

The third principle means that when agreement is reached, the decision is binding on all who have made it. This also holds of the higher-level meeting for all who have sent representatives to it. There is a danger in the fact that each must keep decisions made in a meeting over which he has only an indirect influence. This danger is common to all such decisions, not least in the party system. But it is much less dangerous where the representatives are chosen by common consent and are therefore much more likely to be trusted.

A group that works in this way should be of particular size. It must be big enough for personal matters to give way to an objective approach to the subject under discussion, but small enough not to be unwieldy, so that the quiet atmosphere needed can be secured. For meetings concerned with general aims and methods a group of about forty has been found the most suitable. But when detailed decisions have to be made, a small committee will be needed of three to six [people] or so. This kind of committee is not new. If we could have a look at the countless committees in existence, we should probably find that those that are doing the best work do so without voting. They decide on a basis of common consent. If a vote were to be taken in such a small group, it would usually mean that the atmosphere is wrong.

LEADERSHIP

Of special importance in exercising sociocratic government is the leadership. Without a proper leader, unanimity cannot easily be reached. This concerns a certain technique that has to be learnt. Here Quaker experience is of the greatest value. Let me describe a Quaker business meeting. The group comes together in silence. In front sits the clerk, the leader of the meeting. Beside him sits the assistant clerk, who writes down what is agreed upon. The clerk reads out each subject in turn, after which all members present, men and women, old and young, may speak to the subject. They address themselves to the meeting and not to a chairman, each one making a contribution to the developing train of thought. It is the clerk's duty, when he thinks the right moment has come, to read aloud a draft minute reflecting the feeling of the meeting. It is a difficult job, and it needs much experience and tact to formulate the sense of the meeting in a way that is acceptable to all. It often happens that the clerk feels the need for a time of quiet. Then the whole gathering will remain silent for a while, and often out of the silence will come a new thought, a reconciling solution, acceptable to everyone. It may seem unbelievable to many that a meeting of up to [1,000] people can be held in this way. And yet I have been present at a Yearly Meeting of the Quakers in London, held during war-time (the First World War), at which the much vexed problem of the Quaker attitude to war was discussed in such a manner, no vote being taken. So I believe that if we once set ourselves the task of learning this method of co-operation, beginning with very simple matters, we shall be able to learn this art and acquire a tradition that will make possible the handling of more difficult questions.

This has been confirmed by my experience at Bilthoven in building up the school [that] I called the Children's Community Workshop. Very early on I suggested that we should talk over how we should organize our community life. At first the children objected, saying they wanted me to take the decisions for them. But I insisted, and the idea of the "Talkover," or weekly meeting, was accepted. Later I suggested that one of the children help me with the leadership of the meeting, and from that time on it has become an institution, led by the children, which we should not like to lose.

When I began to hold these Talkovers, I was aware that I was using the procedure of the Quaker business meeting, and I saw in the distance, as it were, the great problem of the government of humanity. It was also curious to discover whether the art of living together, understood as obeying the rule we had all agreed upon, would be simple enough to be learned by children. An experience of some 20 years has shown me that it certainly is.

FOR SOCIETY

But something more is necessary before this method can be applied to adult society. When we are concerned, not with a group of a few hundred people, but with thousands, even millions, whose lives we wish to organize in this way, we must accept the principle of some sort of representation. There will have to be higher-level meetings, and these will have to deal with matters concerning a wider area. Higher-level meetings will also have to send representatives to another higher body, which will be responsible for a still wider area, and so on.

After my hopes for the success of school meetings had been confirmed by practice, I was very curious to know if a meeting of representatives would work also in the school. One day when the number of children had grown too large for one general meeting at which all could be present, I suggested the setting up of a meeting of representatives. At first the children did not like the idea; children are conservative. But, as often happens, six months later they suggested the same plan themselves, and since then this institution has become a regular part of the life of the school.

Of course such meetings, if ever they are to be used by adults for the organization of society as a whole, will have a very different character from those of our children's community. But how in practice could such methods be introduced? First of all, a Neighborhood Meeting, made up of perhaps [40] families, might be set up in a particular district, uniting those who live near enough to one another so that they could easily meet. In a town, it very often happens that people do not even know their neighbors, and it will be an advantage if they are forced to take an interest in those who live close by. The Neighborhood Meeting might embrace about 150 people, including children. About 40 of these Neighborhood Meetings might send representatives to a Ward Meeting, acting for something like 6,000 people. In general it will be true to say that the wider the area the Meeting governs, the less often it will need to meet. The representatives of about 40 Ward Meetings could come together in a District Meeting, acting for about 240,000 people.

In approximately 40 or 50 District Meetings, the whole population of a small country might be covered. The representatives would bring the interests of all the Districts to a Central Meeting. It is an essential condition that representatives have the confidence of the whole group: [I]f they have that, business can usually be carried on quickly and effectively.

[Since] the whole sociocratic method depends on trust, there will be no disadvantage if, alongside the geographical representation of Neighborhood, Ward, District and Central Meetings, a second set of functional groupings [were to] be established. It seems reasonable that all industries and professions send representatives to primary, secondary, and, where necessary, tertiary meetings, and that the trusted representatives of the "workers" in every field should be available to give their professional advice to the government. I have here used the word "government." It is not my intention to put forward a plan according to which the government itself could one day be formed on sociocratic lines. We must start from the present situation, and the only possibility is that, with the government's consent, we make a beginning of the sociocratic method from the bottom upwards; that is, for the present, with the formation of Neighborhood groups. We, ordinary people, must just learn to talk over our common interests and to reach agreement after quiet consideration, and this can be done best in the place where we live. Only after we have seen how difficult this is, and after, most probably, making many mistakes, will it be possible to set up meetings on a higher level. If leaders should emerge in the Neighborhood Meetings, their advice would gradually be seen to be useful in the existing Local Councils. Later, in the same way, the advice of leaders of Ward Meetings would be of increasing value.

The sociocratic method must recommend itself by the efficiency with which it works. When the governing power has learned to trust it enough so as to allow, perhaps even to encourage, the setting up of Neighborhood Meetings, the system will be able to show what possibilities it has, and then the confidence of the governing bodies and of people at large will have a chance to grow. I can well believe that trusted leaders and representatives of Neighborhood Meetings may be allowed, or even invited, to attend Local Meetings. These men and women will of course take no part in the voting, for sociocracy does not believe in voting; but they might be allowed a place in the centre between the "left" and the "right." After a time it may even be deemed desirable to ask them for advice about the matter in hand, since it would previously have been discussed in their Neighborhood Meetings, and a solution sought acceptable to all. It is conceivable that, as confidence grows, certain matters might be handed over to the Neighborhood Meetings with the necessary funds to carry them out. Only when the value of the new system is realized could the higher-level meetings [begin].

Is such a development as this a fantasy? When we consider the possible success of government on the sociocratic principle, one thing is certain; it is unthinkable unless it is accompanied and supported by the conscious education of old and young in the sociocratic method. The right kind of education is essential, and here a revolution is needed in our schools. Only latterly have attempts been made in them to further the spontaneous development of the child and encourage his initiative. Partly because the stated aim of the school is to impart knowledge and skills, and partly because people regard obedience as a virtue in itself, children have been trained to obey. We are only beginning to realize the dangers of this practice. If children are not taught to judge for themselves, they will in later life become an easy prey for the dictator. But if we really want to prepare youth to think and act for themselves, we must alter our attitude to education. The children should not be sitting passively in rows, while the schoolmaster drills a lesson into their heads. They should be able to develop freely in children's communities, guided and helped by those who are older acting as their comrades. Initiative should be fostered in every possible way. They should learn from the beginning to do things for themselves, and to make things necessary in their school life. But above all they should learn how to run their own community in some such way as has already been described.

Finally we must return to the question of representation. We have not gone further than the government of our own country. But the great problem of the government of mankind can never be solved on a national basis. Every country is dependent for raw materials and products on other countries. It is therefore inevitable that the system of representation should be extended over a whole continent and representatives of continents join in a World Meeting to govern and order the whole world. Our technical skill in the fields of transport and organization make something of this kind possible. Finally a World Meeting should invite representatives of all the continents to arrange a reasonable distribution of all raw materials and products, making them available for all mankind. [As] long as we are ruled by fear and distrust, it is impossible to solve the problems of the world. The more trust grows and the more fear diminishes, the more the problem will shrink.

Everything depends on a new spirit breaking through among men. May it be that, after the many centuries of fear, suspicion and hate, more and more a spirit of reconciliation and mutual trust will spread abroad. The constant practice of the art of sociocracy and of the education necessary for it seem to be the best way in which to further this spirit, upon which the real solution of all world problems depends.

Rationale for a New Social Design

GERARD ENDENBURG (1933-)

Gerard Endenburg, a former student of Kees Boeke and a graduate of the Children's Community Workshop, developed the first widely used principles and methods of sociocracy. Beginning with the principles that Kees Boeke developed, Endenburg incorporated what he had learned from cybernetics and systems thinking to structuring and governing all organizations. In this selection from Sociocracy as Social Design, *first published in Dutch in 1995 and in English in 1998, Endenburg talks about how he developed sociocracy in his company, Endenburg Electrotechniek (edited with some re-translation by the authors).*

At the end of the 1960s, I began to look for another way of running a business. With the inequality of individuals in the exercise of power or the making of decisions, traditional organizations with their authoritarian leadership were then seen by many, including myself, to be one of the most important causes of violence. By violence I mean that by which another, I or the other, can be denied or ignored.

From the standpoint of equality, I also distrusted the democratic way of making decisions—the principle of majority rule. The question was, "What should a business look like to avoid this inequality?"

For this reason, whenever anyone developed a new form of organization, I wanted to test it in practice. As a result, a fruitful exchange began between development and application. Having one's own company offered a unique opportunity to do this.

In my view, however, all the experiments with other forms of organization of which I was aware were ultimately authoritarian, or democratic, in character. These included organizations built on a cooperative basis, companies with workers' self-government, as in the former Yugoslavia, the Mondragon project in Spain, the Scott Bader Company and the Glacier Project in England, van Steenis in the Netherlands, and many others. Inequivalence of value was always embedded in the decision-making process in these organizations. Consequently, evaluating these experiments only made sense to me if the manner of decision-making prevailing in the organization was neither autocratic nor democratic. Although at that time, I much preferred the democratic method of decision-making to the autocratic method, as a result of my own experience, I later came to distrust democracy even more. It was not only majority rule that provoked my resistance; there was far more to distrust.

231

My schooling under Kees Boeke served me well here. In fact, my experience of education based on Quaker principles was enormously important.

BOTH I AND THE OTHERS

United in the Religious Society of Friends, Quakers experience their religion each in their own personal way. This involves firstly a fundamental respect for the religious experience and the religious reality of others. The equivalence of each individual derives from this principle. Furthermore, they have never fixed their religion in images, they have no church, and there are no priests. Whenever they come together, silence is the source of their inspiration. Decision-making is by general consensus and non-violence is one of their basic principles. Kees Boeke, for whom these Quaker principles had a universal validity, based his school, De Werkplaats Kindergemeenschap (the Children's Community Workshop), on them, and as a consequence, I had already had in my youth some experience of the "both-and" concept. The test in practice was to see whether one's own interests could be served by serving the interests of the other, in this case both I and the other(s) with whom I worked. I also learned to decide by general consensus to have respect for the ideas of others and to build with the group of which I was a part both my own and my collective world, or reality.

In the group of which I was a part and in other groups at the school, nothing was ever decided by the majority. When majority rule was once tried, the feeling of the group was so altered that we rapidly abandoned it. It seemed as though something violent had happened.

Initially, these experiences formed the only—but essential—data on which my distrust of democracy was based.

LACK OF KNOWLEDGE ABOUT CONTROL OF POWER

I found it enormously irritating that no one could provide any theoretical support for any form of decision-making whatever. Why was democracy the principle on which our whole way of life was based?

I began to form the idea that a great deal of what we experience as problems of power had their root in a lack of knowledge, whether partial or complete, about the control of power or, more specifically, about the control of dynamic processes. It appeared as though nothing from the technical sciences, the area of my own expertise, had managed to penetrate either the social sciences or the practice of organization and control. This was, for me, the point of departure for the process of developing sociocracy.

The various forms of control based on decisively cutting through problems, with which we have become so familiar, are all the result of ignoring the possibilities of integrated control based on circular processes. What all these variations have in common is that an institution of supremacy is created (i.e., a chairperson, major shareholder, representative group, or organ) and allotted a dominant position without this dominance or supremacy itself being in any way open to creation or re-creation using a circular process. If so, it would be self-governing through a mutual exchange of arguments. Indeed, argument and the exchange of arguments in such an institution do not openly cycle, but rather they occur within the process of acquiring and assuming the position of dominance, functioning only to rationalize and legitimize that process. They exist within the framework of a competitive struggle for supremacy to which they are then bound in servitude.

Here, I use the term power in the sense of the ability to influence. (Everything that is, that exists, is a manifestation of power.) Viewed in this way, all the factors capable of influencing our lives are factors of power. Influence is a universal phenomenon that accompanies the actualization of power.

Supremacy is an absolute or authoritarian variant of this power. Supremacy arises where influence can be monopolized or power actualized from an isolated position. Supremacy thus represents the possibility of violence: the ability to deny others and the other.

DELEGATION OF POWER TO THE "ARGUMENT"

The idea of "sociocracy succeeding democracy" began to emerge. At the end of the 1960s, I spoke of the triad—autocracy, democracy, and sociocracy—as methods in an evolutionary sequence to shape and direct our lives and living together. In theory, according to this sequence, in the method of autocracy, a supremacy is granted to an individual or a small select group; in the democratic method, to the majority; and in the sociocratic method, to the argument. What this means is an argument in which the I and the other are so connected that there are no apparent grounds to either party for denying consent to achieve supremacy. Shifting supremacy to the principle of "argument" has practical consequences [because] it precisely precludes the exclusion of the other person and the other from possible influence and contribution. Sociocracy can thus be seen as a social design whose aim is to offer no opportunity for the appropriation or consolidation of supremacy. Because of this, the sociocratic method corresponds more closely and explicitly with the scientific method than is the case with democratic governance. What is proposed here, as a modification of Feyerabend's famous dictum against scientific method (Feyerabend 1975), is to become "Anything goes under the understanding that any thing goes."

Under the principle of consent (the principle of no objection), as I understand it, a decision is only made when no one involved has any strong and argued objection. This is where individual equivalence is determined. By embracing everyone's argument, discussion gives everyone concerned the chance to reach the best solution, one that is practicable for all.

A paramount and argued objection is one that:

◆ Is indisputable by reason of its grounds for withholding consent
◆ Demonstrates a reason or motive that has been ignored or underestimated by those attending and/or the statement presented
◆ Takes the form of a rejection of the proposal because the reason or motive has not been adequately considered in the decision proposed.

Once reasoned consent predominates it governs the process of decision making, subordinating all other ways of reaching a decision, i.e., they are only possible if consent exists for them.

GUIDING OF POWER FOLLOWING PRINCIPLES OF CYBERNETICS

Literally, *sociocracy* means the sovereignty of the *socius*: I myself, the next person, the alter ego, the otherness. From a structural point of view, this corresponds with the definition of sociocracy as a situation where the principle of consent predominates or is socially all–determining in the sense that it governs the making of decisions at all levels of society. The sociocratic circle organization is a cybernetic means of making this possible and then, as a dynamic balance, it maintains, regulates, and develops it.

The definition of sociocracy is a situation where the principle of consent predominates or is socially all–determining in the sense that it governs the making of decisions at all levels of society.

With sociocratic circle organization, there arises the possibility, in fact, to guide power according to cybernetic principles. Sociocracy is in this way also a method, an organizing, a possible ongoing process of construction, reconstruction, and deconstruction. It is a method that in itself is "empty," since every view, ideology, conviction, or method, etc., that might be attached can find its place and influence in it. Only that which serves absolutely to isolate is excluded. Sociocracy is based on the idea that there is no given or permanent base to which social reality can be secured. What is produced as group organization contains an "objective" reality construct: it gives the possibilities that can be inter-subjectively explored. It provides a new basis for our society that will replace the democratic, which in its own turn replaced the autocratic. At the time, I therefore called this the sociocratic circle organization, a basis for living and working together.

With regard to the concept of supremacy, the "one man–one vote" system represents an equality that gives to democracy the appearance of individual equivalence. For the minority, however, the majority means simply a supremacy, a respectable and established means of voting away the interests of the minority. My distrust of democracy only deepened as the sociocratic design developed. The sociocratic way of dealing with power through organizing comprises self-organization in continual relation with that which links that organizing self with the other, the outer world. In this way, sociocracy goes beyond the fixations—the sectarian divisions and limitations—that the democratic way of handling power demonstrably amplifies.

In the early 1970s, I began to apply this design-in-embryo, as a circular process, to the organization of my company. From then on, the process of continuous construction, reconstruction, and deconstruction of the organization became part of the normal routine. Decision-making, investing, ownership—everything was part of the discussion. Every proposal, every argument during the circle meetings had equal value in decision making. Everything that belonged in the circle could be discussed, nothing was excluded, not even salaries or personal matters. The way of electing people, after open discussion with consent, was a part of this.

PROOF THAT THE METHOD WORKS

In the beginning of 1976, the shipbuilding industry collapsed, leading to a crisis that had near catastrophic consequences for the company. By the end of that critical year, once it became clear that the greatest threat to our further existence was over with hardly any layoffs, not only was there rejoicing at our shared success but some considerable amazement, too, at the way that had been achieved. Was the tenacity and creativity of the circles the strength of the sociocratic circle organization?

It was indisputable that sociocracy had contributed to this success, though that contribution is of course difficult to quantify or to demonstrate objectively. The consequence was in any case an unexpected development of the design and, as a result, the sociocratic circle organization acquired a wider significance. Ever since, the possibility of generating, regenerating, degenerating, and repairing starting from chaos has had a recognizable place and function in the sociocratic circle. During this process, which had been generated and sociocratically regulated as result of the crisis, it was discovered that it was vitally important for an organization not only to allow room and influence for the methods of making decisions that is so distinctive of sociocracy, democracy, and autocracy, but also to the decision-making methods characteristic of religion and chaos.

The following suggest themselves as principles for methods of decision-making that characterize respectively these ways of thinking:

- ◆ **Sociocracy**: the principle of consent. Supremacy belongs to the arguments that the individual and the community (with possible inclusion of "the outside world") present to one another.
- ◆ **Democracy**: the principle of the majority. Supremacy is given to the greatest number, the most inclusive representation, the most shares, etc.

◆ **Autocracy**: the principle of the individual or a small, select group. Supreme power is given to the Leader, the Superior, the owner, the aristocratic caste, or the expert.

◆ **Theocracy**: the principle of a totally binding belief or unity. Supreme power is delegated to the "it," the all-inclusive crystallization point in yourself, the other person, and also in the other.

◆ **Chaos**: emergence from possibilities that are not immediately coherent. Supremacy is given to incoherent power phenomenon or possibilities of presence.

A PLACE FOR CHAOS

Starting from chaos, i.e., from a system of possibilities without interconnections understood between them, new ideas are born, problems solved, and the pioneering starts. An organization must literally make room for this—a place for chaos, where there needs to be no connections and where existing connections must be undone and new forms thought up. With sociocracy, that place is the circle meeting, the place where continuous construction, reconstruction, and deconstruction of the work of the organization can occur, where the events and episodes themselves can be looked at and where experiences (intuitions and feelings) can be exchanged. The circle organization should, in this regard, be seen as an infrastructure for reflection. Decision-making in the circle is governed by the principle of consent. Through reflection the application of the principle of consent becomes a process of self-investigation and self-renewal. As a result, the continuance of equivalence in decision-making is possible for those involved. It becomes a reflexive principle of consent.

Application of the principle of consent on its own, without being organically integrated in a circle structure, is not advised, since there is then no provision for reflection, leading to a kind of "equivalence in no-man's land" [that] could be eventually applied as a means of manipulation ... no real human equivalence is possible without organic integration in a circle structure.

During the circle meeting, all possible structural changes and policy proposals are discussed, without there being any necessity to alter the existing structure. After deciding by consent in such a "brainstorming" session on new possibilities, the changes can be carried through. These new possibilities must always link up functionally with the circle members and their collective objective. It can also be proposed that circle members themselves should take a prominent part in expanding the repertoire of new prospects. In the "brainstorming" stage of the circle meeting, their mutual relations and connections that are determined and operative in the workplace can be loosened. The result is to create a forum of chaos and synergy, where each member of the circle can display his or her possibilities, to be able to push further, as much for their own benefit as for the benefit of other circle members. It is a forum in which everyone can freely move without risk of being put down. On the strength of consent alone, structural changes can be developed at the decision-making stage.

Because the circle meeting is preeminently a breeding place for an organization, a business for example, where generation, regeneration, and degeneration can occur, it is by no means an optional luxury but vitally important for organizing. Within a company, the organization of work that is provided with a sociocratic circle organization, shows a capacity to construct, reconstruct, and deconstruct, strongly enhancing continuity. In actual fact, it is the people in a sociocratic circle organization who determine this continuity. The possibility of eternal life? In any case, in principle and excluding unforeseen calamities, there is the possibility of keeping the organization functioning as long as needed.

After chaos, religion. Once a decision is made, with the binding unity formed by consent, the circle can believe in that decision—and necessarily so, for otherwise nothing will succeed. The same is true for those functions and tasks that are delegated to individuals by consent. Cooperation is impossible unless one can believe in this delegation, the embodiment of unity through diversification.

There is then a need for space for independent decision-making (which is authoritarian in the sense that the individual derives the power to dominate through consent) to be able to fulfill the functions and tasks delegated. All forms of decision-making can thus be successfully implemented, provided they are governed by the principle of consent. Within the governing structure that consent decision-making provides, it turns out in practice that there is hardly any use for the democratic way of making decisions—another signal that only confirmed my doubts over the capacity for resolution of the democratic method.

A SELF-CONTROLLING PROCESS

Thus the sociocratic circle organization as a basis for living and working together not only rests on decision-making according to the principle of consent but also allows the possibility for chaos, religion, autocracy, and democracy to exist within it. These possibilities present themselves one after the other, but in actual practice, when organizing decision making, they present themselves at the same time, in what are called parallel processes.

The development [that] accompanies this broadening of the basis also makes it clear that simply laying a basis is not sufficient. More is needed if the process is to be capable of further self-development and of self-direction. Basis here means the starting point from which the process of construction, reconstruction, and deconstruction can take place in a reasonably dignified way. The question remained, however: how can organizing be produced and directed so that equivalence remains integrally present within it, and such that the reciprocal movements of being led and the unfolding of self initiative can maintain a forward momentum?

… because of the speed of developments, permanent education was vital to any company.

By the beginning of the 1980s, I was wondering: "Is there anything known about the shaping and direction of organization as process, and if so, where can I get instruction?" What had so far come to my notice from various disciplines had not produced much of a satisfactory result. This was around the time that the in-company training systems of many companies were folding because of financial constrictions. I, on the contrary, with my awareness tuned by my education at Boeke's school, was coming to the conclusion that, because of the speed of developments, permanent education was vital to any company and that … traditional educational establishments could never in the long run be wholly satisfactory. The term "permanent education" here covers three categories of education:

◆ firstly, vocational education in the relevant field;
◆ secondly, education in the structuring of the organization as process; and
◆ thirdly, education in the organization of decision-making.

In the traditional approach, vocational education is primarily concerned with the first category, but this is of limited value given the speed of developments taking place in the various specialties. It would probably be better to deliver this kind of education within the company.

The two other subjects, to which far too little attention is still given, probably lend themselves ideally to a regular, formal practical education, since they involve the acquisition of skills and practical know-how that is less context- and time-dependent.

In my own company, we began shaping and integrating this permanent education in the early '80s, under the name of "integral education." With a good basis alone, only part of the problem was resolved. It was necessary to develop the lacking knowledge and skills as rapidly as possible.

As a result of the enormous energy that I myself put into the development of this matter of structuring and directing at this stage, I arrived at the discovery with which my intuition of the deficiency of democracy could be given a clear foundation. In retrospect, that discovery provided the legitimation for the decision not to democratize my company but to provide a sociocratic basis.

Sociocracy for One

BY SHARON VILLINES

Each person is capable of creating harmony, resilience, and responsiveness in themselves and their environment. You yourself can implement the principles and practices of sociocracy, whether you are participating in a sociocratic organization or not. These small changes in your behavior and expectations can make a big difference in the decision-making in any group of people.

1. EXPECT CONSENT

Function as if consent is the standard in decision-making.

When a decision is about to be made, ask if there are any remaining concerns or objections before anyone can call for a vote or declare agreement autocratically. If possible, glance at each person as an invitation to speak. If someone tries to dismiss a concern, say, "Let's look at this for a moment." Help clarify and resolve any concerns or objections. Ask if anyone else can do the same.

When unresolved objections remain, emphasize that a decision has not been made. Most small groups function by consent most of the time. With only one objection, however, they may avoid announcing a formal decision and then proceed as if one had been made. The objector will be silent to avoid conflict. Break this cycle and state clearly, "Let's decide not to implement this until we have enough information to resolve this objection."

2. INITIATE ROUNDS

Instead of waiting for open discussion, begin rounds by asking, "What does everyone think? Mary?" Then move around the room to each person.

Doing rounds can completely change the dynamic of a group because rounds:

- ◈ Establish equality in the room as each person is given time to speak.
- ◈ Draw out comments from those who dislike competing for attention or believe their ideas are not important enough to express.
- ◈ Prevent people from using silence to avoid responsibility.
- ◈ Enable everyone to avoid dominating the discussion.

3. DOUBLE LINK

Suggest that two people with differing styles or opinions represent your group when approaching an authority or attending a meeting.

When two people represent a group as equals, the process of representation is more likely to result in:

◆ a shift from an individual viewpoint or benefit to collaboration on behalf of the group;

◆ consultation in a search for solutions, rather than presenting an autocratic decision;

◆ less likelihood of being co-opted with two listening; and

◆ more communication and understanding with the experience and knowledge of two people present.

4. ASSIGN TASKS USING DISCUSSION AND CONSENT

Before anyone can volunteer, ask what the role or responsibility requires and then begin directly by asking one person who thinks they could fulfill those requirements. Convey the expectation that there will be more than one qualified person.

◆ A volunteer may not be the best person for the job, and the person who is may not volunteer.

◆ People often recognize abilities in others that others don't see in themselves.

◆ Self-nominations are acceptable as long as they don't preclude discussion of other possible candidates or a consideration of the volunteer's ability to fulfill the task requirements. One ability demonstrated by volunteering, however, is the desire to fulfill the task!

5. ACTIVELY SOLICIT OBJECTIONS

After presenting an idea, welcome objections by asking, "Now how is this going to work? What's wrong with it? Let's make it better and get all the chinks out now."

Resolving objections builds a stronger proposal. Don't allow concerns and objections to slide away. Taking them seriously builds the commitment and focus necessary for collaborative decision-making and effective action. Even when an objection cannot be resolved, everyone may be more willing to move forward and test the decision if it is thoroughly understood.

6. RESOLVE OBJECTIONS IN THE GROUP

Treat the objection as an issue the group needs to resolve, not as an attempt to convince the objector privately. Objections should be content-focused and consent is not a bargaining chip as votes are often used in majority vote decisions.

7. MEASURE & REPORT

Build measurements into plans and proposals so you will know if they have accomplished their purposes. If the group doesn't want to include these in the proposal, keep a list of purposes and measurements yourself, letting everyone know you are doing it and that you would like to bring it back for discussion in a certain number of months. If the group doesn't consent to a group review, refer to what you have learned when discussing related topics. Share openly. Transparency builds trust and invites more information.

Measurements don't have to be complicated. Match the amount of data needed to the complexity of the decision. Burdensome measurements may not be kept accurately.

8. PRACTICE & ENCOURAGE SELF-ORGANIZATION

Self-organize by taking control of your assigned or assumed responsibilities. Be self-generating by producing new ideas and solutions. Create a plan for growing personally and professionally. Include learning more about your organization and your industry or profession. Expect the same of others by asking questions that expect a positive answer.

Self-organization is often discouraged, but even in the most-controlled, autocratic workplaces and organizations, there may be small opportunities to take more responsibility and initiative.

Take responsibility for your own development, continuing to learn about your work and your organization.

Sociocracy is based on values and practices that encourage inclusiveness, self-organization, development, productivity, and effectiveness. By applying those values and practices in your daily life, you will create a sociocracy.

Bylaws for a Sociocratic Business

The following example is adapted from the operating agreement for a Limited Liability Company (LLC) incorporated in Delaware. It contains the key clauses that can be used in many forms of sociocratic operating agreements and bylaws including nonprofit organizations, associations, local government agencies, etc.

Appendix F is an example for nonprofit organizations that will also work well for small businesses.

In the United States, LLCs are now legal in all 50 states and the District of Columbia, and currently provide the most-efficient mechanism for establishing a fully sociocratic company that owns and governs itself. While a sociocratic company is allow to have investors and protects the interests of investors, it does not grant the investors the exclusive right to sell or to control the company.

The key clauses can also be used as the basis of bylaws for a C or S corporation, but in these cases, a "double corporation" strategy is required to enable the company to raise capital without giving stockholders the right to override consent decision-making. A full explanation of the double corporation is outside the scope of this book, but it involves setting up a foundation to hold the controlling stock. The members of the board of the foundation and the board of the corporation are defined as identical and the decisions of one to be those of the other.

A digital version is posted at:

http://www.sociocracy.info/bylaws-for-a-sociocratic-business/j

This operating agreement is an example only and does not constitute legal advice. Because laws vary widely between jurisdictions, professional legal advice is required to address specific circumstances.

OPERATING AGREEMENT

FOR A SOCIOCRATIC LIMITED LIABILITY COMPANY (LLC)

Article 1 The Sociocratic Circle-Organization Method

1.1 Organizational Model

The LLC shall be structured and governed in accordance with the sociocratic Circle-Organization Method, the underlying principles of which are:

1.1.1 The Principle of Consent

The principle of consent governs decision-making. This means that not every decision requires consent, but that there will be consent about the policies by which decision-making takes a different form. Consent means there are no argued and paramount objections. In other words, a policy decision can only be made if no member of the circle raises a argued and paramount objection to it.

1.1.2 The Principle of Circles

The organization is composed of a hierarchy of semi-autonomous, self-organizing circles. A circle is a group of people who are operationally related. Each circle has its own aim and the authority and responsibility to execute, measure, and control its own activities and to maintain an appropriate level of knowledge and skill, assisted by a program of development conducted by the circle.

1.1.3 The Principle of Double-Linked Circles

All circles are double-linked. A lower circle is always linked to a higher circle so at least two people—that is, the operational leader and at least one elected representative from the lower circle—belong to and participate in the decision-making of the next-higher circle.

1.1.4 The Principle of Election of People

People are elected to functions and tasks exclusively by consent after open discussion.

1.2 Structure

The organization of the LLC shall be a hierarchy of double-linked circles, in the following order, from top to bottom:

1.2.1 Top Circle

The top circle shall be the highest circle of the LLC, the powers and responsibilities of which are set forth in the articles of organization and this operating agreement. The composition of the top circle is defined in Article 2.

The top circle shall manage and direct the business and affairs of the LLC, with full power to engage in any lawful act or activity under the General Limited Liability Company (LLC) Law of [name of jurisdiction] unless otherwise limited by the provisions of this operating agreement.

1.2.2 General Circle

The general circle shall consist of the chief executive officer (CEO), operational leaders of the department circles, and at least one representative from each department circle. The general circle shall manage the operations of the LLC within the limits set by the top circle.

The general circle shall:

(a) determine and control policy to realize its own aim(s) within limits set by the top circle;

(b) delegate part of its decision-making authority to the department circles so their aims can be achieved;

(c) assign functions and tasks to its own members to execute its own policy; and

(d) decide, in its sole discretion, whether new department circles should be created or existing circles should be split up, combined, or dissolved. The department circle in question may not participate in the decision to dissolve its circle. The consent of the representative of the department circle in question shall not be required for the general circle to act, but such representative may participate in such discussions in the general circle.

1.2.3 Department Circles

Each department circle shall consist of (1) either an operational leader and the members of the department circle or an operational leader and the operational leaders of the section circles and (2) at least one representative from each section circle. The department circle shall:

(a) determine and control the policy to achieve its aim within the limits set by the general circle;

(b) assign tasks to its own members to execute its own policy; and

(c) decide, in its sole discretion, whether a new section circle should be set up or whether existing circles should be dissolved. The section circle in question may not participate in the decision to dissolve its circle. The consent of the representative of the section circle in question shall not be required for the department circle to act, but such representative may participate in such discussions in the department circle.

1.2.4 Section Circles

Each section circle shall consist of (1) either an operational leader and the members of the section circle or an operational leader and operational leaders of the unit circles and (2) at least one representative from each unit circle. The section circle shall:

(a) determine and control policy to achieve their aims within the limits set by the department circle;

(b) assign tasks to its own members to execute its own policy; and

(c) decide, in its sole discretion, whether new unit circles should be set up or whether existing circles should be dissolved. The unit circle in question may not participate in the decision to dissolve its circle. The consent of the representative of the unit circle in question shall not be required for the section circle to act, but such representative may participate in the discussions in the section circle.

1.2.5 Unit Circles

Each unit circle shall consist of an operational leader and its own members. Unit circles shall:

(a) determine and control policy to achieve its aim within the limits set by the section circle, and

(b) assign tasks to its own members to execute its own policy.

1.2.6 Further Subdivision

The hierarchical pattern established in sections 1.2.2–1.2.5 shall be repeated for any levels below unit circles.

1.3 Investing and Working Partners

People can become members of the LLC by investing money or by performing active labor or both. People or organizations having made investments in the LLC shall be called hereafter "investing partners." Those who perform labor shall be called hereafter "working partners."

Members of the general, department, section, and unit circles, and any circles below unit circles, shall be working partners. A natural person can be both a working partner and an investing partner. A legal person, for example, another LLC, S corporation, or C corporation, can be an investing partner but not a working partner.

[The decision to have "working partners" or "employees" has tax and other implications that require legal advice. The intention is that everyone be able to participate in decision-making on an equivalent basis. The term "partner" is not intended to infer greater authority nor "employee" less authority.]

ARTICLE 2 TOP CIRCLE

[Top Circle is the generic term for the highest governing level of the organization. It retains the circular process connotations and links to the primary sociocratic theory. Organizations may wish to adopt other terms to reflect their culture and environment.]

2.1 Composition and Number

The top circle shall consist of no fewer than six (6) nor more than twelve (12) members, as such number may be established from time to time by resolution of the top circle. This number shall include:

(a) external experts,

(b) the CEO of the LLC, and

(c) one or more representatives of the general circle of the LLC.

2.2 External Experts

[The importance of the title "board of directors" varies among legal jurisdictions and not all organizations are required to have a board. When a board is required, there may also be a requirement that it be composed entirely of people from outside the organization—the external experts. If that is the case, the following clause can be used: "The top circle shall totally encompass all the duties of the board of directors. Every meeting of the top circle shall be considered a meeting also of the board of directors. The board of directors shall not meet separately from the top circle." If a board is required by law, it may also be necessary to have a separate article defining the board and its responsibilities. If so, it can be modeled after the clauses used for the top circle.]

The external experts, chosen from outside the organization, shall represent each of the following roles:

(a) a person with expertise in financial matters relating to the business of the LLC.

(b) a person with expertise in the area of human resource, small business, or other management specialties;

(c) a person with expertise in sociocratic (dynamic self-governance) or other technical areas in which the LLC may choose to conduct its business; and

(d) a representative of the governmental or legal community.

2.3 Separation of Roles

The CEO, elected representatives from the general circle, and the person with expertise in financial matters must be separate people. These people and other members of the top circle who are not working partners of the LLC may fulfill one or more than one of the other above roles at the same time, unless this could result in a statutory, operational, or legal incompatibility.

2.4 Designation of Roles

The top circle, by resolution, shall designate the roles that each of its members fulfills.

2.5 Election, Terms, and Reimbursement

The members of the top circle, except for the financial expert, may be proposed by an external organization with consent from the CEO and elected representative(s). If such external organizations are not available, the top circle may elect people with expertise in these areas to participate in the top circle for specified terms. The experts' terms shall be staggered and up to two years in duration, renewable at the invitation of the top circle. The top circle may choose to reimburse these experts for their services.

2.6 Resignation; Vacancies

Any member of the top circle may resign from the top circle at any time by submitting a letter of resignation to the secretary of the top circle.

Any newly created membership or any vacancy occurring in the top circle for any cause may be filled by a person selected by the consent of the remaining members of the top circle. Each member so elected shall hold office until the expiration of the term of office of the member of the top circle whom he or she has replaced or until his or her successor is elected and qualified.

The CEO shall be elected or re-elected at two-year intervals at the first top circle meeting after the annual investors' meeting. The representative(s) from the general circle shall be elected at intervals of up to two years on a schedule set by the general circle.

2.7 Regular Meetings

Regular meetings of the top circle may be held at such places in or outside of the [name of jurisdiction] and at such times as the top circle may from time to time determine. If so determined, notices thereof need not be given.

2.8 Special Meetings

Special meetings of the top circle may be held at any time or place in or outside of the [name of jurisdiction] whenever called by any member of the top circle. Notice of a special meeting of the top circle shall be given by the person or people calling the meeting at least forty-eight (48) hours before the special meeting.

2.9 Telephonic Meetings Permitted

Members of the top circle may participate in a meeting by means of conference telephone or similar communications equipment by means of which all persons participating in the meeting can hear each other, and participation in a meeting pursuant to this operating agreement shall constitute presence in person at such meeting.

2.10 Consent Decision Required for Action

The principle of consent by all parties shall be organized as follows: At all meetings of the top circle, one-half of the members of the top circle or at least two (2) members of the top circle, whichever number is the greater, shall constitute a quorum for the transaction of business. All decision-making by the top circle, however, shall be according to the principle of consent; that is, whether or not a member of the top circle is present, consent is required of all the members of the top circle to all proposed decisions.

Any member of the top circle absent from a meeting of the top circle shall be notified within forty-eight (48) hours of the proposed decision(s) of the top circle. Unless the absent top circle member objects to a decision of the top circle within seventy-two (72) hours of receipt of such notice, he or she will be deemed to have consented to such decision.

If an absent top circle member objects to any action of the top circle in a timely fashion, the matter will be placed upon the agenda for the next meeting of the top circle, which meeting shall be held within seventy-two (72) hours of the receipt of such objection. Any member absent from such top circle meeting shall be deemed to have consented to the decision that the top circle reconsiders.

2.11 Organization

Meetings of the top circle shall be presided over by the president of the top circle or another person chosen by consent of the top circle. In the absence of the president or other chosen person, a chairperson chosen at the meeting shall preside over the meeting. The secretary shall act as secretary of the meeting, but in his or her absence, the person presiding may appoint any person to act as secretary of the meeting.

2.12 Informal Actions

Any decision required or permitted to be made at any meeting of the top circle may be made without a meeting if all members of the top circle consent thereto in writing, and the writing or writings are filed with the minutes of proceedings of the top circle.

ARTICLE 3 EXECUTIVE OFFICERS OF THE TOP CIRCLE

3.1 Executive Officers; Election; Qualifications; Term of Office; Resignation; Removal; Vacancies.

The top circle shall elect executive officers annually from among its members: a president, secretary, and treasurer. It also may, if it so determines, choose a chairperson (or facilitator) of the top circle and a vice chairperson (or second facilitator) of the top circle from among its members. The top circle may also choose one or more vice presidents, one or more assistant vice presidents, one or more assistant secretaries, and one or more assistant treasurers. Each such officer shall hold office until the first meeting of the top circle after the annual meeting of investing partners next succeeding his or her election, and until his or her successor is elected and qualified or until his or her earlier resignation or removal.

Any officer may resign his or her executive office at any time upon written notice to the secretary of the LLC. The secretary may resign at any time upon written notice to the president. The top circle may remove any officer from his or her executive office at any time without necessarily removing him or her from the top circle. Such removal shall be without prejudice to the contractual rights of such officer, if any, with the LLC.

Any number of executive offices may be held by the same person unless prohibited by governing law. At any regular or special meeting, the top circle may fill any executive officer vacancy in any office of the LLC occurring by death, resignation, removal, or otherwise for the unexpired portion of the term.

3.2 Power to Require Security

The top circle may require any of its members, and any officer, agent, working member, or employee of the LLC, to give security for the faithful performance of his or her duties.

ARTICLE 4 CIRCLE MANAGEMENT

4.1 General Provisions

Management of all circles of the LLC, with the exception of management of the top circle, shall be in accordance with the following procedures only to the extent that such procedures are not inconsistent with Article 2 or Article 3 hereof, or any other provisions of this operating agreement, the articles of organization, or the laws of [name of jurisdiction].

4.1.1 Circle Regulations

Each circle shall be a separate organ of the LLC and shall be empowered to draft its own regulations with respect to the tasks, authority, and responsibilities of the circle, which regulations shall not be in conflict with this operating agreement or any regulations that the top circle may adopt.

4.1.2 Assisting Circles

A circle is authorized to form assisting (or helping) circles to prepare decision-making recommendations for the circle. The assisting circle may be composed of people from the circle, members of other circles, and external advisors.

4.1.3 Circle Decisions and Limits

A circle may make decisions within certain limits agreed on in the next-higher circle; individual members may make independent decisions within the limits drawn up by their own circles.

4.2 Decision-making

4.2.1 The Principle of Consent

Decision-making shall be in accordance with the principle of consent or "no objection." Decision-making does not require consent to be used for every decision of the circle, but it must be used to establish an alternative means of decision-making for a specific decision or for a specific class of decisions.

4.2.2 Objections

Should there be a paramount objection to a decision, arguments for the objection must be given. An objection without reasoned argument will not be considered.

4.2.3 Second Meetings

If a circle is unable to reach a decision on a particular matter, a new meeting of the circle shall be convened after at least forty-eight (48) hours, with the same subject on the agenda.

4.2.4 Referring Decisions

If a circle is unable to reach a decision on a particular matter in a second meeting of the circle, the chairperson may refer the matter to the next-higher or -lower circle for decision or recommendation.

4.2.5 Annual Decision-making Audit

An independent auditor shall review the decision-making process in each circle annually and shall report to the top circle whether the decision-making of the circles conforms to this operating agreement.

4.2.6 Assuming Decision-making Authority

The next-higher circle is responsible for assuring that decision-making in a circle functions according to this operating agreement. If the next-higher circle concludes that the decision-making within a circle does not function according to this agreement, the next-higher circle may take over the decision-making of that circle on an interim basis.

The circle shall continue to make recommendations to the next-higher circle concerning its area of responsibility. The next-higher circle shall take such action(s) as it deems necessary to re-establish the circle's performance according to sociocratic (dynamic self-governance) principles as soon as possible. The next higher circle shall restore decision-making authority to the circle as soon as either the next-higher circle or the independent auditor determines that decision-making is functioning according to sociocratic (dynamic self-governance) principles.

4.3 Selection of People

4.3.1 Officers and Representatives

Each circle shall elect a chairperson (or facilitator) of circle meetings and a secretary from among its members. Each circle shall also elect one or more representatives of the circle in the next-higher circle, whether or not that person is a member of the circle, provided the representative is in some way connected to the LLC. These elections shall be conducted annually, or as deemed necessary by the circle, at a meeting convened for this purpose, according to the consent principle and after open discussion.

4.3.2 Multiple Functions

A person may fulfill more than one function at the same time, unless this could result in a statutory, operational, or legal incompatibility, provided that the operational leader (elected by the next-higher circle) and the representative may not be the same person.

4.3.3 Procedures for Appointment and Dismissal

Each circle shall determine procedures for the appointment and dismissal of members of the circle, in accordance with the law, this operating agreement, and the articles of organization. A circle shall make decisions about the appointment or dismissal of its members only after the person involved has been given an opportunity to present his or her arguments. However, the person involved may not participate in the making of this decision.

In the absence of a written agreement to the contrary between an individual working partner and the LLC, these procedures shall not constitute a contract between any person and the LLC, and all working partners of the LLC shall continue as working partners at the will of the LLC.

4.3.4 Objections to Appointments or Dismissals

In the event a circle objects to the appointment of or seeks to dismiss a representative of the next-lower circle, the circle shall submit objections to the next-lower circle concerning the functioning of its representative in the circle. Should the consideration of these objections not result in consent between the higher circle and the next-lower circle, the higher circle may deny the representative the right to represent the lower circle in the higher circle.

Such denial of representation is an extreme remedy and the higher circle should only undertake it as a final resort, and should take all necessary action to restore representation of the next-lower circle as soon as possible.

4.4 Circle Meetings

4.4.1 Frequency

Circles shall meet at regular intervals, at least six times per year.

4.4.2 Convening and Notice

Regular circle meetings shall be convened by the chairperson (or facilitator) of the circle. All members shall receive notice of the meeting, the agenda, and any relevant information necessary to make decisions on matters to be discussed at the meeting within a reasonable time before the meeting.

4.4.3 Special Meetings

The chairperson shall convene a special meeting within seven (7) days of a request therefore from any member of the circle.

Should the chairperson fail to convene such a meeting within seven (7) days after the receipt of such a request, the circle member who made the request may convene the meeting.

4.4.4 Members Present (Quorum)

It is not necessary for all the members of the circle to be present to hold a meeting; however, consent is required from all members of a circle before a decision can take effect. Each circle shall establish its own written policy defining a quorum for conducting business and its procedures for obtaining consent from absent members.

4.4.5 Delegation of Participation

Members who are unable to be present can delegate their right to participate in decision-making to another member of the circle. The right to participate, however, does not constitute a proxy consent or veto. The delegated right to participate is the right to present arguments on behalf of another circle member.

4.4.6 Recording Decisions

Any decision made during a circle meeting shall be recorded in circle minutes or notes to be circulated to all members of the circle and to other circles with which the circle is linked within three (3) days of the meeting in the format determined by the organization.

4.4.7 Amending or Repealing a Delegated Decision

Amending or repealing a delegated decision is possible, provided the consent of the circle involved has been obtained.

ARTICLE 5 COMPENSATION AND PROFIT-SHARING

5.1 Fixed Compensation

Both investing partners and working partners engaged in active operations shall receive fixed compensation to be reimbursed only from earnings from operations. The fixed part of the investing partners' reimbursement will be calculated at the end of fiscal year at the then-prevailing prime lending rate. Working partners will be reimbursed throughout the business year at a fixed rate analogous to wages or salaries.

5.2 Variable Compensation

Both investing partners and working partners will receive variable reimbursements to be reimbursed only from earnings from operations. The reimbursements will vary depending on profitability. Variable compensation will be in the form of short-term measurement (STM) and long-term measurement (LTM) payments. STM payments will be made only when profits for the month exceed the targeted profit percentage. If profits for a month fall below the targeted profit percentage, that shortfall must be covered before any STM payments can be made. LTM payments will be made once or twice annually at the discretion of the top circle.

5.3 Determining Fixed and Variable Payments

5.3.1 At least annually, the top circle shall determine the amount targeted for company reserves and the targeted profit percentage.

5.3.2 At least at the end of each fiscal year, the top circle or person(s) delegated by the top circle will normally deduct the targeted reserve from the profits, calculate the amount of fixed payments due to investors per Section 7.1, and subtract that amount and the amount of the targeted reserve from the profits available for variable payments to the parties. The variable payments, however, are so important to the measurement process, a key component of the LLC management, that the top circle can choose to make variable payments before fully paying investors' fixed payments.

5.3.3 The top circle or person(s) delegated by the top circle will calculate an STM payment for the investing and working partners each month and an LTM payment once or twice a year.

5.3.4 The top circle shall decide whether to have the company pay taxes on retained earnings at the corporate tax rate or to pass all earnings through to the partners.

OTHER ARTICLES

[Additional articles may be necessary to address such issues as indemnification, conflict of interest, fiscal year, corporate seal, and so forth. Care must be taken to ensure that these clauses do not contradict or undermine the provisions of Articles 1 through 6.]

ARTICLE X MISCELLANEOUS

Amendment of This Operating Agreement

This operating agreement may be altered or repealed and new agreements made by the top circle, applying the principle of consent in accordance with the provisions of these agreements, with a minimum of thirty (30) days' notice to all members of the LLC, including investing partners, working partners, and board of directors members, of intent to amend this operating agreement. The purpose of such notice shall be to allow all levels of the circle structure, including the investing partners, time to call special meetings if necessary, to deliberate, and to select representatives to attend the deliberations of the next-higher circle.

ADDENDUM
CONDUCT OF MEETINGS OF INVESTING PARTNERS

ARTICLE 1 MEETINGS OF INVESTING PARTNERS

Meetings of investing partners shall be conducted in accordance with the sociocratic (dynamic self-governance) method. By consent, the investing partners may choose methods and structures of decision-making other than consent for a meeting of investing partners.

ARTICLE 2 NOTICE OF MEETINGS

Whenever the investing partners are required or permitted to take any action at a meeting, a written notice of the meeting shall be given to investing partners that shall state the place, date, and hour of the meeting, and, in the case of a special meeting, the purpose or purposes for which the meeting is called. Unless otherwise provided by law, the articles of organization, or this operating agreement, the written notice of any meeting shall be given not less than ten (10) nor more than sixty (60) days before the date of the meeting to the investing partners. If mailed, such notice shall be deemed to be given when deposited in e-mail or mail, postage prepaid, directed to the investing partner at its address as it appears in the records of the LLC.

2.1 Annual Meeting of Investing Partners

The investing partners shall meet annually for the purpose of electing a representative(s) to the top circle and determining the date and time of the next meeting. Only those who have made monetary investment in the LLC, plus the CEO plus the representative(s) from the general circle to the top circle, shall participate in said meeting.

2.2 Special Meetings of Investing Partners

Special meetings of the investing partners may be called with at least 15 days' notice by one or more of the investing partners, the CEO, or elected representative to the top circle. Only the investing partners, the CEO, and the representative(s) to the top circle from the general circle shall be entitled to participate in such meetings. Special meetings will be for the sole purpose of considering the removal and/or replacement of the investing partners' representative(s) to the top circle.

2.3 List of Investing Partners Entitled to Participate in Annual and Special Meetings of Investing Partners

The secretary of the top circle, upon notice of an annual or special meeting of the investing partners, shall prepare and make, at least ten (10) days before such meeting, a complete list of the investing partners entitled to participate in the meeting, arranged in alphabetical order and showing the address of each investing partner and the percentage of equity registered in the name of each investing partner. Such list shall be open to the examination of any investing partner in a designated electronic location.

ARTICLE 3 QUORUM

Except as otherwise provided by law, the articles of organization, or this operating agreement, at each meeting of the investing partners, the presence in person or by electronic means of a person or persons representing at least one-half of the total investment in the LLC plus the CEO or a representative of the general circle shall constitute a quorum. The investing partners may, at their sole discretion, form a legal entity.

ARTICLE 4 ORGANIZATION OF INVESTING PARTNERS MEETING

Meetings of the investing partners shall be presided over by the CEO, a representative of the general circle, or another person elected at the meeting by consent. The meeting attendees shall elect a secretary or direct the CEO to appoint a person to act as secretary of the meeting.

ARTICLE 5 PARTICIPATION IN MEETINGS

Each investing partner in attendance shall be entitled to participate in the consent decision-making process in the investing partners' meeting. Members who are unable to be present can delegate their right to participate in decision-making to another member of the investing partner's circle. The right to participate, however, does not constitute a proxy to consent or veto. The delegated right to participate is the right to present arguments on behalf of another circle member.

ARTICLE 6 FIXING DATE FOR DETERMINATION OF INVESTING PARTNER OF RECORD

6.1 Fixed Record Date

So that the LLC may determine the investing partners entitled to notice of or to participation in any meeting of investing partners or any adjournment thereof; or entitled to receive payment of any funds or other distribution or allotment of any rights; or entitled to exercise any rights in respect of any change, conversion, or exchange of partnership equity; or for the purpose of any other lawful action, the top circle may fix a record date. The record date shall not precede the date upon which the resolution fixing the record date is adopted by the top circle. The record date:

(a) shall not be more than sixty (60) nor less than ten (10) days before the date of the next scheduled meeting of the investing partners;

(b) nor in the case of any other action, shall not be more than sixty (60) days before such other action.

6.2 No Fixed Record Date

If no record date is fixed:

(a) the record date for determining investing partners entitled to notice of or to participate at a meeting of investing partners shall be at the close of business on the day preceding the day on which the meeting is held, and

(b) the record date for determining investing partners for any other purpose shall be at the close of business on the day preceding the day on which the top circle adopts the resolution relating thereto.

A determination of investing partners of record entitled to notice of or to participate at a meeting of investing partners shall apply to any adjournment of the meeting; provided, however, that the top circle may fix a new record date for the adjourned meeting.

ARTICLE 7 LIST OF INVESTING PARTNERS ENTITLED TO PARTICIPATE

The person or people responsible for calling an annual or special meeting of the investing partners must give the secretary of the top circle notice of the meeting at least fifteen (15) days in advance of the date of the meeting.

Bylaws for a Sociocratic Nonprofit Organization

This example is based on the bylaws of a membership advocacy organization incorporated in Washington, DC. It includes the key clauses for establishing a sociocratic governance structure and consent as the basis of decision-making and may be adapted for associations, intentional communities, condominiums, cooperatives, etc.

Depending on the organization, some clauses may not apply and others will have to be amplified or added. For example, your organization might be membership-based or have no members, or be a condominium homeowner association or a cooperative food coop.

One of the most-common requirements is for a board of directors with certain powers. This can be accommodated by stating that the board of directors is identical to the Top Circle. The second usual requirement is for majority vote. Since the minimum majority vote is usually 51%, or 50% plus one when 50% produces a fraction, this is included in the requirement of consent that would be equal to 100%.

This document is for reference only and does not constitute legal advice. Because laws differ between jurisdictions, professional legal advice is required to ensure that all the legal requirements for your organization are included and properly worded.

It can be helpful, however, to draft your own bylaws for your lawyer to review and then add and modify as advised. This allows you to make many decisions before becoming overwhelmed with the legalese in which many legal documents are written. If you receive sample documents, insist that they be written in Plain English. Plain English has been the standard for decades, although many lawyers are still using standard legal phrases from the 19th century. *Plain English for Lawyers* by Richard C. Wydick has been the accepted reference for over 25 years and may be helpful.

(Appendix E is an example for incorporated or limited liability businesses.)

BYLAWS FOR A NONPROFITSOCIOCRATIC ORGANIZATION

1. Description
2. Principles of Governance
3. Governance Structure
4. Circle Governance
5. Decision-making
6. Board of Directors
7. Elections & Terms
8. Meetings
9. Members
10. Advisory Council
11. Financial Practices
12. Annual Report
13. Indemnification
14. Amendments
15. Dissolution
Addendum: Conflict of Interest and Confidentiality Agreement

1. DESCRIPTION

1.1 Name & Affiliations

The name of the organization is the [name]. The Organization is [description of the organization].

Wherever "Organization" appears, substitute the name or shortened name of the association. A definition of terms should also be added— what does "member" mean, for example.

1.2 Legal Structure

The Organization is a nonprofit organization incorporated under the laws of [jurisdiction] exclusively for charitable and educational purposes within the meaning of Section 501(c)(3) of the Internal Revenue Code of 1986, as now enacted or hereafter amended, including making distributions to similar organizations for the same purposes.

1.3 Vision, Mission, and Aim

The strategy and policies of the Organization will be directed toward realizing its vision, mission, and aim.

1.3.1 Vision

The vision of the Organization, the dream that inspires it, is a [vision statement].

1.3.2 Mission

The mission of the Organization—that which will make the vision tangible—is to [statement of mission].

1.3.3 Aim

The aim of the Organization—the products and services that realize its mission—shall be to [statement of aim].

1.4 Governance

The Organization shall be governed according to the principles of sociocratic governance as specified in §2, Sociocratic Governance.

2. SOCIOCRATIC GOVERNANCE

2.1 Definition

Sociocratic governance shall be defined as a method of governance that delegates policy-making to all levels of the organization and establishes equivalence between its members within their domains of responsibility.

2.2 Benefits

The principles and methods of sociocratic governance develop:

    a. strong leadership and clear delegation;
    b. self-governance, self-organization, and cooperation;
    c. the ability to apply scientific theory and methods; and
    d. responsibility for continuing profession development.

2.3 Governing Principles

Three principles are essential to sociocratic governance:

2.3.1   The Principle of Consent

Consent governs policy decision-making. Except as required by law and as otherwise stated in these bylaws, policy decisions shall be made with the consent of those they directly affect. Consent shall be defined as having "no reasoned objections" and as further defined in §§5.2, Consent, and 4.2, Limitations of Consent.

Policy decisions are defined in §5.3, Definition of Policy.

2.3.2 The Principle of Circles

The Organization shall govern itself through a circular hierarchy of semi-autonomous, self-organizing circles that are responsible for policy decisions within their domain. Circles and the circular hierarchy are further defined and described in §3, Governance Structure.

2.3.3 The Principle of Double Links

In the hierarchical structure of circles, a lower circle shall be double-linked to the next higher circle by the operations leader and one or more representatives of the lower circle as described in §§3, Governance Structure, and 4.2, Circle Officers.

2.3.4 The Principle of Consent Elections

Except as required by law, circle members shall elect people to functions and tasks by consent as described in §2.1, Election Process.

3. GOVERNANCE STRUCTURE

3.1 A Circular Hierarchy of Circles

The governance of the Organization shall be structured as a circular hierarchy formed by double-linked, semi-autonomous circles that reflect the operations of the organization. A circular hierarchy shall be defined as one in which each circle, by means of representative participation in the next higher circle, must consent to the policy decisions that affect its domain. Circles are thus linked in an apparently linear hierarchy, but policy decision-making forms a feedback loop, with each circle occupying a place in the loop.

3.2 Circle Definition

A circle includes every person with a common aim who has a significant role in the operations of a department or unit of the Organization.

Circle members meet to make policy decisions within their domains of responsibility. Circle responsibilities are further defined in §§5.1, Domain of Decision-making, and 4, Circle Governance.

3.3 Circle Limitations

No circle's policies shall conflict with the law, these bylaws, the principles and methods of sociocratic governance as defined in these bylaws, or the policies of other circles.

3.4 Circle Membership

3.4.1 Definition

Except for the Board of Directors as defined in §6, Board of Directors, a circle shall include all members of the organization who have significant roles in the circle's operations, whether they are paid or volunteer staff. Each circle shall define "significant roles" and shall be as inclusive as possible while ensuring (1) the stable functioning of the circle and (2) the ability of its members to deliberate with a consistent membership.

3.4.2 Consent to Members

Circle members shall have the right to consent to new members.

3.4.3 Equivalence

Within the circle meeting, the principle of consent shall be used to ensure that all circle members are equivalent in decision-making.

3.4.4 Size

Circles shall be of a size that allows inclusive and efficient deliberations; generally no larger than 40 members, with 20 being the optimal maximum.

3.5 Board of Directors or Top Circle

The Board of Directors shall be identical to the Top Circle, the highest circle in a sociocratically governed organization. Except as required by law or as otherwise stated in these bylaws, the board shall function according to the provisions of §4, Circle Governance, and be subject to any provisions of these bylaws and all the Organization's rules and regulations.

Board-specific requirements for composition, powers, and

responsibilities as required by [state] are specified in §5.6, Decisions of the Board of Directors, and §6, Board of Directors.

3.6 General Management Circle

The general management or coordinating circle shall manage the operations of the Organization within the limits set by the board. It shall consist of the managing director, the operations leader, and one or more representatives from each department circle.

3.7 Department Circles

Each department circle shall consist of the operations leader and members of the department circle and, if it has responsibility for other circles, the operations leaders and at least one representative of those circles.

3.8 Further Subdivision

The hierarchical pattern established in §§3.2–3.3, shall be repeated throughout the Organization.

3.9 Circle Names

Circle names are for illustration only and may be changed as desired and appropriate, as long as the hierarchical chain of leadership, representation, and delegation is clear.

4. CIRCLE GOVERNANCE

4.1 Circle Responsibilities

Each circle, within the limits set by the next higher circle, shall:

    a. determine and control its own policies to achieve its aim as defined by the next higher circle;
    b. assign the leading, doing, and measuring of circle roles and responsibilities to its own members to achieve its aim and execute its own policies;
    c. maintain a record-keeping system of policy decisions and other information, as specified in §4.4, Circle Record-Keeping;
    d. assume responsibility for the professional development of the circle and its members;
    e. elect one or more representatives from its members to serve as the circle's representative(s) to the next-higher circle;
    i. decide how to allocate the resources included in its budget,

including the hiring and firing of personnel;

f. create lower circles as it determines appropriate, assigning an aim and allocating part of its resources to those circles;

g. with the participation of the representative(s) of that circle, elect the operations leader of the next-lower circle; and

h. decide whether lower circles shall be subdivided, combined, or dissolved.

4.2 Limitations of Consent

The principle of consent shall not apply to all circle members in two classes of circle decisions.

4.2.1 Circle Elimination or Redefinition

The operations leader and representative(s) of the lower circle may participate in any discussion of dissolution or restructuring of their circle, but their consent shall not be required for the higher circle to make a decision.

4.2.2 Personnel Decisions

A circle member or members about whom decisions are being made may participate in any discussions, but shall be excluded from participation in consent decisions related to their own benefits of employment, compensation, or service.

4.3 Circle Officers

Except for the board of directors as defined in §6.4, Executive Officers, each circle shall have the following officers:

a. Operations Leader

The operations leader shall be elected by the next higher circle to manage the day-to-day operations within the lower circle's domain. The operations leader shall be a member of both the higher and lower circles, but shall not serve as the representative of the lower circle.

b. Facilitator

A facilitator shall be elected by each circle to conduct circle meetings, provide leadership in decision-making, and ensure that the circle is functioning according to the principles and methods of sociocratic governance.

c. **Executive Secretary**

Each circle shall elect an administrative secretary to manage the affairs of the circle and perform tasks related to its functioning, such as:

1. arranging and announcing circle meetings;
2. preparing the agenda in consultation with the facilitator and operations leader, and other circle members;
3. distributing study materials and proposals;
4. taking and distributing minutes; and
5. performing any other tasks assigned by the circle.

d. **Logbook Keeper**

A logbook keeper shall be elected by the circle to maintain the circle logbook as defined in §4.4, Circle Record-Keeping. Depending on the size of the circle and the complexity of its work, the office of the logbook keeper may be combined with that of the administrative secretary.

e. **Representative(s)**

One or more representatives, other than the operations leader, shall be elected by the circle to participate in the next-higher circle. The circle representative(s) participates as a full member in both the lower and higher circles, but cannot be the same person as the operations leader. Otherwise, any member may fill more than one office and offices may be combined.

4.3 Circle Meetings

All circles shall meet at least quarterly to review their policies, evaluate their effectiveness, adopt new policies if necessary, and review development plans and progress.

4.4 Circle Record-Keeping

Each circle shall create and maintain a logbook that includes, but is not limited to:

a. organization's vision, mission, and aim statements
b. organization's bylaws, rules, and procedures;
c. organization's strategic plan;
d. diagram of the Organization's circle structure;

e. budgets of both the Organization and the circle;

f. circle aims;

g. circle policy decisions and meeting notes;

h. circle development plans;

i. individual members' aims, roles and responsibilities, and development plans; and

j. any other documents that record the business of the circle.

Circle members shall have a copy of, or easy access to a copy of, the circle logbook. Circle members shall maintain their personal logbooks with their aims, roles and responsibilities, development plans, and any other documents related to their individual roles and responsibilities as circle members.

5. DECISION-MAKING

5.1 Aim & Domain of Decision-Making

A circle's aim shall be determined by the next-higher circle and defines the circle's domain of responsibility. To accomplish their aim, circles shall be responsible for making the policy decisions governing operations within their domains.

5.2 Consent

The principle of consent shall be applied to all circle decisions. Objections to a proposed decision must be:

a. based on the decision's adverse affect on the circle member's ability to fulfill their roles and responsibilities in achieving the aim of the circle, and

b. reasoned, meaning that reasons for the objection must be explained clearly enough for the objection to be resolved.

For all or some decisions, other methods of decision-making can be used by the circle if like all policy decisions the decision is made by consent and reviewed on a regular basis.

5.3 Definition of Policy

Policy decisions govern the day-to-day operations activities of the Organization and include, but are not limited to:

a. setting aims,

b. defining the scope of work,

c. designing the work process,

d. allocating resources,

e. delegating functions and tasks,

f.   evaluating group and individual performance,

g. determining compensation, and

h. planning professional development.

5.4 Operations Decisions

Day-to-day operations in a circle's domain shall be governed by the circle's policy decisions and directed by the operations leader. A circle shall establish policies that determine which methods of decision-making will govern operations decisions. These methods may include autocratic decisions by the operations leader.

5.5 Operations Decisions without a Policy

If a necessary operations decision is not covered by an existing policy, the operations leader shall make the decision and request that it be reviewed at the next circle meeting or at a special circle meeting called for this purpose, as described in §8, Meetings.

The operations leader, or other person acting as an operations leader, shall determine at his or her sole discretion that such a decision is necessary.

5.6 Decisions of the Board of Directors

Decisions of the board shall also be made by consent, and consent, as a higher standard than majority vote, shall be considered satisfaction of the legal requirement that board decisions be made by majority vote of the directors present and eligible to vote.

5.7 Failure to Reach Consent

If after all options have been exhausted, a circle, other than the board, cannot achieve consent on a proposed action, the decision shall be referred to the next higher circle.

If after all options have been exhausted, the board cannot achieve consent on a proposed action, the decision shall be referred to the appropriate expert director, and if necessary, that director's organization.

5.8 Proxies

The right to participate in decision-making or any other action of any circle, including the board, may not be delegated or exercised by proxy unless required by law.

6. BOARD OF DIRECTORS

6.1 Authority

Within the requirements of the laws of [jurisdiction], the board, as the top circle of the Organization, shall manage and direct the business of the Organization with full power to engage in any lawful act unless otherwise limited by these bylaws.

6.2 Responsibilities

The board is responsible for ensuring that the Organization, as a nonprofit organization, is acting in accordance with the public trust and any laws that govern nonprofit corporations. Other responsibilities include, but are not limited to:

   a. setting and overseeing the execution of a strategic plan;
   b. ensuring fiscal responsibility;
   c. maintaining long-term viability;
   d. generating new ideas and directions; and
   e. maintaining connections with external persons, organizations, agencies, and any other bodies necessary to the development and functioning of the Organization.

6.3 Composition

The Board of Directors shall include:

   a. the managing director (chief executive officer);
   b. one or more representatives of the general management circle;
   c. three or more expert directors as defined in §6.5, Expert Directors; and

d. other directors as determined by the board.

6.4 Executive Officers

6.4.1 Number and Titles

As required by law, the board shall elect from its members a minimum of three executive officers: a president, executive secretary, and treasurer. In accordance with the law and at its own discretion, the board may use other names to designate the executive officers.

6.4.2 President

The president shall:

a. oversee board compliance with the law, the Articles of Incorporation, these bylaws, the principles and methods of sociocratic governance, and the board's own decisions;

b. ensure that the board functions as a circle in accordance with the provisions of §4, Circle Governance, including ongoing professional development;

c. execute all instruments requiring a signature on behalf of the Organization;

d. serve as or designate a public spokesperson for the Organization;

e. perform other duties necessary to the office or as required by the board; and

f. perform the duties of other executive officers if they are unable or unwilling to complete them as stated in these bylaws or at the direction of the board.

6.4.3 Executive Secretary of the Board

The executive secretary of the board shall perform all the functions specified for executive secretaries of all circles in §4.3.b Executive Secretary.

In addition, the executive secretary of the board shall:

a. give, or cause to be given, any notices required by law or by these bylaws;

b. assume responsibility for corporate and board circle records;

c. maintain custody of the seal of the organization, if any, and validate documents by affixing the seal as authorized by the board or the president;

d. perform the duties of the president if he or she is unable or unwilling to complete them as stated in these bylaws or at the direction of the board; and

e. perform such other duties as may be assigned by the board or the president.

6.4.5 Treasurer

The treasurer shall:

a. Oversee financial affairs
b. Have custody of all funds and securities until otherwise assigned
c. Establish or cause to be established appropriate financial records, accounts, and practices to ensure judicious use and care
d. Prepare or cause to be prepared budgets, fundraising plans, and financial reports
e. Make the financial records available in accessible format in accordance with the practice of sociocratic organizations for transparency as required by § 11 Financial Practices
f. Perform the duties of the executive secretary if he or she is unable or unwilling to perform them
g. Perform other duties as required by the board

6.5 Expert Directors

A minimum of three (3) directors shall be elected by the board to provide expertise in specific areas and to serve as independent connections to the larger social, financial, governmental, and sociocratic environment.

6.5.1 Sociocratic Expert Director

Unless none is available to serve, one or more of the expert directors shall have expertise related to the application and teaching of the principles and methods of sociocracy.

6.5.2 Other Expert Directors

To the extent possible, other areas of expertise shall include:

a. education of the public on issues related to governance,

b. financial management of nonprofit organizations,

c. fundraising and development,

d. legal affairs, and

e. social and environmental concerns.

Expert directors may have more than one designated area of expertise as determined by the board. Expert directors are full members of the board and participate fully in decision-making and the affairs of the board.

6.6 Accountability

Each director shall exercise independent judgment in good faith and in the best interests of the organization with the care of an ordinarily prudent person under similar circumstances.

6.7 Compensation

With the exception of the managing director, the general management circle representatives if employed by the organization, and any expert directors who are otherwise providing contracted professional services to the organization, directors shall not receive compensation for their services, although they may be reimbursed for ordinary and necessary expenses incurred in fulfilling their responsibilities.

6.8 Conflict of Interest and Confidentiality

Each director shall sign and the secretary shall retain or cause to be retained in the files of the organization a copy of the conflict of interest and confidentiality policy.

6.9 Transparency

Whenever possible, the board shall ensure compliance with the practice of sociocratic organizations to make records of all transactions transparent and available to the members, staff, and other interested parties.

To address a reasoned objection to any information being classified confidential, the board shall establish policies providing for examination that protects the information and makes it available for review.

7. ELECTIONS & TERMS

7.1 Election Process

Board members, board officers, and circle officers shall be elected applying the principle of consent elections as required in §2, The Principle of Consent Elections. Elections may be conducted as an item of business on any meeting agenda or in a meeting called for this purpose. The process shall include, but is not limited to:

   a. nominations with rationales;
   b. discussion and resolution of objections, if necessary; and
   c. consent.

The facilitator or another person elected for this purpose shall conduct the process and may propose what appears to be the best choice, given the reasons presented in the nominations and discussion.

Consent to the facilitator's proposal must be confirmed.

7.2 Date of Elections

Election of directors, executive officers, and other circle officers shall be conducted at the circle's annual meeting, as specified in §8.2, Annual Meeting, and as necessary to fill vacant positions.

7.3 Terms of Office

7.3.1 Incorporating Directors

Incorporating directors shall begin their terms on the date of incorporation and continue until the first annual meeting of the board.

7.3.2 Directors and Officers

Except as limited by §7.6, Completion of Terms, directors and circle officers shall be elected for one-year terms in the first annual meeting of each circle and annually there after, and shall be eligible for re-election.

7.4 Resignation

Resignations must be in writing and received by the circle secretary.

7.5 Removal

A director or circle officer may be removed on the decision of the circle without his or her consent as required by §4.2, Limitations of Consent.

Such removal shall be without prejudice to the contract rights, if any, of the person so removed. Election shall not itself create contract rights.

7.6 Completion of Terms

7.6.1 Directors

As required by law, any director elected to complete the term of a director who has left the board shall be elected to serve the remainder of that term only.

7.6.2 Circle Officers

Circles other than the board may establish their own rules for the completion of terms, including electing for the remainder of the term plus one year.

7.6.3 Vacant Positions

The executive officers of the board, as required by law, and other circle officers shall be replaced as soon as possible. Other than officers, circles may decide not to fill a vacant position.

8. MEETINGS

8.1 Annual Meeting

One circle meeting a year shall be designated the annual meeting for purposes of conducting elections, as specified in §7, Elections & Terms. Other business may also be conducted at this meeting as determined by the circle.

[An annual meeting of stakeholders is required by many jurisdictions for both for-profit and nonprofit corporations, as well as membership organizations, condominiums, etc.]

8.2 Circle Meetings

Circles shall meet at least quarterly at an agreed-upon time and place, including by any telephonic or digital electronic means, or any other method that allows circle members to deliberate, resolve objections, and consent to decisions.

8.3 Special Circle Meetings

Special meetings may be held at the request of any circle member at a time convenient to a sufficient number of other circle members to constitute a quorum, if required by the circle's policies. Such a request should be made to the executive secretary of the circle or as otherwise determined by the circle.

8.4 Notice

At least seven (7) days' advance notice must be given to each circle member for any meeting in which decisions or other actions are to be made, subject to §8.5, Waiver of Notice. Methods of notification include a note in the records of the last circle meeting; notification by mail, facsimile, telephone, or digital/electronic; or any other method as determined by the circle.

When possible, such notice shall include proposed agenda items and any supporting documents.

8.5 Waiver of Notice

The circle may determine in its policies when notice of meetings, including special meetings, may be waived.

Presence at a meeting or failure to pay attention to methods of communication established by the circle shall constitute waiver of notice.

8.6 Quorum

Members present by telephonic or other means that allow them to participate in the discussion, resolve objections, and consent or vote, as appropriate, shall be included in the quorum.

8.6.1 Board of Directors

As required by law, unless written consent is given by absent members and is presented to the secretary before the meeting, one-third of all board members must be present for business to be conducted or actions taken. In no case, however, shall business be conducted or actions taken with fewer than three directors participating.

8.6.2 Circles other than the Board

Circles other than the board may determine their own quorums for all meetings, for a specific meeting, or for a class of meetings.

8.5 Actions without a Meeting

8.5.1 Board of Directors

Any action required or permitted at a meeting of the board may be taken without a meeting if written consent is granted by all directors entitled to vote or consent as appropriate. Written consent may include notices by mail, facsimile, electronic means, or other methods as determined by the board and such notices shall be filed with the minutes of the board.

By law, consent to an action without a meeting shall have the same force and effect as consent or unanimous vote given in a meeting.

8.5.2 Other Circles

Any action required or permitted at a circle meeting may be taken without a meeting by consent of all members as specified in this section for the board of directors or according to any process set by circle policy.

9. MEMBERS

[For membership organizations, this section should define members and their privileges and obligations.]

9.1 Classes

The board shall establish at least one class of membership in the Organization.

9.2 Non-voting

All members will be non-voting members because conducting meaningful elections or other decision-making processes in a diverse and geographically distributed membership would be impractical.

9.3. Participation in Governance

The circles shall establish appropriate means by which members who are participating in the work of the Organization can also participate in the policy-making related to that work.

10. ADVISORY COUNCILS

The board may establish one or more advisory councils to achieve the purposes of the Organization.

11. FINANCIAL PRACTICES

11.1 Financial Practices

The financial practices of the Organization shall follow the highest standards of accountability and transparency. Unless doing so would reveal personal information of employees, donors, or other persons; or otherwise compromise the stability of the Organization, financial records will be available to all members and employees of the Organization, and to other such people as the board determines.

11.2 Use of Funds

Organization funds shall only be used for activities related to the Organization's mission as stated in §1.3, Mission, and exclusively for charitable and educational purposes.

11.3 Fiscal Year

The fiscal year shall begin on the first day of January and end on the last day of December unless otherwise determined by the board.

11.4 Compensation

The Organization shall follow the sociocratic practice of fixed and variable compensation for all employees.

12. ANNUAL REPORT

The Organization shall publish, in any media, an annual report that shall include, but not be limited to, a summary of the Organization's activities and a financial report for the previous year. The annual report shall be available to the public.

13. INDEMNIFICATION

13.1 Rights

Except as otherwise limited by law and these bylaws, each director, employee, or volunteer of the Organization shall be indemnified by the Organization and shall not be held liable for damages or the costs of their defense for any acts or omissions as a result of providing services or performing duties on behalf of the Organization.

These rights of indemnification shall, in the case of the death of a director, employee, or volunteer, exist to the benefit of his or her heirs and estate.

13.2 Limitations

Indemnification, as specified in § 13.1, Rights, shall not include:

a. any act or omission that is not reasonably included in the services or duties requested or approved by the Organization;
b. the willful misconduct of the director, employee, or volunteer;
c. a crime, unless the director, employee, or volunteer had reasonable cause to believe that the act was lawful;
d. a transaction that resulted in an improper personal benefit of money, property, or service to the director, employee, or volunteer; or
e. any act or omission that is not in good faith and is beyond the scope of authority of the Organization.

13.3 Professional Services

With the exception of expert directors functioning in their roles as directors, the limitation of liability in § 13.2, Limitations, shall not apply to any licensed professional employed by the Organization in his or her professional capacity.

14. AMENDMENTS

These bylaws may be altered or repealed and new bylaws adopted by the board with a minimum of thirty (30) days' notice to all circle members of intent to amend, including the wording of such amendment. The purpose of such notice shall be to allow circles to call special meetings, if they consider it necessary, to deliberate on such amendment and to select a representative(s) to participate in the deliberations in the next higher circle.

No amendment shall be made that would adversely affect the Organization's qualification under Section 501(c)(3) of the Internal Revenue Code of 1986 (or any successor provision).

15. DISSOLUTION

15.1 Notice

Acting in accordance with the laws of the District of Columbia, the Organization may be dissolved by the board with a minimum of thirty (30) days' notice to all circle members of the intent to dissolve, including the reasons for the proposed dissolution. The purpose of such notice shall be to allow all levels of the circle structure time to call special meetings, if they consider it necessary, to deliberate on the proposal and to select a representative(s) to participate in the deliberations of the next higher circle.

15.2 Distribution of Assets

On dissolution of the Organization, any remaining assets shall be distributed to one or more charitable, educational, scientific, or philanthropic organizations qualified for a tax exemption under Section 501(c)(3) of the Internal Revenue Code of 1986, as amended. Such organization will be recommended by members, employees, and volunteers of the Organization and determined by the board.

ADOPTED [date]

Addendum

Conflict of Interest and Confidentiality Policy

Each member of the top circle and board of directors shall sign and the secretary shall retain in the files of the Organization a copy of this conflict of interest and confidentiality policy:

As Director of the Organization, I realize that I owe duties of care, loyalty, and obedience to the Organization so that:

1. To avoid conflicts of interest, I agree to disclose to the board any situations in which it might appear that I have conflicting duties to other organizations or persons in which my allegiance might be split between the Organization and other personal, professional, business, or volunteer positions or responsibilities. Such a conflict may warrant withdrawal from debate, vote, or, if necessary to protect against legal liability, my position with the Organization.

2. I understand that I will have access to confidential information about the Organization, its programs, activities, employees, and transactions, and I agree to maintain the confidentiality of that information where unwarranted disclosure could jeopardize the success of the endeavor or damage the Organization.

Signature: Date:

Printed Name:

Notary:

Guides to Organizing Sociocratically

This section of the appendix includes guides for using a variety of sociocratic practices and processes as explained in Part II, "Organizing Our Strengths." They are intended to be used when you are organizing circles, conducting circle meetings, and making decisions.

PRINCIPLES, NOT RECIPES

The guides are designed to help apply the principles effectively. They are not intended to be prescriptive. They may be changed, modified, and sometimes ignored as long as the result achieves the purposes of the three principles: consent, the circular hierarchy, and double links. This will allow you to establish and maintain a coherent structure and express the values of equivalence, transparency, and effectiveness.

The Implementation Process

Implementing sociocracy is a process of planning, implementing, measuring, and planning again. Where this process starts and how fast it moves depends on the organization—its size, current structure, openness to change, leadership acceptance, etc. Sociocratic experts are trained to help with this implementation.

A TYPICAL IMPLEMENTATION

1. **Form an implementation circle that includes key decision-makers and representatives from all levels of the organization. The circle should:**

   a. define the circle structure and circle aims;

   b. decide which circle or circles will be activated first;

   c. arrange training for members of the activated circles;

   d. develop an in-house trainer(s);

   e. establish a process for developing and maintaining the circle structure; and

   f. develop a compensation system in which everyone experiences both the profits and the losses.

2. **Activate the top circle, if not activated first:**

   Some organizations may be required to have a distinct board of directors. If so, the top circle may be constituted as the board by specifying in the bylaws that any decision of the top circle is a decision of the board, and any decision of the board is made in a meeting of the top circle.

   Members of the top circle would be:

   a. general manager of operations, whether called a chief executive officer (CEO), director, or president;

   b. elected representative(s) from the general circle; and

   c. external experts.

   External experts—usually four—are:

   1. a legal advisor or representative of local government;

   2. an expert in finance,

287

3. a sociocratic or management expert, and

4. an expert on the aim of the organization.

3. First Actions and Responsibilities of the Top Circle

These actions and responsibilities include:

    a. elect or affirm the general manager of operations;

    b. adopt or affirm the aim statement, overall budgets, and policy plans;

    c. confirm the form of incorporation and bylaws;

    d. connect the organization's aim to the environment;

    f.   exercise legally mandated fiduciary responsibilities; and

    e. pro-actively generate and introduce new ideas.

4. First Actions and Responsibilities of General Managing Circle

These actions and responsibilities include:

    a. elect or affirm leaders of operations circles;

    b. adopt, adjust, or affirm budgets for operations circles;

    c. review and adjust aims for the operations circles;

    d. review or establish long-term plans; and

    e. establish an agenda for addressing policies related to decisions that affect more than one operations circle.

5. Operations Circles Self-Organize

Following the same process as the General Managing Circle, circles and sub-circles self organize.

6. Dissolve the Implementation Circle

Once the circle structure is in place, the implementation circle is no longer necessary, although some members may continue to provide administrative support for internal training and oversight of the governance system.

Circles & Officers

CIRCLES

All members of an operations unit—teams, departments, committees, working groups, etc.—meet as necessary to decide the policies that will govern the day-to-day operations in their domain.

They make decisions by consent as equals and elect officers to do the governance work of the circle.

CIRCLE OFFICERS

Circle members elect officers who have specific roles and responsibilities in circle meetings. (See Guide 3, "Elections Process.")

1. Operations Leader

The operations leader supervises the circle's daily work, is elected by the next higher circle with the circle representative's participation, and is responsible for the circle's development.

The operations leader may be elected to fill any circle role except that of the circle representative.

The operations leader is responsible for communicating information from the larger organization to the circle, functioning as the "down" link in the feedback loop formed by the double link.

2. Facilitator

The facilitator leads circle meetings, works with the secretary to prepare agendas and materials for meetings, and may or may not be the operations leader of the circle.

3. Secretary

Serving as the circle administrator, the secretary:

  a. records and publishes meeting minutes;
  b. works as a partner with the facilitator to formulate proposals and plan facilitation and meeting process;

    c. announces and makes arrangements for meetings;

    d. either prepares the meeting agenda in consultation with the facilitator, operations leader, and other circle members as appropriate, or organizes proposed items for spontaneously generated agendas records according to circle policies; and

    e. prepares handout materials.

4. Logbook Keeper

Maintains records of minutes, policy decisions, detailed descriptions of work processes and instructions, financial records, etc. This role is often combined with the secretary, particularly in small circles or circles with less-complex responsibilities.

5. Elected Representative or Representatives

This(these) individual(s) represents the circle in the next-higher circle; participates in both circles as a full member whose consent in decision-making is required; and is not a "vote carrier," but a full participant representing circle's best interests.

The representative(s) communicate information from the circle to the higher circle, functioning as the "up" link in the feedback loop formed by the double link.

6. Other Circle Officers

Other circle officers may be elected for defined roles, particularly in large circles with complex tasks.

The Elections Process

Circles elect their members to roles and responsibilities by consent following an open nominations process that includes arguments to support the nominations. The circle facilitator may conduct elections or another person may be elected to facilitate elections.

1. Read Description of the Role or Responsibility

This may require defining and consenting, or reaffirming the description. The description should include the length of service and the means of measuring performance.

2. Nominations

Each member of the circle, including the facilitator, submits a written nomination to the facilitator containing the name of the nominator and the name of the person nominated. Members of the circle may nominate other members or themselves, or indicate "no nomination" or "outside hire."

Nominations Form

```
          [Your Name ]
            nominates
        [Nominee's Name ]
```

3. Presentations

The facilitator reads each of the nomination forms and asks each nominator for the reasons (arguments) for their nomination. Reasons should address the roles and responsibilities in the description.

4. Changes after Nominations are Explained

Based on the other presentations, the facilitator asks the nominators if they want to change their nominations and if there are new nominations. If none are given, the facilitator requests reasons for any changes

291

[handwritten margin notes:]
CC: Kat
Heather T?
Liliane
✱ Jenny M
Lori U?
Pam W
Sally P

JM – calm, kind open, able to see thru difficulty, stay hopeful or new nominations. This can be done in a round or in a simple invitation to change.

5. Consent Round(s)

   a. Based on the reasons given and the role description, the facilitator chooses a person from those nominated, gives reasons for the choice, and asks each circle member, in turn, if they consent. Important: The proposed person is asked last and also gives reasons.

   b. If there is an objection, the circle may try to resolve the objection.

   c. If there is an unresolved objection or the person him-/herself objects, the process repeats from Step 4, "Changes," until there is a choice with no objections.

   d. If there are objections to all the nominees, including from the nominees themselves, the vacancy continues until a resolution is found.

   e. Completing the process may require redefining the role description to address objections or hiring a new circle member with the required knowledge and skills.

   f. If someone is hired from outside, the operational leader is normally responsible for initiating and conducting the process, subject to the consent of the circle.

CAUTIONS

   1. **Specify term limits**, a date when the person must be reconfirmed or re-elected.

   2. **Listen without discussion or comment** while reasons are given for nominations.

   3. **Do not ask for volunteers** or ask who is interested. Assume everyone is a candidate until the end of the process.

   4. **Remember that choices are "more or less."** No one will be perfect and everyone can learn.

Circle Meetings

Circles typically meet every 4-6 weeks or as necessary to make and review the policy decisions that govern the planning and execution of day-to-day operations within their domain.

MEETING FORMAT

Meetings are led by the facilitator and recorded by the logbook keeper/ secretary, unless otherwise determined by the circle.

Preparation

1. **Opening Round**

   A time to attune to each other and to the aim of the circle, similar to musicians tuning to the same note before a performance.

2. **Administrative Concerns**

   Meeting support items that require little or no discussion or decision. Announcements, housekeeping, consent to minutes of last meeting, date of next meeting, introduction of guests, etc.

3. **Consenting to the Agenda**

   Acceptance of the agenda, including any additions, clarifications, etc. (Does not require a round.)

   Some businesses and organizations have adopted spontaneous agenda generation at the beginning of the meeting. Others have agenda items submitted in advance. Others do a combination of the two.

Content

   The content part of the meeting may include any or all of the following, or any other item the circle decides.

4. **Consideration of Proposals**

   See Guides 6, "Policy Development," and 7, "Resolving Objections."

5. **Discussion of issues or concerns**

6. Circle development activities

Closing Round

The closing round concludes the meeting and serves as a transition out of the meeting in the same way that a function of the opening round is to attune members to each other. The evaluation serves as a "feed-forward loop" and focuses on the future, not the past.

The closing round may include an evaluation of the meeting and its results as a measurement of its effectiveness, suggestions for future agenda items, review of tasks to be done, how individuals experienced the meeting, etc. It may also include the "takeaway" from the meeting: "What happens tomorrow?" "How did this meeting affect the circle member's future?"

CIRCLE MEETING MINUTES

Circle meeting minutes include:

1. details of the meeting (date, time, who was present, etc.);

2. clearly recorded decisions and reasons for the decisions;

3. text of adopted proposals;

4. next meeting date; and

5. other information as appropriate.

The secretary:

1. reviews the minutes with the facilitator,

b. distributes them to each member,

c. adds them to the circle's logbook and tracks dates on which they are to be reviewed, and

d. includes text of decisions to the policy and procedure manuals, if any.

Also see Guide 9, "Logbooks."

Rounds

The purpose of a round is to encourage each circle member to participate equally in decision-making and to establish and re-establish equivalence in the meeting. Rounds may be conducted multiple times to collect information, connect circle members, and resolve objections.

CONDUCTING A ROUND

The facilitator starts a round by asking a person to begin, followed by each person moving alternately clockwise or counter-clockwise. The person may be chosen randomly or for a specific reason, for example, because the person is recognized as an expert on the topic. The purpose is to alternate which person speaks first, last, before, or after another person. If the group is not sitting in a circle, the facilitator indicates with a nod who should speak next.

In a round, there is generally no cross-talk or interruptions by members or the facilitator. The focus is on listening to each person in the round.

If the circle meeting is conducted by telephone or by video conferencing, it is helpful if the facilitator assigns circle positions to the participants using a virtual clock: "George is at 1 o'clock, Marsha is at 2 o'clock," etc., so there is no need to call names and the round can move quickly.

KINDS OF ROUNDS

1. Opening Rounds

These are the very first actions in every circle meeting and create energy and re-connect each person to other circle members. People share work or non-work–related events or feelings. They bring themselves into the meeting.

2. Reaction Rounds

These occur when a proposal is presented and involve a quick round of one or two words or a sentence on whether the proposal is ready for consideration. A reaction round will quickly reveal problems, move the proposal to discussion, or indicate that it is ready for consent.

3. Information-gathering Rounds

These are done before a proposal is written to solicit information and suggestions and can occur at any time to clarify issues and objections, and to obtain more information after a negative reaction round.

4. Consent Rounds

These are intended to ensure that there are no further objections and the proposal has the consent of each circle member.

5. Closing Rounds

A circle meeting always closes with a round. It includes an evaluation of the meeting and its results as a measurement of its effectiveness, suggestions for future agenda items, review of tasks to be done, what individuals gained, etc.

The closing round is more than an evaluation of the facilitation or the meeting. It includes the takeaway from the meeting: "What happens tomorrow?"

CAUTIONS

1. **Do not ask for volunteers** to start. People may compete or a person with a private agenda may deflect the purpose of the round.

2. **Balance rounds with open discussion and dialogue.** Open discussion allows ideas to build quickly, but some people may remain silent and others dominate. This discourages the equivalence that is crucial to self-organizing.

3. **A long queue is an indication that a round is needed.** This will balance all the issues or points of view.

4. **If a very new idea or reaction is expressed at the end of the round, repeat the round** to give all circle members an opportunity to react to or consider this information.

5. **Remember to listen to each person.** There is a tendency in some groups to focus on the facilitator.

Policy Development

Policies are statements of principles or strategies for accomplishing the aim of the circle. They set requirements and permissions for future actions. A policy may be narrow, covering one budget item, or broad, changing a whole work process. It may define one person's role, or rearrange everyone's roles.

Proposals are developed and adopted differently depending on the complexity of the proposed action.

A proposal should normally include:

1. the purpose of the policy;

2. the conditions or issues it addresses;

3. its scope or range of application;

4. the implementation process, including budget and other resource requirements;

5. dates for implementation; and

6. dates for review.

SIMPLE CONSENT

Simple consent can be used to set meeting dates, accept reports, approve the minutes, make a simple change in a previous decision, or make other routine decisions.

The facilitator proposes a decision and asks if there are any objections. If so, the facilitator conducts a round to resolve objections. If the issue is more complex than originally believed, the facilitator can proposes that the decision be delegated for the development of a satisfactory proposal.

A formal round is usually not necessary for routine decisions or when there have been no objections.

DEVELOPING A PROPOSAL

The process of developing a proposal for a policy decision, sometimes called "picture forming," begins with information gathering, often in a round, to identify needs and ideas for resolving a problem or taking advantage of an opportunity.

The facilitator delegates proposal development to an appropriate person or people, or the circle may choose to conduct an election. An election usually isn't necessary because the most-appropriate people are often apparent.

The proposal process includes:

1. Information Gathering (Input)

2. Proposal Development (Transformation)

3. Consent (Output)

Long and Short Processes

When all these steps are performed in the circle meeting, it is referred to as the long process. After an initial round to identify issues, however, the proposal development, and sometimes information gathering, are done outside a circle meeting. This is the short process.

Whether the whole process is done in the circle meeting or not, the steps in the process are the same:

1. Information Gathering (Input)

a. Explain the need for a decision on a policy.
b. Identify, question, explore the problem or opportunity.
   This may be done using rounds, dialogue, or other discussion methods.
c. Consent to a list of the identified issues.

2. Proposal Development (Transformation)

This step can be done in the circle meeting, delegated and done in a meeting, or a combination of both.

a. Collect ideas for taking action.

For complex issues, this step includes doing inside and outside research and consultations.

b. Combine the ideas and draft a proposal.

c. Confirm that the draft proposal addresses all the issues.

3. Consent (Output)

The consent process includes presentation, clarification, possible changes or additions, and acceptance.

a. Proposal review

The secretary or proposal writer distributes the proposal, before the meeting if possible. If members have studied the proposal before the meeting, only a brief summary would be given.

b. Clarifying questions

Participants ask questions to understand the proposal. These are "clean" questions that do not reveal personal preferences or judgments. If there are many questions, this may be done in a round.

c. Quick-reaction round

Circle members make brief comments to determine whether the proposal needs more work, or it is ready for consideration and if the circle is ready to consider it.

If the reaction round is negative, a quick round may be done to collect a list of concerns.

d. Consent rounds

Each person in turn consents or states concerns or objections. Rounds may be repeated and other discussion methods used to resolve objections. See Guide 9, "Resolving Objections."

If consent is not reached, the facilitator may propose a fate for the proposal. It can be returned for redrafting, re-delegated, set aside, etc. A round may be done to determine this.

e. When consent is reached, confirm that a decision has been made. If appropriate, celebrate.

CAUTION

Gathering information outside the circle meeting:

When information gathering is done outside the circle meeting, it may not sufficiently involve the whole circle in listening to each member's concerns. It also doesn't begin the process of uniting the circle around the needed action.

But circle involvement is not always necessary, particularly with technical decisions, and when the greater value is holding when shorter or fewer meetings. Of course, research is best done outside a meeting.

Resolving Objections and Building Consent

Achieving consent is a process. It begins with explaining the need for a policy and ends when objections are resolved. The requirement to resolve objections is unfamiliar to many who are new to consent decision-making but it is essential.

An objection is not a veto. It is the beginning of a creative process. Objections have to be explained so they can be understood and resolved. Once an objection clarified, everyone "owns" it. Both the raising and resolving of objections is necessary to improve a proposal and ensure the ability of all circle members to function optimally when the policy is implemented.

IMPROVING THE PROPOSAL BY RESOLVING OBJECTIONS

After the objection is stated and clarified so everyone in the circle understands it, any or all of the following may be done by:

1. **a round** asking, "How might we resolve this?" Invite amendments to the proposal;

2. **a brief dialogue** between two or three people to explore the issues and their ramifications;

3. **a free-form discussion** to build energy around the process of resolving the objection or finding a new direction;

4. **shortening the timeframe** of the proposed action to test the policy and then improve the decision;

5. **limiting application** of the policy—does it really have to affect everyone? can the policy be limited to fewer people, activities, spaces, etc.;

6. **dividing the proposal** and make a decision on each piece independently so the circle can move forward;

7. **deferring** the decision to gain perspective; or

8. **reevaluating** whether a decision is necessary—perhaps the discussion and serious consideration were enough to change the situation.

If the circle cannot resolve an objection:

9. **Take a short break** to stretch and confer.

10. **Take a step back** and review the reasons the policy was proposed. Briefly review the process, the aim, the changes made in resolving concerns, and the unresolved objections.

11. **Exempt some people or processes** from the policy, if possible. Can they be "grandfathered" in without causing resentment or affecting the work of others?

12. **Refer the objection to a subgroup** for further consideration.

13. **Refer the objection to a higher circle** where there might be more information and a broader perspective.

The top circle can refer the decision to an expert and the expert's company. It should also have the option to refer the decision to mediation and, if necessary, arbitration.

CAUTIONS

This is a list of suggestions, not a list of steps that have to be done in order or in combination. Each policy and objection may have to be addressed in a different way. Three of these steps may be needed, and another six.

There is rarely a need to do all of them, or to do them in order. The facilitator suggests the next step or another activity that might help resolve an objection. Circle members may also make suggestions.

Designing the Work Process

The work process is a detailed plan for achieving the vision, mission, and aim. Operations are directly controlled by the aim and often more clearly understood. Thus, it is generally easier to start with the aim and then revisit the vision and mission.

Organizations, circles, and role descriptions all have visions, missions, and aims. This example uses the circle.

1. Define the Aim

The aim describes the product or service in a way that differentiates it from others, and in terms the client, customer, or recipient will easily understand. An aim is tangible and measurable; the result of doing.

2. Determine the Vision

The vision is that inspires circle members; their dream of a better world, for example. Visions are typically outward-looking.

3. Determine the Mission

The mission is what the circle will do to realize the vision. The mission motivates the circle to action and is typically inward looking.

4. Plan the Work Process

The work process is a detailed plan for producing or achieving the aim.

a. **Design the doing process.** Include the input, transformation, and output steps.

b. **Create the steering network** of leading and measuring. Establish the policies that will govern, or steer, the work and the methods of measuring its results.

c. **Elect people by consent** for each role or responsibility.

d. **Plan for development.** This includes researching, learning, and teaching for each person, in relation to each step in the doing process and the leading and measuring.

CAUTIONS

The work process is a circular process. It is dynamic, always evolving. Don't try to perfect it before putting it into operation, or expect to be able to follow it exactly. It will change as soon as you begin testing it.

The circular process moves from planning to doing, to measuring, and then back to evaluating and planning again. It will circle around several times before it is ready to test.

And will be regularly updated.

Guide for Logbooks

Transparency is an essential value and practice in sociocracy. If everyone is expected to participate in budget planning, for example, everyone needs to see the finances of both the circle and the organization. Equivalence also requires that everyone have equal access to information.

Each circle and each circle member should have a logbook that both is unique and overlaps with those of others.

MAINTAINING THE LOGBOOKS

Each member of a circle maintains their own logbook that includes relevant documents distributed by the secretary. The operational leader of each circle is responsible for the logbook of the circle, which is maintained with the help of the secretary and/or logbook keeper.

FORMAT

Each logbook has a common part that is the same for every circle in the organization, a unique part for each circle, and a unique part for each individual.

1. **Common Content includes:**

   a. statement of the organization's vision, mission, and aim(s);
   b. bylaws;
   c. strategic policy plan; and
   d. diagram of the circle organization.

2. **Rules and Procedures**

   The general circle and all sub-circle logbooks should contain the rules and procedures approved by the general circle that apply to the whole organization.

   Each circle logbook should also include all the rules and procedures the circle needs to accomplish its aim. The general circle logbook should include copies of all the circle-specific procedures.

   The top circle logbook does not need the kind of operational detail kept in the general circle logbook, but it does need the complete text of the articles of incorporation and any related legal documents. Both sets of documents are available to all members of the organization.

3. Meeting Records

Each circle logbook and the logbook of each person in a circle should have a complete set of circle minutes, etc.

4. Circle Members and Their Work

The logbook should contain the names of all members of the circle and their roles and responsibilities, and those of the chair, the secretary and/or logbook keeper, and the elected representative(s) to the next-higher circle, with all their terms in those offices.

This section should also include flow charts summarizing the leading, doing, and measuring activities of the circle.

5. Circle Development Plan

Development includes any training, experience, teaching, and research that circle members need to continue functioning effectively. The operations leader is responsible for organizing development activities for circle members.

Training is needed in:

    a. knowledge and skills required to accomplish aims;
    b. governance and decision-making methods;
    c. methods of organizing work and work processes; and
    d. knowledge of developments in their operations field.

6. Individual Work Plan

Each person's logbook should include descriptions of assigned roles and responsibilities, the work process for specific assignments, and a unique development plan

Glossary

A glossary is a reference intended to provide information and clarification, as well as definitions. Some of the terms and definitions included are not used in the main text because they refer to more-specialized or complex processes. They are used in works by Gerard Endenburg and the Sociocratic Norms, published by the international Sociocracy Group. Since those documents are not easily accessible, we have included the definitions here.

*Words in **bold** in the text are defined elsewhere in the glossary.*

⇒ A B ⇐

aim. A product or service that an organization completes or produces to accomplish its **vision** and **mission**. Unlike the vision and mission, which state the desired effects, the aim is a product or a service that is **measurable** and can be described as different from other products and services. It is tangible in that it can be traded or exchanged with a client or customer. Also see **exchange**.

aim realization. The process of producing or accomplishing the aim. Both the **primary work process** and **supporting work processes** are designed to ensure aim realization.

argued, arguments. Reasoned statements of fact, as in mathematical arguments, used to explain an **objection** so it can be resolved. A skilled **facilitator** and other members of the circle will help clarify arguments. Also see **consent** and **objections**.

assisting circle. See **helping circle**.

audit. A systematic, independent examination of an organization by a certified sociocratic **auditor** to determine whether the organization has implemented the method correctly and efficiently, and is obtaining the desired results.

autocratic decision-making, governance, hierarchy. When one person or a small number of people make **policy decisions** without meaningful consultation with those who are affected by them, such as monarchies and dictatorships. Traditionally, government agencies, businesses, and many other organizations have been governed autocratically, without benefit of **feedback loops**. Also see **linear hierarchy**.

"basis rule." The literal translation of the Dutch term *basis regeling*, translated here as "principles." See **governing principles**.

base wage. See **Guaranteed Base Wage (GBW).**

both-and. Inclusive, win-win decision-making rather than oppositional, exclusive, and win-lose. Most often used as "both-and thinking" in opposition to "either-or thinking" that requires the choice of one alternative.

≋ **C** ≋

certification. A guarantee of expertise in compliance with **sociocratic norms.** Sociocratic certification is granted to people and to organizations. People can be certified in facilitation, training, and consulting. Certified consultants are trained to implement sociocracy in corporations and large organizations. Also see **audits.**

chair, chairperson. Top circle meeting leader, who may or may not be the same person as the **general manager** or CEO. Also see **circle officers.**

chaos theory. The study of **systems** that develop unpredictably, such as hurricanes. The initial state can be measured and short-term development predicted, but the longer-term outcomes are influenced by minute variations that can produce widely variable results. Chaotic systems are **self-organizing** and create their own energy.

Chaos is often confused with **random.** Random events are unpredictable because they have no measurable patterns or characteristics, do not generate energy, and are not self-organizing. Without external intervention, random activity stays random.

chaos in decision-making. Unpredictable elements introduced purposefully when discussing solutions to encourage creative thinking and **self-organizing.** Brainstorming, for example, is a technique that introduces chaos into the decision-making process and can unleash great energy.

circle, circle meetings. Members of **operations** units, departments, or teams who share a common aim meet as equals in circle meetings to make the **policy decisions** that determine how they will accomplish their aims.

Operations units are **semi-autonomous** and **self-organizing.** They set the policies that govern their areas of responsibility or their **domains.** They maintain their own memory systems in **logbooks,** assume responsibility for their own **development,** and can generate new circles with different aims.

Elected **circle officers** conduct circle meetings. Circles meet as often as necessary to make policy decisions to guide the **operations leader** and the work of the team. In a circle meeting, the interests of the individual and the interests of the group become mutual concerns. See also operations meetings.

circle decision. See **policy decisions.**

circle meeting leaders. See **facilitator, secretary,** and logbook keeper.

circle representative(s). See **representative(s)**.

circle structure. A **circular hierarchy** of **double-linked circles** that corresponds to the **operations structure** makes the **policies** that guide the daily work of the circle. The circle structure is composed of circles connected by **double links** to the next higher and lower circles. Each link participates in the decision-making of both of the circles and forms part of a **feedback loop** that carries information to and from other circles, connecting the entire organization. Also see **autocratic hierarchy**.

circular process. The functions of **leading-doing-measuring** that govern or steer **policy** and **operations** decisions. Also see **input-transformation-output**.

circular hierarchy. As opposed to a linear **autocratic hierarchy** in which all communication is top down, in a circular hierarchy power are balanced throughout the whole organization. For example, the game of rock-scissors-paper is a circular hierarchy because each element controls another element in a structured relationship.

closed system. An organization with no relationship to its environment. Thus, it lacks the information necessary to adapt to change. Sociocratic organizations are purposely structured as **open systems**.

closing round. A **round** completed at the end of a **circle meeting** in which each person is given an opportunity to make final comments. It often includes an evaluation of the meeting in terms of its productivity, relationship to aim realization, what has been gained personally, etc. Also see **opening round**.

compensation. Wages or other benefits received in exchange for services rendered. Compensation in a sociocratic organization consists of the **Guaranteed Base Wage** (GBW), **Short-Term Measurement** (STM), and **Long-Term Measurement** (LTM). While the GBW is generally calculated based on market rates, the STM and LTM are variables based on profits and distributed to all employees. This structure ensures both a basic income and an income based on organizational performance. Variable compensation involves all members of the organization as co-entrepreneurs.

consent. Consent is defined as "no **objections**." An individual consents to a proposed decision when all their **argued and paramount objections have been** resolved. If no objections are raised, consent is assumed. See also **principle of consent**.

consent round. A **round** in which the circle members, in turn, explicitly indicate their **consent** by stating they have **no objections** to a proposed decision. Consent does not imply agreement or **solidarity**. It is consent to move forward.

cybernetics. The study of communications and control in systems that have **aims** or purposes, of how they affect their environment and change in response to **feedback** from their environment. Cybernetics is related to information theory, control theory, and systems theory, and is applicable to both social and physical systems. It is an interdisciplinary field, including electrical and mechanical engineering, evolutionary biology, neuroscience, anthropology, and psychology.

 D

decision confirmation round. See **consent round.**

democratic governance. The governance structure of an organization functioning as a democracy, as opposed to a monarchy or a theocracy, in which the decision-making power is vested in its members collectively. In practice, members usually make decisions using majority vote or delegate decisions to officers or representatives who are elected by majority vote. This results in majority rule.

development. A process involving researching, teaching, and learning. Each circle is responsible for its own development and the development of its members. Sociocratic literature often refers to development as "integral education," "permanent education," and "schooling." Also see **sociocratic engineering.**

domain. A defined area of authority or responsibility in relation to the realization of an aim. The limits of the circle's domain are set by the next higher circle. The limits of an individual's domain are set by the **circle.**

double-link, double-linking. The linking of a circle with the next higher circle in which at least two persons, the **operations leader** and at least one elected **representative**, are also members of the next higher circle. The double-link (1) makes attuning between circles possible, (2) facilitates top down and bottom up communications, and (3) creates a **feedback loop** between circles. All circles **double-linked** form the **governance structure.**

double-linked circles. Two circles connected by two people, the operations leader and at least one elected representative. Also see **circle structure.**

dynamic. The ability or the condition of changing. Not static. In physics, a dynamic element is one that is changing and self-organizing. Also see **dynamic steering.**

dynamic governance, dynamic self-governance. Alternative names for **sociocracy** that reflect its use of **dynamic steering** in applying the **circular process** to the **governance** and **operations** of the organization.

dynamic steering. A governing or guiding process in an organization that allows it to **self-correct** in response to its changing environment. See also **circular process.**

➣ E ➢

elections process. People are elected to assume circle and operations roles and responsibilities using the elections process, which includes open nominations and discussion. Also referred to as a *sociocratic election*.

empty method. How sociocracy is sometimes described because it is universally applicable.

enfranchised. To have legal voting rights, to control one's own destiny. All members of a sociocratic organization are enfranchised.

engineering. The application of scientific, mathematical, economic, and social knowledge to the design and development of devices, machines, materials, structures, systems, or processes. As an electrical engineer, Gerard Endenburg applied engineering principles to the design of his company to develop the **Sociocratic Circle-Organization Method (SCM)**. At the time, the social sciences were not applying scientific methods to the same extent as the physical sciences.

equivalence. The equal valuing of individuals rather than valuing people from one socioeconomic class or ethnic group more highly than another. Equivalence is a primary value in sociocracy and central to its vision, mission, and aim. The **principle of consent**, **round**s, and other practices is designed to establish and maintain equivalence.

exchange object, partner, process, relationship. The aim of an organization is the object, service, or financial compensation that will be exchanged by mutual agreement between a client and a provider. To accomplish its mission, an organization forms **exchange relationships** with **exchange partners** in an exchange process. Ideally, the exchange partnership will be mutually profitable and have a synergistic effect on both **partners**.

Existence Possibility Guarantee (EPG). See **Guaranteed Base Wage (GBW)**.

external expert. A member of the **top circle** who has professional expertise and current knowledge of developments in the external environment of the organization.

external expert. A member of the **top circle**, who has professional connections and knowledge in a field relevant to the organization's aim. They usually include an economic or financial expert, a legal expert, a social or community expert, and an expert in the organization's aim or field of operation.

➣ F ➢

facilitator. One of four **circle officers elected to lead circle meetings**. Works with the **operations leader, secretary,** and **logbook keeper** to determine agendas and oversees the process of **policy development**. The facilitator is not necessarily the **operations leader** but may be.

feedback loops. Elements in an organization or other system that provide information about how a system is functioning. **Double links** establish feedback loops between circles. The **circular process** of **leading-doing-measuring** establishes a feedback loop. Also see **dynamic steering**.

feed-forward loops. A chain of **cause-and-effect** actions established to control responses to anticipated future events. See also **dynamic steering** and **circular process**.

free organization. An organization that is not owned. In order to ensure that **consent** is the basis of decision-making and not ownership, sociocratic organizations may have investors but they are not owners. There are a variety of legal structures with which this can be accomplished.

⇒ G ⇐

governance structure. The policy decision-making authority in an organization. The governance structure determines who, what, when, and how decisions will be made to accomplish the organization's aims. In sociocratic organizations, the governance structure is the circle structure and it includes all members of the organization. Within the whole organization's policies, each circle sets policy in its **domain of responsibility**.

governing principles. Sociocratic governance is based on three principles:

1. Consent governs policy decisions, including elections for assignment to roles and responsibilities, distribution of resources, strategic plans, etc.

2. A circular hierarchy of **semi-autonomous** and **self-organizing circles** forms the governance structure of the organization. Each circle has its own **aim** and **domain of responsibility**, controls its own **work process** of **leading-doing-measuring**, maintains its own memory system or **logbook**, and is responsible for its own **professional development**.

3. Double links interconnect circles, which consist of the **operations leader** and one or more **representatives** who participate fully in the decision-making of both circles.

Guaranteed Base Wage (GBW). A level of **compensation** that may include goods, services, benefits, and wages and is guaranteed to every member of the organization entitled to compensation. This wage is set as opposed to a variable wage and is generally established based on industry standards. Also referred to as an

Existence Possibility Guarantee (EPG). Also see **Short-Term Measurement (STM)** and **Long-Term Measurement (LTM)**.

⇒ H I ⇐

helping circle. A temporary **circle** established for developing a **policy proposal**. A helping circle may consist of members of the same circle; members of other circles; and/or external experts. A helping circle does not make policy decisions. Also called an assisting circle.

higher circle. In the circular hierarchy, the higher circle creates the lower circle, assigns its domain, and elects its leader. The lower circle then makes decisions within its domain, and its representative and operations leader must consent to any further changes in the domain or functioning of the lower circle. "Lower" and "higher" refer only to power-with relationships, not to power-over relationships.

hierarchy. A coherent arrangement of people or things in grades, orders, or classes, according to their roles and relationships. Hierarchies are characteristic of all natural systems and organize the actions of semi-autonomous sub-systems. Sociocratic hierarchies, like natural hierarchies, include bottom-up as well as top-down communications and control. Also see **circular hierarchy** and **linear hierarchy**.

ignoring as violence. Sociocracy regards ignoring individuals as a form of violence, and possibly the source of all violence. Requiring the **consent** of each individual within a **domain** of responsibility makes it impossible to ignore individuals, thus avoiding this form of violence.

incentives, short-term and **long-term.** See **Short-Term Measurement (STM)** and **Long-Term Measurement (LTM)**.

input-transformation-output. The process that guides the production of a product or service. One obtains an order (input), makes the product or provides the service (transformation), and receives compensation (output). See also **exchange process**.

integral education. See **development**.

⇒ J K L ⇐

linked circles. See **double-linked circles**.

linear hierarchy. A governance structure in which authority flows from top to bottom, typically in a **power-over** relationship. Autocratically governed organizations are typically linear hierarchies.

logbook. The **memory system** of the **circle** and of each circle member. It contains all the **policy decisions**, meeting notes, and other data important to the functioning of the circle and to measuring the results of its decisions. Individual logbooks contain both the circle's records and the records relating to the person's responsibilities.

logbook keeper. The officer of a **circle** who is responsible for keeping the circle's **logbook** up to date. Is often combined with the role of the circle **secretary.** The **operations leader, facilitator,** or **representative** may also be elected logbook keeper.

Long-Term Measurement (LTM). Part of **compensation** in a sociocratic organization based on long-term profits, generally distributed semi-annually or annually. Also see **compensation, Guaranteed Base Wage (GBW),** and **Short-Term Measurement (STM).**

leading-doing-measuring. The three functions of the **circular process** on which the sociocratic **circle structure** is based. See also **leading, doing, measuring, feedback loops,** and **feed-forward loops.**

⇒ M N O ⇐

magical decision-making. See **theocratic decision-making.**

measuring. One function of the **circular process** of **leading-doing-measuring** used for steering organizations toward their aim. During **doing** or execution, **measuring** produces data that provides the information required for **leading** or planning. Measurement and evaluation are separate functions.

measurement. See **Short-Term Measurement (STM)** and **Long-Term Measurement (LTM).**

memory system. See **logbook.**

mission. What the organization intends to do to realize its **vision** of the future. While the vision looks outward to the world the organization wishes to create, the mission defines the organization and what it will do to realize the vision. Also see **aim.**

nine-block chart, plan. A diagram of nine blocks for planning a **work process.** It charts the three **leading-doing-measuring** functions vertically and the **input-transformation-output** processes horizontally. It can be expanded in detail to the 27-block chart, 81-block chart, 243-block chart, etc.

note taker. See **secretary.**

objection. An argument against a proposed decision, stated clearly enough to be resolved. **Consent** is based on the absence of **argued and paramount objections**.

open system. In sociocratic governance, an organization that is linked to its environment. An open system has the ability to self-correct and self-renew, to gain energy from outside itself, as opposed to a **closed system** that cannot self-correct or benefit from new energy. Also see **dynamic steering**.

opening round. A **round** that begins a **circle meeting**. Members attune themselves to the **aim** of the meeting and the **circle** as they share feelings, expectations, potential agenda issues, etc. Roughly analogous to an orchestra tuning to a note. This focuses circle members on their common interest, which is the basis for **consent decision-making**.

operations decision. A decision affecting the day-to-day work or activities of the organization, governed by **policy decisions** made in **circle meetings** and normally delegated to the **operations leader,** who executes them.

operations leader. The circle member responsible for day-to-day **operations** management and decisions within the circle's and the larger organization's policies. Operations leaders are elected by the next-higher circle with the participation of the circle they will lead. See also **operations structure**.

operations meetings. Staff meetings conducted by the **operations leader** to plan the execution of policies adopted in **circle meetings**. These are typically conducted autocratically, or as the circle has determined, rather than by consent. If a member believes an operations leader has acted in violation of circle policy or a policy does not cover the situation, the operations leader makes the decision. Then it will be discussed at the next circle meeting or a special meeting called for this purpose.

operations structure. The structure of the organization that performs the **doing** function in the **circular process** of **leading-doing-measuring**. The operations structure reflects the **circle structure** that performs the **leading** and **measuring** functions.

output. The third step in the **input-transformation-output** process, in which the client or customer receives the product or service and makes a payment for it, completing the **exchange process.**

outside expert. See **external expert**.

≈ P Q ≈

paramount. Of overriding importance, as in **argued** and **paramount objections**. A paramount objection is one that would prevent a circle member from being able to work toward the **aim** of his or her circle, to do their job. Also see the **principle of consent** and **objections**.

pattern language. How sociocratic **norms** are formulated; a structured method of describing good design practices. In addition to naming the processes and elements, describing effective solutions, and structuring solutions in a logical way, pattern languages allow designers to construct many models using the same methods and processes. Pattern languages formalize decision-making values and structure fundamentally complex systems without oversimplification. The structure and pattern reveal the interrelationships between processes and functions as part of the larger whole.

policy, policy decision, policy determination, policy plan. A decision or group of decisions that govern or constrain future **operations decisions**. A policy sets aims, standards, and limits. It may allocate resources, clarify values, establish plans, or specify general procedures. Policy decisions are the responsibility of the **circle,** as opposed to **operations decisions** that are normally delegated to the **operations leader**. Policy decisions are made by the **circles** in the **domains** they affect by **consent**.

policy preparation or development. The process of developing a **policy** proposal that includes circle members providing requirements and ideas. Usually delegated to a few circle members or to an assisting or **helping circle** that studies and researches the issue.

power-over. An autocratic concept in which one person or group dominates another. Also see **power-with**.

power-with. A concept of power as shared. The circle structure and the principle of consent ensure that power is shared in a sociocratic organization and cannot become "**power over**."

primary work process. The operations directly related to realizing an **aim**, in generating a service or product, in contrast to a **secondary process** such as marketing or human resources that support delivery or production. An organization can engage in several primary processes. Also see **exchange process**.

principle of consent. The first organizing principle in sociocracy: *The principle of consent governs decision-making*. All members must consent to **policy decisions** made by their **circle**. This is the primary mechanism for establishing and maintaining **equivalence**. It also ensures greater commitment to the organization and that all available information has been considered before a decision is made.

R

representative(s). A **circle** member or members chosen by the circle to participate in the next-higher circle. Representatives participate in decision-making with full authority to make decisions; they are not vote carriers. The **operations leader** may not serve as a representative.

reaction round. A quick **round** in which each member of the circle gives a one or two word response to a proposed decision. Used to quickly determine if a proposal is ready for discussion or **consent**.

round. A process used in meetings in which each member in turn is given an opportunity to speak. Doing a round maintains or reestablishes **equivalence** after a period of open discussion or when beginning or closing a meeting. See also **opening round**, **closing round**, **reaction round**, and **consent round**.

S

SCM. See **Sociocratic Circle-Organization Method**.

SCN. See sociocratic norms.

secretary. Circle officer who is responsible for the administration of the circle's decision-making process. Collects agenda items and documents for circle meetings, distributes the agenda and documents to circle members, takes notes of the meeting, and distributes decisions. This function is often combined with the **logbook keeper** in smaller circles.

self-organizing systems. A concept arising from chaos theory where natural systems are found to emerge out of chaos into organized patterns, achieving equilibrium. In sociocracy, it is used to refer to the expectation that **circles** and individuals will organize themselves and their own work in interaction with and contributing to the aim of the larger organization.

semi-autonomous. Semi-independent, as in "circles are semi-autonomous and self-organizing." Circle policies can't contradict or interfere with the policies of the organization or other circles but within its domain, each circle decides how it will accomplish its assigned aim.

Short-Term Measurement (STM). Part of the **compensation** in a sociocratic organization based on profits, generally distributed several times a year or when a project is completed. It is a measurement of productivity. Also see **Guaranteed Base Wage (GBW)** and **Long-Term Measurement (LTM)**.

sociocracy. An inclusive, collaborative method of **governance** based on the **equivalence** of all members of an organization. Equivalence is ensured by the **principle**

of consent. Steerability of the organization is ensured by applying the **circular process** in its **operations** and decision-making.

Sociocratic Circle-Organization Method (SCM). The formal name of what is generally referred to as sociocracy. Various names are used in English-speaking countries, including sociocracy, dynamic governance, dynamic self-governance, direct democracy, and sociocratic governance. The Sociocratic Center Norm SCN 500 defines it as "a compilation of rules and procedures that make it possible for people as unique persons to work and live together in equivalence." See also **governing principles**.

sociocratic election. See **election of people** to functions and tasks.

sociocratic engineering. Analysis, design, construction, and planning for development of an organization based on sociocratic principles and practices.

sociocratic hierarchy. A structure of interlinked circles that govern a sociocratic organization. In contrast to linear autocratic hierarchies, it is a circular hierarchy in which all parts are equivalent and linked with feedback loops. The structure is a steering mechanism designed to maintain communications and control between all units of an organization. It is a steering mechanism based on power-with relationships. Also see **hierarchy.**

sociocratic norms. The Sociocratic Center Norms (SCN) are established, published, and revised by the circles of the international Sociocracy Group based in the Netherlands. They provide unambiguous definitions and arguments for the principles and methods of **sociocracy** to ensure accurate understanding and application. See also **pattern language.**

sociocratic organization or company. A legal entity with (1) the **governing principles** of **sociocracy** incorporated into its statutes, bylaws, or operating agreements, and (2) a separation of ownership and authority structure; in other words, a **free organization**.

sociocratic consultant. Person certified to advise organizations about the introduction and implementation of the sociocratic method.

sociocratic trainer. Person qualified to teach the sociocratic method in seminars and workshops.

sociocratic structure. In the sociocratic method, the structure of an organization is "a configuration of transformation points which, as a whole, has the characteristic of letting specific processes take place." In other words, the structure reveals the points at which change—transformation—can happen.

sociocratic vision. A society in which people live together as unique individuals who are equivalent in policy decision-making.

solidarity. Total commitment to a shared aim, as is often required by resistance fighters or other groups risking their lives. Sometimes confused with **consensus**.

strategy. A long-term plan for accomplishing an aim. See also **strategic planning process**.

strategic planning process. The process of developing a long-term, all-encompassing plan that describes the methods and means an organization will use to achieve its **aim**. In a sociocratic organization, the strategic planning process, as part of the governance process, involves the whole circle structure but is the responsibility of the **top circle**. See also **tactics**.

steering. Governing. To govern means to steer or guide. Also refers to the **circular process** of **leading-doing-measuring**. See also **dynamic steering**.

supporting process(es). The organization's operations functioning in support of the primary process of **aim** realization; for example, administration, accounting, etc.

system, systems theory, systems thinking. A dynamic and complex whole that interacts as a structured functional unit with a common aim. Systems are often composed of entities seeking equilibrium, but can exhibit oscillating, chaotic, or exponential growth or decay.

⇒ T U ⇐

tactics. The short-term actions taken to implement a longer-term **strategy**. Also see **strategic planning process**.

theocratic decision-making. A method of decision-making in which decisions are made on the basis of faith in a supernatural power or an unquestionable set of rules or beliefs.

top circle. The element that connects the organization to its environment and prevents it from becoming a **closed system**. The top circle consists of the officers of the organization; elected **representative(s)** from the **general circle;** an **external financial** or **economic expert;** an **external legal expert;** an **external social or organizational expert;** and an **external expert on the purpose or operations of the organization**. The top circle complements the information gained by the organization in its **exchange relationships** by predicting changes in the environment and correcting the exchange relationship when necessary.

transformation. The second step in the process of **input-transformation-output** that guides production of a product or service. A product or service is created by changing the state of assets such as land, labor, capital, and materials into a new form. See also **input-transformation-output**.

➤ V W X Y Z ◄

vision or vision statement. An organization's description of the future as desired by the organization; distinct in nature from the **mission** and **aim**. Best described as the organization's desired image or dream for the future.

Selected Bibliography

Ackoff, Russell Lincoln. 1989. "The Circular Organization." *Academy of Management Executive*, 3:11–16.

———. 1981. *Creating the Corporate Future: Plan or Be Planned*. NY: Wiley.

———. 1979. *The Democratic Organization*. NY: Oxford University Press.

Amar, Akhil Reed. 2005. *America's Constitution: A Biography*. NY: Random House.

American Society of Cybernetics. Accessed 27 July 2017. http://asc-cybernetics. org/ASC.

Ansoff, Igor. 1956. *Corporate Strategy: An Analytical Approach to Business Policy for Growth and Expansion*. NY: McGraw-Hill. (Revised edition: *The New Corporate Strategy*. 1989. NY: Wiley.)

Argyris, Chris. 1957. *Personality and Organization: The Conflict Between the System and the Individual*. NY: Harper.

———. 1960. *Understanding Organizational Behavior*. Homewood, IL: Dorsey Press.

Avery, Michel, et al. 1981. *Building United Judgment: A Handbook for Consensus Decision Making*. The Center for Conflict Resolution. (Reprinted by the Fellowship for Intentional Community. 1999.)

Babbage, Charles. 1832. *On the Economy of Machinery and Manufacturers*. London: C. Knight.

Barnard, Chester I. 1938. *The Functions of the Executive*. Cambridge, MA: Harvard University Press. (30th Anniversary Edition. 1971.)

Blackwell, Christopher W. 2006. *Demos: Classical Athenian Democracy*. A publication of the Stoa: a Consortium for Electronic Publication in the Humanities. Accessed 27 July 2017. http://www.stoa.org/projects/demos/ home.

Boeke, Kees. 1957. *Cosmic View: The Universe in 40 Jumps*. Introduction by Arthur H. Compton. NY: John Day. Also available online, accessed 25 July 2017. http://www.vendian.org/mncharity/cosmicview/.

———. 1945. "Sociocracy: Democracy as It Might Be" as edited by Beatrice C. Boeke, accessed 30 July 2017. http://www.sociocracy.info/ sociocracy-democracy-kees-boeke.

Bohm, David. 1980. *Wholeness and Implicate Order.* London; Boston: Routledge & Kegan Paul.

———, and B. J. Hiley. 1993. *The Undivided Universe: An Ontological Interpretation of Quantum Theory.* London: NY: Routledge.

Boulding, Kenneth. 1958. *Principles of Economic Policy.* Englewood Cliffs, NJ: Prentice-Hall.

———. 1950. *A Reconstruction of Economics.* NY: Wiley.

———. 1985. *The World as a Total System.* Beverly Hills, CA: Sage Publications.

Buck, John. 2003. "Employee Engagement in Sociocratic versus Conventional Organizations." Master's thesis. Washington, DC: George Washington University.

———, and Gerard Endenburg. 1987. "The Creative Forces of Self-Organization." The Netherlands: Sociocratisch Centrum.

Buhl, J., et al. 2006. "From Disorder to Order in Marching Locusts." *Science,* 312:1402–1406.

Burns, James MacGregor. 1978. *Leadership.* NY: Harper & Row.

Butler, C.T., and Amy Rothstein. 1991. *Conflict and Consensus: A Handbook of Formal Consensus Decisionmaking.* Second edition. Portland, ME: Food Not Bombs.

Chandler, Alfred. 1962. *Strategy and Structure: Chapters in the History of the Industrial Enterprise.* Cambridge: MIT Press.

———. 1980. *The Visible Hand: The Managerial Revolution in American Business.* Cambridge: Harvard University Press.

Charest, Gilles. 1996. *La Gestion par Consentement: Une Novelle Facon de Partager le Pouvoir* [*Management by Consent: A New Way of Sharing Power*]. Montreal: Les Editions Transcontinental.

———. 1988. *Du Management à l'Écogestion* [*Management by Consent*]. Montreal: L. Courteau.

Chomsky, Noam. 2012. *Occupy.* NY: Zuccotti Park Press.

———. 2014. *Requiem for the American Dream: The 10 Principles of Concentration of Wealth & Power.* NY: Seven Stories Press. (New edition. 2017.)

Clausewitz, Carl von. 1968. *On War.* Edited with an introduction by Anatol Rapoport. Mattituck, NY: Aeonian Press. Originally published as *Vom Kriege.* 1832. First English translation, 1908.

Collins, Jim. 2001. *Good to Great: Why Some Companies Make the Leap ... and Others Don't.* NY: HarperCollins.

Comte, Auguste. 1853. *Positive Philosophy.* English translation of *Cours de Philosophie. Six volumes, 1830–1842.* Translated and condensed by Harriet Martineau.

Corning, Peter. 1996. "Synergy, Cybernetics, and the Evolution of Politics," *International Political Science Review*, 17:1, 91–119.

Couzin, Iain D. 2005. "Effective Leadership and Decision-Making in Animal Groups on the Move." *Nature*, 433:513–516.

Cyert, Richard and James March. 1963. *A Behavioral Theory of the Firm.* Englewood Cliffs, NJ: Prentice-Hall.

Dechert, Charles R. 1965. "The Development of Cybernetics," *American Behavioral Scientist*, 8:10, 15–20.

Deming. W. Edwards. 1984. *Chain Reaction: Quality, Productivity, Lower Costs, Capture the Market.* Cambridge, MA: MIT Center for Advance Engineering Study.

————. 1986. *Out of the Crisis.* Cambridge, MA: MIT Press.

Drucker, Peter F. 1954. *The Practice of Management.* NY: Harper.

Eames, Charles and Ray. 1978. *The Powers of Ten: A Film Dealing with the Relative Size of Things in the Universe and the Effect of Adding Another Zero.* Based on the book *Power of Ten* by Kees Boeke. Made by the office of Charles and Ray Eames for IBM. Video release: Santa Monica, CA: Pyramid Media.

Endenburg, Gerard. 1974. *Dictatuur, Democratie, Sociocratie.* Rotterdam: Endenburg Elektrotechniek.

————. 1998. *Kennis, Macht en Overmacht: De Lerende Organisatie, in het Bijzonder de Sociocratische Kringorganisatie.* Delft: Eburon.

————. 1981. *Sociocratie: Het Organiseren van de Besluitvorming : een Waarborg voor Ieders Gelijkwaardigheid.* Alphen aan den Rijn: Samsom. [*Sociocracy: The Organization of Decision-Making.* 1998. Delft: Eburon.]

————. 1997. *Sociocratie als Sociaal Ontwerp in Theorie en Praktijk.* Delft: Eburon. [Translated from the Dutch by Murray Pearson. 1998. *Sociocracy as Social Design: Its Characteristics and Course of Development, as Theoretical Design and Practical Project.* Delft: Eburon.]

————. 1975. *Sociocratie: Een Redelijk Ideaal [Sociocracy: A Reasonable Ideal].* Zaandijk [Lagedijk 169]: Woudt.

Feyerabend, Paul K. 1975. *Against Method: Outline of an Anarchist Theory of Knowledge.* London: Humanities Press.

Fletcher, Ronald. 2002. *The Making of Sociology: A Study of Sociological Theory.* From a reprint of the original 1971 edition. 2 volumes. Jaipur: Rawat Publications.

Follett, Mary Parker. 1940. *Dynamic Administration: The Collected Papers of Mary Parker Follett.* Edited by Henry C. Metcalf and L. Urwick. NY: London: Harper.

Gilbreth, Frank B., Jr., and Ernestine Gilbreth Carey. 1948. *Cheaper by the Dozen.* NY: Grossett & Dunlap.

———. 1950. *Cheaper by the Dozen.* Directed by Walter Lang. Hollywood, CA: 20th Century Fox. Film.

Gitlin, Todd. 2012. *Occupy Nation: The Roots, the Spirit, and the Promise of Occupy Wall Street.* NY: It Books.

Haken, H[erman]. 1978. *Synergetics: An Introduction: Nonequilibrium Phase Transitions and Self-Organization in Physics, Chemistry, and Biology.* Springer Series in Synergetics, volume 1. Berlin; NY: Springer-Verlag.

Hamel, Gary. 2000. *Leading the Revolution: How to Thrive in Turbulent Times by Making Innovation a Way of Life.* Cambridge, MA: Harvard University Press.

Holocaust Encyclopedia. "Joop Westerweel." United States Holocaust Museum, accessed 20 July 2017. https://www.ushmm.org/wlc/en/article.php?ModuleId=10005777.

Jaques, Elliott. 2002. *The Life and Behavior of Living Organisms: A General Theory.* Westport, CT: Praeger.

———. 1998. *Requisite Organization. A Total System for Effective Managerial Organization & Managerial Leadership for the 21st Century.* Revised second edition. Arlington, VA: Caslon Hall. (Originally published 1986.)

Jantsch, Erich. 1980. *The Self-Organizing Universe: Scientific and Human Implications of the Emerging Paradigm of Evolution.* Oxford; NY: Pergamon Press.

Jay, Antony. 1967. *Management and Machiavelli: An Inquiry into the Politics of Corporate Life.* London: Hodder & Stoughton.

Joseph, Fiona. 2012. *Beatrice: The Cadbury Heiress Who Gave Away Her Fortune.* Birmingham, UK: Foxwell Press.

Juran, J. M. 1964. *Managerial Breakthrough: A New Concept of the Manager's Job.* NY: McGraw-Hill. Revised edition. 1995. *Managerial Breakthrough: The Classic Book on Improving Management Performance.* NY: McGraw-Hill.

———. 1951. *Quality Control Handbook.* NY: McGraw Hill. Reprinted as *Juran's Quality Control Handbook* beginning in 1968.

———, and Frank M. Gryna, Jr. 1970. *Quality Planning and Analysis: From Product Development Through Use.* NY: McGraw-Hill.

Klarreich, Erica. 2006. "The Mind of the Swarm." Science News. 25 November 2007. 170:347.

Knight, Douglas E., and Herbert W. Robinson. 1972. *Cybernetics, Artificial Intelligence, and Ecology.* Proceedings of the Fourth Annual Symposium of the American Society for Cybernetics. NY: Spartan Books.

Koestler, Arthur. 1976. *Bricks to Babel.* First American edition. Includes a postscript by the author. NY: Random House.

———. 1980. *Bricks to Babel: A Selection from 50 Years of His Writings, Chosen with a New Commentary by the Author.* NY: Random House.

Kramer, Jeffery. 2008. *Inside Drucker's Brain.* NY: Portfolio Penguin.

Laloux, Federic. 2014. *Reinventing Organizations.* Brussels: Nelson Parker.

Levitin, Michael. 2015. "The Triumph of Occupy Wall Street," *The Atlantic Monthly.*

Likert, Rensis. 1967. *The Human Organization: Its Management and Value.* NY: McGraw-Hill.

———. 1961. *New Patterns of Management.* NY: McGraw-Hill.

———, and Jane Gibson Likert. 1976. *New Ways of Managing Conflict.* NY: McGraw-Hill.

Machiavelli, Niccolò. 1980. *The Prince.* Introduction by Christian Gauss. Oxford University Press "World's Classics" translation by Luigi Ricci, revised by E.R.P. Vincent. NY: New American Library.

Manville, Brook, and Josiah Ober. 2003. *A Company of Citizens: What the World's First Democracy Teaches Leaders about Building Great Organizations.* Boston: Harvard Business School Press.

Maslow, Abraham H. 1968. *Toward a Psychology of Being.* NY: Van Nostrand.

Mayo, Elton. 1933. *The Human Problems of an Industrial Civilization.* NY: Macmillan.

Meadows, Donella, et. al. 2004. *Limits to Growth: The 30-Year Update.* VT: Chelsea Green.

———. 2008. *Thinking in Systems: a Primer.* VT: Chelsea Green.

Naím, Moisés. 2013. *The End of Power.* NY: Basic Books.

Mooney, James D., and Alan C. Reiley. 1931. *Onward Industry! The Principles of Organization and Their Significance to Modern Industry.* NY: Harper & Brothers.

Morgan, Gareth. 2006. *Images of Organization.* Updated edition. Thousand Oaks, CA: Sage Publications.

Morieux, Yves. 2014. *Six Simple Rules: How to Manage Complexity without Getting Complicated.* Cambridge, MA: Harvard Business Review Press.

Naisbitt, John. 1982. *Megatrends: Ten New Directions Transforming Our Lives.* NY: Warner Books.

Nash, John F., Jr. 1997. "Equilibrium Points in n-Person Games." "The Bargaining Problem." "Non-Cooperative Games." In *Classics in Game Theory,* edited by Harold W. Kuhn. Princeton, NJ: Princeton University Press.

———. 1996. *Essays on Game Theory.* Cheltenham, UK; Brookfield, VT: E. Elgar.

Nauta, D. 1984. "Defensie in Sociocratisch Perspectif. Hoofdstuk 8" in M.H.K. van der Graaf, *De crisis van de Technocratie en het alternatief van de sociocratie.* De Horstink.

———, and E. van der Verlde. 1987. "Informatisering en arbeid." In *Wijsgerig Perspectief.* 27:5, 156-162.

New York State General Assembly. "Occupy Wall Street." Website of the New York State General Assembly, accessed 26 June 2017. http://occupywallstreet.net.

Nye, Joseph S. 2011. *The Future of Power.* NY: PublicAffairs Perseus.

Ober, Josiah. 1989. *Mass and Elite in Democratic Athens: Rhetoric, Ideology, and the Power of the People.* Princeton, NJ: Princeton University Press.

Ohmae, Kenichi. 1990. *The Borderless World: Power and Strategy in the Interlinked Economy.* London: Collins.

———. 1995. *End of the Nation State: The Rise of Regional Economies.* London: HarperCollins.

———. 1982. *The Mind of the Strategist: The Art of Japanese Business.* NY; London: McGraw-Hill.

Owen, Robert. 1815. "Observations on the Effect of the Manufacturing System." Reprinted in *The Voice of Toil: Nineteenth-Century British Writing about Work,* 2000, edited by David J. Bradshaw and Suzanne Ozment. Athens, OH: Ohio University Press.

Pascale, Richard Tanner and Anthony G. Athos. 1981. *The Art of Japanese Management: Applications for American Executives.* NY: Simon and Schuster.

Piketty, Thomas. 2016. *Capital in the Twenty-First Century.* Translated from the original French by Arthur Goldhammer. Cambridge, MA: Harvard University Press.

———. Thomas. 2015, *The Economics of Inequality.* Translated from the original French by Arthur Goldhammer. Cambridge, MA: Harvard University Press.

Prigogine, Ilya. 1997. *The End of Certainty: Time, Chaos, and the New Laws of Nature.* NY: Free Press.

———, and Isabelle Stengers. 1984. *Order Out of Chaos: Man's New Dialogue with Nature.* Toronto; NY: Bantam Books.

———. 1977. *Self-Organization in Nonequilibrium Systems: From Dissipative Structures to Order through Fluctuations.* NY: Wiley.

Principia Cybernetica Project (PCP). *Principia Cybernetica Web.* Accessed 1 July 2017. http://pespmc1.vub.ac.be.

Quarter, Jack. 2000. *Beyond the Bottom Line: Socially Innovative Business Owners.* Westport, CT: Quorum Books.

Rapoport, Anatol. 1986. *General Systems Theory: Essential Concepts and Applications.* Tunbridge Wells, Kent, UK; Cambridge, MA: Abacus Press.

Robertson, Brian. 2015. *Holacracy: The New Management System That Redefines Management.* NY: Holt.

Rogers, Everett M. 2003. *Diffusion of Innovations.* Fifth edition. NY: Free Press.

Rawson, Wyatt. 1956. *The Werkplaats Adventure.* London: Stuart.

Romme, A. Georges L. 1994. "Continuous Self-Renewal: The Case of Sociocracy." *Research Memorandum, RM/0/94-039.* Maastricht: Maastricht Research School of Economics of Technology and Organizations.

———. 1996. "Making Organizational Learning Work: Consent and Double Linking Between Circles." *European Management Journal,* 14(1): 69–75.

———. 2016. *The Quest for Professionalism.* Oxford, UK: Oxford University Press.

———. 1997. "Work, Authority, and Participation: The Scenario of Circular Organizing." *Journal of Organizational Change Management,* 10(2):156–166.

———, and Gerard Endenburg. 2006. "Construction Principles and Design Rules in the Case of Circular Design." *Organization Science: a Journal of the Institute of Management Sciences.* 17(2):287.

———, and Annewick J.M. Reijmer. 1995. *Sociocracy in Endenburg Elektrotechniek.* Winner of the 1995 European Case Writing Competition, sponsored by the European Foundation for Management Development.

Schein, Edgar H. 1997. *Organizational Culture and Leadership.* Second edition. San Francisco: Josssey-Bass.

Seeley, Thomas D. 2010. *Honeybee Democracy.* Princeton, NJ: Princeton University Press.

Senge, Peter M. 1990. *The Fifth Discipline: The Art and Practice of the Learning Organization.* NY: Doubleday.

———, 2008. *The Necessary Revolution: How Individuals and Organizations Are Working Together to Create a Sustainable World.* NY: Doubleday.

Sheeran, Michael J. 1996. *Beyond Majority Rule.* Philadelphia: Philadelphia Yearly Meeting of the Religious Society of Friends.

Simon, Herbert A. 1957. *Administrative Behavior: A Study of Decision-Making Processes in Administrative Organization.* Second edition. NY: Macmillan. First edition, 1947.

Stanley-Jones, D., and K. Stanley-Jones. 1960. *Kybernetics of Natural Systems, A Study in Patterns of Control*. London: Pergamon Press.

Sun-tzu. 1994. *The Art of War*. Translated with introduction by Ralph D. Sawyer with the collaboration of Mei-chün Lee Sawyer. Boulder, CO: Westview Press. Original edition, Fifth-century BCE.

Taylor, Fredrick Winslow. 1911. *The Principles of Scientific Management*. NY: London: Harper.

Tuchman, Barbara. 1978. *A Distant Mirror: The Calamitous 14th Century*. NY: Knopf.

Ward, Lester F. 1902. *Dynamic Sociology*. Second edition. NY: Appleton.

———. 1907. *Pure Sociology*. Second edition. NY: Macmillan.

———. 1893. "Sociocracy." From *The Psychic Factors of Civilization* (Boston: Ginn & Co., 1893), pp. 315–331. As reprinted in *American Thought: Civil War to World War I*, edited by Perry Miller. 1954. NY: Holt, Rinehart and Winston. 306–320.

United Nations Economic and Social Commission for Asia and the Pacific (ESCAP) *"What Is Good Governance,"* Available for download. Accessed 12 August 2017. http://www.unescap.org/sites/default/files/good-governance.pdf

Wheatley, Margaret J. 1992. *Leadership and the New Science: Learning about Organization from an Orderly Universe*. San Francisco: Berrett-Koehler.

Weber, Max. 1947. *The Theory of Social and Economic Organization*. London: Free Press of Glencoe; Collier-Macmillan.

Weiner, Norbert. 1948. *Cybernetics; or Control and Communications in the Animal and the Machine*. NY: Wiley.

———. 1954. *The Human Use of Human Beings: Cybernetics and Society*. Boston: Houghton Mifflin.

Whyte, William Foote, and Kathleen King Whyte. 1988. *Making Mondragon: The Growth and Dynamics of the Worker Cooperative Complex*. Cornell International Industrial and Labor Relations Reports, no. 14. Ithaca, NY: ILR Press.

Zuboff, Shoshana. 1988. *In the Age of the Smart Machine*. NY: Basic Books.

———, and James Maxmin. 2002. *The Support Economy: Why Corporations Are Failing Individuals and the Next Episode of Capitalism*. NY: Viking Penguin.

Index

14th Amendment to the Constitution, 125
"27 Block Chart for Producing Organization,"
    189–191

⊸ A ⊸

A Beautiful Mind, 134
A Behavioral Theory of the Firm, 74
accountability, 18
activation of circles. *See* implementation
active-dynamic steering, 106
active-passive steering, 105
Administrative Behavior by Herbert Simon, 74
Affordable Care Act, 126
agreement. *See* consent
aim, aim statement, vi, viii, 18, 154, 166
    accomplishing of, 184
    named product or service, 184
    basis for exchange, 133
    cybernetics and, 56
    definition and requirements, 93, 142, 184–188,
        195
    frequency of review, 195
    strategic planning process, 123
    Examples: 185–187
alienation, effect of, 67
alignment, 67
allocation of tasks
    See roles and responsibilities
American Federation of Teachers, 122
American Society for Cybernetics, 55
analogical thinking, 47, 52
    physical sciences to social sciences, 47
anticipatory steering
    advantages, 106
    unpredictability, 107
    See also steering; feed-forward
application of sociocratic methods
    See implementation
Appreciative Inquiry, 156
argued and paramount. *See* objections; arguments
arguments, 180

defined, 81
    Example: glass of water, 81
    See also objections
aristocracy, 17
Art of War by Sun Tzu 121
Ashby, W. Ross, 55
assembly line production, 71, 121
    I love Lucy, 71
    Modern Times, 71
    See also Fordism
authoritarian decision-making, 68–69, 84, 117
autocratic decision-making, 59, 141
    See also majority-vote
        autocracy, autocratic organizations, 18, 20,
            37, 38, 92, 69, 138, 175
    as objects, 140
    distribution of profits in, 139
    employee-owned companies, 139
    employees as servants in, 23–26, 140,
    feedback in, 109
    leadership, vii, 121
        limits on, 116
    retention rate, workers, 71
    structure, 135, 139
    Example: Fordism, 70–71
    See also ownership, owners

⊸ B ⊸

Babbage, Charles, 70
Beer, Stafford, 55
A Behavioral Theory of the Firm, 74
    by Richard Cyert and James March
behavior and decision-making, 84
beyond democracy, 18
Bilthoven, the Netherlands, 41, 42, 79
board of directors, 76, 68, 115, 147
    See also top circle
Boeke, Cornelius "Kees," 41–45, 49
    education, progressive, 42
    international peace activist, 42
    Jewish refugees, 44

majority rule, 43

political party system, 43

Quaker missionary, 42

"Sociocracy: Democracy as It Might Be," 45, 223–231

See also Children's Community Workshop

bonuses, 135

See also compensation; variable compensation

"both-and" thinking, 46

bottom-archy 119. *See also* hierarchy

"bounded rationality," 74

See also Herbert Simon

BP Global. *See* Deepwater Horizon oil spill

Brown University, 40

Buck, John, xv, 23–27, 34–35, 210

about, xv

Gerard Endenburg, and, 23–24, 26–27

sociocracy, and, 23–27

"Why We Need Another -ocracy," 23–27

budgets, budgeting process, 154, 199–206

weighting factors, 200–202

calculating variables, 200–203

nonprofits, 205

proposals and approval, 199

transparency, 206

See also compensation; general management circle; money as measurement; top circle

Building United Judgment, 31

Burwell v. Hobby Lobby Stores, 126

Affordable Care Act, 126

See also corporations as persons

Butler, C. T., 32

Conflict and Consensus, 32

formal consensus, 32

Bylaws for a Sociocratic Business

Operating Agreement for a Sociocratic Business," 243–260

"Bylaws for a Sociocratic Nonprofit Organization, 261–283

Conflict of Interest and Confidentiality Agreement, 283

bylaws, constitutions, 148

⇜ **C** ⇝

Cadbury, Beatrice "Betty" Cadbury, 41–44, 49

education, progressive, 42

international peace organizations, 42

Jewish refugees, 44

majority rule, 43

peace activist, 42

political party system, 43

Quaker missionary, 42

See also Children's Community Workshop

Cadbury Chocolate, 41

Capability Maturity Model, 189

capital. *See* investment capital; market economy

C corporation, 241

CEO. *See* general manager

changing conditions, managing.

See circular process

chaos, chaos theory, 19, 160

power and energy of, 19

Chaplin, Charlie, *Modern Times*, 71

charismatic leaders, 115

Jack Welch as, 115

Cheaper by the Dozen, 70

Children's Community Workshop, 41, 42–45

See also Beatrice "Betty" Cadbury; Cornelius "Kees" Boeke

China, 209

circle, 90–92, 145, 151, 153–154

assign roles and responsibilities, 60

common aim, 153

control over operations, 90

delegation, 154

"organizes its production," 92

second principle, the, 90–91

self-organizing, 153

semi-autonomous, 153

size of, 91

See also circle development; circle meetings; circle types

circle types

implementation, 145–158

full circle. See full circles

general management circle, 149

helping circle, 113

operations circles. See department level circles

top circle. *See* top circle

circle development, 96, 147, 157, 195

5% of resources 195–196
Examples::
    Great Recession, 96
    loading dock, 195
    See also logbook
circle logbook. *See* logbook
circle officers, 151-163
    facilitator, 50, 151–152, 166
        participant, as, 50
        responsibilities, 151
        role in election process, 177, 178
        techniques, 159
    secretary, 151, 156–157, 162–163,
        distributing documents, 162–163
        meeting logistics, 151
        minutes, 156–157
    logbook keeper 151
    See also circle representative(s); logbooks;
        operations leader
circle representative(s), 61, 100–101, 151–152
    abilities needed, 101
    measuring function, 100
    roles and responsibilities, 101, 151
    Example: shipping crisis, 152
    See also circle structure; double-linking
circle meetings, 60, 89, 151–155, 159
    "Circle Meetings," guide for 293–294
    frequency, of 91
    operations circles, 150–151
    meeting format, 154
    responsibilities, 90, 153
    rounds, discussion, and dialogue, 155,160
    special meetings of, 102
    topics for, 91, 153
    See also staff meetings; consent; policy pro-
        posals; rounds, elections process
circle structure, 145, 146
    communication and control, 99
    designing, 145
    diagrams, 111
    levels of circles, 110
    strategic planning process, and, 123
    system, as a, 95
    See also circular process, feedback loop, imple-
        mentation process

"Circles & Officers," guide for, 289–290
circular hierarchy, 100
    See also circular process; feedback
circular process, 78, 92, 99, 100, 102, 103, 131,
        136, 145
    diagram, 95
    leading-doing-measuring, 193–194
    types of steering, 103
    Examples: heating system, 78, 103
citizen-government relationship, 21, 79
Citizens United v. Federal Election Commission,
    126
clarifying questions, 163
Clausewitz, Carl von, 120–122
    On War, 120–121
    strategic planning, 120
closing round. *See* rounds
coherent structure, 57
cohousing, 29–33
collaborative, collaboration, vi, vii, 79
    consent, and, 79
    governance, 18
Collins, Jim, 119–120, 122
    Good to Great, 119-120
communication and control, 21
    circle structure, 99
    double-link, 99
    See also cybernetics; circular process
communications, coordination, 60, 64, 128, 130
    between circles, 60
    communications, lack of, 128-131
    Examples:
        multi-national corporations, 128
        Deepwater Horizon oil spill, 129–131
        Veteran's Administration (VA) hospitals,
        132l
    See also: general management circle
compensation as measurement, 135–136
    Guaranteed Base Wage (GBW), 137–138, 199
    Long-Term Measurement (LTM), 137–138
    Short-Term Measurement (STM), 136–137
compensation structure, 137–138,199.
    sharing profits, losses, 137
    applies to everyone, 137
    See also budget process

competition, 127, 135, 214
complexity theory, 121
    See also: chaos theory
computing, 70, 74
Comte, Auguste, 37–41, 62
    Father of Sociology, 37
    metaphysical understanding, 38
    Positivism, 38
    quantitative and mathematical methods, 38
    science, and, 30
    sociocracy, idea of, 37
    Ward and, 39
Conflict and Consensus by C. T. Butler, 32
"Conflict of Interest and Confidentiality Agree-
    ment," 283–4
    Also see "Bylaws for a Sociocratic Nonprofit
      Organization"
consensus decision-making, full-group 43, 49, 50,
    51, 59
    Building United Judgment, 31
    cohousing, 29–30
    Conflict and Consensus, 32
    consensus community, 50
    definitions of, 29
    delegation, 31, 50
    dependence on facilitator, 33
    dissension, 50
    impracticalities, inefficiency, 50
    lack of leadership, 31
    large organizations, in, 50
    Quaker practices as model, 33
    trust-based, values-based, 49
    Example: Occupy Wall Street, 50–51
    See also consent; supra-majority vote
consent decision-making, vi, vii, 68–84, 159, 135
    advantages, 84
    Declaration of Independence (US), 79–80
    defined, 78, 80
    not agreement, 81
    solution to full-group consensus, 59
    Examples:
      heating system 78
      Sara's Story, 169–173
    See also consent, principle of; rounds; objec-
      tions; domain of decision-making

consent decision-making process, 161–169
    achieving consent, 161–165
    clarifying questions, 163
    complex or controversial decisions, 161
    consent rounds, 165
    facilitating and, 161–165
    improving the proposal, 163
    objections, seeking out, 165
    presenting the proposal, 162
    quick reaction rounds, 162
    refer proposals back, 162
    resolving objections, 163–165
    simple decision, 161
    Example: Sara's Story, 169–172
    See also consent, principle of; consent deci-
      sion-making; rounds
consent, principle of, 58, 79-81
    basis of decision making, 148
    defined, 80
    facilitating and, 161–165
    in election process, 117, 175–181
    no objections, 79
    not about veto, 84
    right to reason or argue, 84
    See also consent decision-making; objections
"consent of the governed," 79
constitutions
    policy, as, 20
    sociocratic, 20
    See also bylaws.
Constitution of the United States of America, 17,
    20, 80
    as experimental, 17
consultants, trainers, 210-211
consultative decision-making, 72–73
continuous improvement, 21
contracts, 205
coordinating circle
    See general management circle
coordination. *See* communications, coordination
co-responsibility, 43
Corning, Peter, 55
corporations, 69, 125
    14th Amendment to the Constitution, 125
    abuse of power, 125–127

control, lack of ability to, 64
history of, 125
resources of, 126
social impact, 132
social responsibility, 127
sociocracy, and, 127
Tobacco Master Settlement Agreement, 126
See also corporations as persons
corporations as persons
Burwell v. Hobby Lobby Stores, 126
Citizens United v. Federal Election
  Commission, 126
"persons under the law," 125–126
Santa Clara County v. Southern Pacific
  Railroad, 125
correcting, correction
See steering process; circular process
creating organization
See producing organization
customers as judges of quality, 87
See also aim
cybernetics, 19, 21, 49–62, 232
aim, 56
consent, 79
definitions of, 55
first-order cybernetics, 56
interdisciplinary study, 53, 54, 56
Plato, 53
purpose, unique to, 56
questions it asks, 52
second-order cybernetics, 56
  learning organizations, 57
See also steering; circular process
cybernetics of cybernetics
See second-order cybernetics
Cybernetics by Norbert Weiner, 53
Cyert, Richard, 74
A Behavioral Theory of the Firm, 74
circles, 95
changing and unpredictable circumstances, 74
"power-with," 74

⇒ **D** ⇐

debate, sociocratic
focus on argument, 142

decision-making
authoritarian, 68
changing and unpredictable circumstances, 74
distributed, 68
history of, 68–72
inclusive, 20, 67–83
leadership and, 33
operations leader, 80
See also delegation
decision-making methods
autocratic, 80
belief system, 80
consensus, full group, 80
effect on behavior, 84
in sociocratic organizations, 80
listed, 80
majority vote, 80
methods compared, 234
solidarity, 80
theocratic, 80
Declaration of Independence of the United
  States, 18, 79
and consent, 79
Deepwater Horizon oil spill, 129–131
delegation, delegate, 15, 20
power, and, 67
Deming, W. Edwards, 25, 86, 132
Total Quality Management (TQM), 87
Veteran's Administration (VA) hospitals, 132
creating organization
See producing organization
democracy, vii, 17, 96
deficiencies of, 17
  general elections, 18
  ineffective, ensuring high performance, 18
  political alliances, 18
definitions, 18
differences from sociocracy, 18
majority rule, 17
precondition to sociocracy, 96
scientific method, 17
word origin, 18
"Democracy as It Might Be," 223–230
  by Kees Boeke
democratic elections, 175

department-level circles, 111–112, 123
  composition, 149
  elect representative(s), 150
  establish unit circles, 151
  meeting frequency, 150–151
  responsibilities, 151
  set policy for operations, 150
  short-term planning, 150
  See also circles; elections process
"Designing the Work Process," guide for, 301
development, professional
  See circle development
Dewey, John, 41
dialogue, 155, 164. *See also* rounds
dictatorships, dictators, 18
difference-controlled
  See passive-dynamic steering
direct client, 134.
  See also for-profit organizations
dissatisfiers, 198
distribution of profits, 139
distrust, 135
disturbances. *See* unpredictable events
diversify, inability to, 71
dividends, 139.
  See also compensation
doing. *See* circular process, hierarchy
domains, 81-82
  defined, 81
  of responsibility, 90
  See also circles
donors, 138.
  See also non-profit organizations
donors, sponsors, 136
double corporation, 241
double-links, double-linking, 99–103, 148
  communication and control, as, 99
  creating strong systems, 102
  diagram, 101
  downlink. *See* operations leader
  feedback loops, 60
  prevents autocratic decision-making, 100
  uplink. *See* representative(s)
  See also operations leader; representative(s)
Drucker, Peter, 72

Inside Drucker's Brain, 72
  praising Mary Parker Follett, 72
dynamic, changing, adaptable, 19
dynamic governance, viii, 99
dynamic organizations, 58
dynamic steering. *See* steering, dynamic

⇒ E ⇐

economic motive, 134
education, progressive, 40–44
  John Dewey, 41
  Montessori Method, 43
  Ward, Lester Frank, 40
  See also Betty Cadbury, Kees Boeke, Children's Community Workshop
"either-or" thinking, 46
election process, 95, 116, 175–181, 195
  arguments in, 178–180
  description of roles, responsibilities, 176–177
  electing to roles and responsibilities, 146, 148
  facilitator role, 177, 178, 180
  nominations, 175, 177–178
  precautions, 179
  used for other decisions, 181
"Elections Process," Guide to, 291–292
employees. See workers
employee-owned company, 139
Endenburg, Anna and Gerardus, 46
  "both-and" thinking, 46
  "either-or" thinking, 46
  market economy, 46
  socialism, 46
Endenburg Electrical Engineering, 46, 46–48, 52
  as a laboratory, 47, 61
  free organization 62
  ISO 9000, 89
  shipping crisis, 60
  worker council exemption, 47
Endenburg Elektrotechniek
  See Endenburg Electrical Engineering
Endenburg Foundation, x
Endenburg, Gerard, 45–48, 51–52, 79, 121, 141
  Buck, John, 23
  cybernetics, 57–58
  Children's Community Workshop, 45–46

Philips Electronics, 46
"Rational for a New Social Design," 231–238
social vs. physical sciences, 46
Sociocracy: A Reasonable Ideal, 48
Sociocracy as Social Design, 48
Sociocracy: The Organization of Decision-Making, 48
University of Maastricht, 48
enfranchisement, 66
entrepreneurs, entrepreneurial, 58, 20, 197
equivalence, 18, 142, 155, 156, 159, 160
transparency, and, 123, 124
establishing new circles, 149
exchange process
"basis for the exchange," 133
exchange value, 185
Examples: 133, 185
Existence Possibility Guarantee
See compensation, Guaranteed Base Wage

⟾ F ⟽

facilitator, facilitation
See circle meeting facilitator
family meetings and sociocratic methods, 207
feedback, 58, 103, 120, 141, 119.
profit as, 131
rejection of, 70
See also measuring
feedback loop, 54–55, 130
cause-and-effect, 54
communication, 54
controlling, 20
defined, 54
equilibrium, maintain, 54
See also circular process
feed-forward loops, 54, 105–108.
Example: heating system, 105
See also feedback loops; circular process
financial reporting systems, 135
first governing principle. *See* consent
fixed compensation. *See* Guaranteed Base Wage
Foerster, Heinz von, 55, 57
Follett, Mary Parker, 72–73
co-active control, 73
"group networks," 73

Hawthorne Experiment, 72
Peter Drucker praises, 72
"power-with," 73
Ford, Henry, 70–71, 116, 121
See also Fordism, Ford Motor Company
Fordism, 85, 100, 108
autocratic quality control, 85
de-skilling, 85
linear process, 100
minute management, 70
standardization, 85
Ford Motor Company, 70
assembly line, first moving, 71
Modern Times, 71
profits and wages, 71
worker dissatisfaction, 71
Formal Consensus, 32
fractals, 98
freedom and equality, 17, 18, 20
free organizations 62
Endenburg Electric, 62
protected from hostile takeovers, 61, 62
French Revolution, 38
friction, 77
See also harmony
full circle, full circle meetings, 113–114, 156
See also circle, circle meetings
functions and tasks. *See* roles and responsibilities
furnace analogy. *See* heating system

⟾ G ⟽

game theory. *See* Nash, John Forbes
General Electric, 115, 119
GBW. *See* compensation: Guaranteed Base Wage
general management circle, 60, 110–111
budgeting process, 199
roles and responsibilities, 60
operations budgets for departments, 149
elects operations leaders, 150
establishing new circles, 149
See also communications; coordination
general manager, 112, 113, 139, 208
roles and responsibilities, 62
General Motors, 86
generativity, 149

George, Frank Honywill, 55

Gilbreth, Frank and Lillian
  Cheaper by the Dozen, 70

Glasersfeld, Ernst von, 55

global economy, 130

globalization, 87–89

Good to Great by Jim Collins, 119–120

governance, governing, 19, 21, 37–38
  characteristics of good governance, vii
  definition, vii
  history of, 68–72
  Quaker, 49
  structures, 66
  word origin, meaning, 53

government, responsibilities of, 79

Grant, Ulysses S., 122

Guaranteed Base Wage, 135, 136-138, 199
  See also compensation

Gulf of Mexico. *See* Deepwater Horizon oil spill

≈ H ≈

harmony, harmonious, xii, 37, 43, 50, 62, 142

harnessing energy, 20, 21

Hawthorne Experiment, Elton Mayo, 72

health care, 209

heating system example, 78–80, 83, 103–104,
    105, 106

helping circle, 113

Henry Ford, 85

hierarchy, 73, 100, 117–120, 123–124, 146
  autocratic, 73, 100
  bottom-archy, 119
  communications, 119
  complex tasks, 119
  circular, 100
  military and ecclesiastic, 118
  networks vs., 73
  work, of, 118–119
  strategic planning process, 123–124
  Example: garden, 118–119
  See also Arthur Koestler

Hilbert, David, 53

history of governance, 68–72

Hobby Lobby.
  See Burwell v. Hobby Lobby Stores

Holacracy, viii

holons, holarchy 118
  See also Arthur Koestler

Honeybee Democracy by Thomas D. Seeley vii

honeybees, vii-viii

horizontalism, 51

human capital, strength of the organization, 121

≈ I ≈

idea of a sociocracy, 37–47

implementation process, 142–143, 145–158
  activation of circles, 147
  equivalence training, 150
  "Implementation Process," guide to, 285
  order of activation of circles, 147
  top circle, 147
  Example: structural changes, 146

implementation circle, 145-147
  composition, 145
  continuing as internal trainers, 147
  functioning sociocratically, 146
  transitioning into organization, 147

"Implementation Process," guide to, 287–288

inclusive, inclusive decision-making, viii, 18, 38

India, 208

indirect client, 134
  See also nonprofit organizations

individualism, 39

self-interest, 62

Industrial Revolution, 38, 69, 69

innovation, 21

input-transformation-output process, 188–189

Inside Drucker's Brain by Jeffrey Krames, 72

installation. *See* implementation

integral education. *See* development

internal trainers, 147. *See also* implementation

International Fellowship for Reconciliation, 42

International Institute of Sociology, 40

International Monetary Fund, vii

International Organization for Standardization
    (ISO), 88

investors, investment capital, 136–137, 200
  attracting capital, 137
  rights protected, 62
  shareholders rights, 139

ISO 9000. *See* quality certification
Jack Welch, 115
Japan, 86, 121
    Japanese Union of Scientists and Engineers
        (JUSE), 86
    See also W. Edwards Deming, Joseph Juran
John Dewey, 41
Juran, Joseph, 86–87
    "freedom from trouble," 87
    Japanese Union of Scientists and Engineers
        (JUSE), 86
    Managerial Breakthrough, 87
    Pareto Principle, 87
    Total Quality Management (TQM), 87

≡**K**≡

Kepner-Tregoe Matrix, 156
Koestler, Arthur, 117–118
    holarchy, 118
    holon, 118
Krames, Jeffrey, *Inside Drucker's Brain*, 72
kring. *See* circle

≡ **L** ≡

labor, 136, 200
    as investment, 200
    labor-management relationship, 21
    labor movement, 69
    See also workers
languages, sociocracy taught in, 211
leadership, 20, 21, 62, 76, 115–124, 141, 193
    charisma and power, 119
    constricted by authoritarian structures, 116
    responsibility of everyone, 115
    systems problems and, 194
    skills as predictors of success, 121, 122
    transparency, 76
    work as, 115–120
    See also Good to Great, leading function, oper-
        ations leaders
Leadership and the New Science, 128
        by Margaret Wheatley
leading-doing-measuring.
    See circular process
leading function, 193–196

learning organizations.
    See second-order cybernetics
Lee, Robert E., 122
Limited Liability Company (LLC)
    operating agreement for, 241
linear command structure
    advantages, 107
    benefits in doing, 107
    Examples: 107
linear steering structures, 107–108
    authoritarian leaders, 100
    autocracies, 100
    Fordism, 100
    lacking feedback, 103
logbooks, 91, 124, 147
    access, 156
    contents, 156
    development program, 196
    "Logbooks," guide for, 305
    See also circle officers; circle meeting minutes
"Logbooks," guide for, 305
Long-Term Measurement (LTM), 136, 137
long-term planning, 120
LTM. *See* compensation; Long-Term
    Measurement

≡ **M** ≡

majority rule, vote, vii, 43, 59, 75, 80, 117, 141
    deficiencies of, 17, 18, 84
    super-, supra majority vote, 50
    Example: heating system, 78
management circle
    See general management circle
management theory, 70
    Babbage, Charles, 70
    Drucker, Peter, 27
    Follett, Mary Parker, 72
    human relations, 72
    objective data, based on, 70
    by objectives, 26
    participatory management, 92
    Drucker, Peter (1909–2005), 72
    Juran, Joseph, 87
    March, James, 74
    Mayo, Elton, 72

Simon, Herbert, 73-74
    sociocracy and, 19
    Taylor, Frederick Winslow, 70
    Also see autocratic
Managerial Breakthrough by Joseph Juran, *87*
March, James, 74
    A Behavioral Theory of the Firm, 74
    and circles, 95
    changing and unpredictable circumstances, 74
market economy, 20
    and socialism, 46
    investor rights, 62
    See also investors, investment
master-servant relationship, 66
mastery. *See* optimization
Maslow, Abraham, 198
Mayo, Elton, Hawthorne Experiment, 72
McCulloch, Warren, 55
measurement, measurability, 18, 86, 136, 141,
        194, 199
    Babbage, Charles, 70
    Comte, Auguste, 38
    compressed data, 197
    define and quantify, 131–132
    "experience the measurement," 135
    feedback and, 197
    improperly defined, 131, 132
    numerical, 130
    non-monetary, 132
    objective data, 70
    Examples:
        hair dressing salon, 195
        Wright Brothers, 194
        shipping, 194
    See also circular process, compensation
mechanical models, 20
memory system. S*ee* logbook
metaphysics, metaphysical, 38
military strategy, 120–122
Mill, John Stuart, 135
    Chapters on Socialism, 220
    inadequate distribution, 135
minute management, 70
    See also Fordism
minutes, circle meetings, 152, 154, 156–157

objections to, 154
mission, 93
    definition, 93
    vision, mission, and aim examples:, 187
Models of Man by Herbert Simon, 74
Modern Times, 71
    inspired by Ford's River Rouge plant, 71
monarchies, monarch, 17, 18, 38
monetary exchanges. *See also* exchange processes
money as measurement, 197–206
    compressed labor, as, 200
    demotivate, ability to, 198
    information, as, 127–128
    motivate, ability to, 198–199
    produce power, ability to, 199
    measure of effectiveness, 127
    See also: budgeting; compensation
monopolies, 199, 214
Montessori Method, 43
motivation, self actualization, 198
    See also Abraham Maslow; Daniel Pink
Motorola, 86

⇒ N ⇐

Nash, John Forbes, 134
    A Beautiful Mind, 134
National Education Association, 123
neighborhood circles, 208
networks, hierarchy versus, 73
nominations. *See* elections process
nonlinearity theory, 121
non-monetary
    exchanges, 132
    measurements improperly defined, 132
nonprofit organization, 128, 131, 141
    "Bylaws for a Sociocratic Nonprofit Organiza-
        tion," 261–284
    misnamed, 133
    profit and, 133
"no objections," *see* consent; objections
"no owners, no slaves," 140
    See also ownership

⇒ O ⇐

objections, 81–82, 84, 154

definition of consent as, 59
  basis for, 82
  importance of, 84
  problem solving opportunity, as, 84, 165, 166
  reasoned, argued, 81
  systems problem, evidence of, 165
  See also consent
Occupy Wall Street, 50–51
  hand gestures, 50
  horizontalism, 51
  impartial facilitators, 50
  leaderless, 51
  See also consensus, full group
officers. *See* circle meeting officers
ongoing development. *See* development
On War by Carl von Clausewitz, 120–121
opening rounds. *See* rounds
Open Space Technology, 156
"Operating Agreement for a Sociocratic
    Business," 243–260
operations, 124
  decision-making, 59
  strategic planning, 120, 124
operations budget
  See general management circle
operations circles
  See circles; department-level circles
operations decisions, 75, 77
  defined, 75, 76
  without a policy, 102
  Examples: 76
operations general manager, 80, 89
  circle structure, 61
  leading function in circular process, 100
  requesting special meetings, 102
  roles and responsibilities, 99, 116
  See also double linking
optimization, 134
O'Rear, Tena Meadows. Sara's Story, 169–173
organizational design, 67
  for power, 78
  "group networks," 73
  productivity, reduce friction, 78
organizations, organizing, viii, 20
  designing and redesigning, 184

free & self-optimizing, 125–139
  powerful, 77
  power, in, 67
  self-observing, 97
  social impact, 127, 132
  sociocracy used by, viii–ix
  word origin, meaning, 63
organizing work, 183–195
  organizing production, 183
  "Designing the Work Process," guide for,
      303–304
  See also producing organization
"outside the range of tolerance," 82
Owen, Robert, 69
ownership, owners
  autocratic power, 69
  free organizations, 62, 140
  reframing, 66
  See also master–servant

⟳ P ⟳

Pangaro, Paul, 55
paramount and argued objections.
    See argued; objections
Pareto Principle, 87
parliamentary procedure, 141
  See also Robert's Rules of Order
participatory management
    See management theory
passive-dynamic steering, 104
    Example: Eastman Kodak company, 104–105
    Also see steering
passive steering. *See* steering, passive
permanent education. *See* development
physical and natural sciences, 141
physics, 49
"picture forming," *see* policy development
piece work, 137
Pink, Daniel, 198
Plato, cybernetics, 53
*A Pocket Manual of Rules of Order
    for Deliberative Assemblies*, 141
points of information, 141
police department, 208
policy decisions, 60, 74-84, 138, 145, 153

aims, 60
board of directors, 76
consent of all circle members, 145
consequences, 76
control operations, 145
defined, 75, 76
distributed, 76, 89
foundation of governance, 145
names used for, 80
roles and responsibilities, as, 60
within the policies of organization, 145
work process, as, 60, 192
Examples: 76
See also policy development; circle meetings;
    consent
policy development, 124, 155–156
circulating proposal, 162
developing in circle meeting, 162
information gathering, 192
improving, 166–167
"picture forming," 192
presenting, 162
writing process, 161
input-transformation-output process, 192
"Policy Development," guide for, 299–300
political and social conflict, 37, 37–48
political party system, 39, 43
political theory. *See* social and political theory
positivism, positive knowledge, 38, 40
power, 142
defined, 77
history of, 68
money as, 199
organization, of, 62
physics, 77
power as energy, 21
chaos, 19
powerlessness, 68
power, organizational, 67
delegated, 67
restructuring, rewiring, 63–66
power-over, 73, 109, 117
coercive, as, 73
Follett, Mary Parker, 73
"pseudo power," 73

power-with, 73, 109
co-active control, 73
creates a whole, 73
integrative, 73
Prince Charles, 64
principle of consent. *See* consent
principle of "no objection"
See consent; objections; double linking
principles
circles, 90
consent, 59
double linking, 99–101
not "rules," 141
principles and practices, 141
how to apply, 142
"Principles, Not Recipes," 285
producing organization, production process,
    92–98, 183–196.
addresses doing, 183
"Designing the Work Process," guide for, 303
diagram of, 92, 185
functioning and adapting, 184
input, transformation, and output, 188.
organizational engineering, 184
planning production process, 188–196
Examples:
    car analogy, 183
    garden, 118–119
See also steering process
productivity, 77
workers, 47
professional development. *See* development
profit and losses, 58, 127–140, 200
distribution of, 136, 200
feedback, as, 131
measurement, as, 131, 136
measures of success, 131–132
See also transparency; money as measurement
property rights, 69
proposal development.
    See policy proposal process
proprietary
formulas, 135
information, 90
Psychic Factors of Civilization by Lester Frank

Ward, 213
public schools, 208
purpose, viii, 142
    See also aim
purpose or aim in science 56
    unique in cybernetics, 56

⇛ Q ⇚

Quakers Society of Friends, 41–44, 49–50
    meetings, 41, 42, 43, 44, 49
    missionaries, 42
    model for consensus decision-making, 33
    principles, 41
    sense of the meeting, 33
quality management, 85–97, 142, 193-194
    circles and, 89–94
    consumers and market, by, 85
    Deming, W. Edwards, 86
    Fordism, 85
    history of, 85–88
    international trade, 86, 87–88
    Japan, 86, 121
    Juran, Joseph, 86
    majority vote as, 142
    Pareto Principle, 87
    Six Sigma, 86
    statistics in, 86
    See also circular process; producing organiza-
        tion; quality certification
quality certification, 87–89, 193-194
    ISO 9000 International Organization for
        Standardization, 88
    Endenburg Electrical Engineering, 89

⇛ R ⇚

random activity
    of linear systems, 103
range of tolerance, 82
"Rationale for a New Social Design," 231–238
    by Gerard Endenburg
reaction rounds.
    See rounds
reasoned consent, 232
reasoned objection, 82
    See also arguments; objections

Reijmer, Annewiek, 211
representatives
    See circle meeting representatives;
        double-links; circle structure
resilience, 57
resolving objections, 163–164
    common methods for, 164
    "Resolving Objections and Building Consent,"
        guide for, 301–302
    Example: Sara's Story, 169-172
    See also objections
revolution, revolutionary, 20
    Industrial Revolution, 38
    Roman Catholic Church, 38
River Rouge, Ford plant at
    as inspiration for *Modern Times*, 71
Robert, Henry M., 141
    *A Pocket Manual of Rules of Order
        for Deliberative Assemblies*, 141
    Robert's Rules of Order, 141
Robert's Rules of Order, 141
    deficiencies, 141
    majority rule, 141
    regulating and recording debate, 141
    value in large bodies, 141
roles and responsibilities, 119, 142.
    assigned, 95
        autocratically, 95,151
        in circle meetings, 60, 95
        by elections, 95
        policy decisions, as 95
    consent required, 95
    relation to aim, in, 142
    use of election process in, 195
    Example: hair dressing salon, 195
    See also circle meetings; elections process;
        operations leader; representative(s)
Roman Catholic Church, 38
Röntgen, Frants Edvard, 42
rounds, about, 159–167, 160
    alternating with open discussion, 160
    establishing equivalence, 160
    facilitator's role, 159, 161
    improving proposals in, 166–167
    purpose of, 154

resolving objections in, 165–167
teleconferencing, 159
when needed, 160
See also circle meeting facilitator; circle
 meetings; elections process; rounds, types
rounds, types, 159
 opening, 160–162
  before other actions, 160
  passing in, 161
  purpose of, 160-161
 consent, 165–166, 178
  Sara's Story, 169–173
 closing, 157, 166–167
  evaluation of meeting, 166
 refer proposals back, 162
 quick-reaction, 162
 See also policy proposal process
"Rounds," guide for, 297
Russell, Bertrand, 53

≋ **S** ≋

Santa Clara County v. Southern Pacific Railroad,
 125
Sara's Story, 169–172
satisfice, 74
satisfiers, 198
scientific management, 70
 Babbage, Charles, 70
 Taylor, Frederick Winslow, 70
 Taylorism
 Cheaper by the Dozen, 70
scientific method, 17, 18, 37–39, 62
 Comte, 38
 democracy, 17
 replacing the mechanical model, 20
 Ward, 39
 See also cybernetics
Second Governing Principle.
 See circles
second-order cybernetics
 cybernetics of cybernetics, 57
Seely, Thomas D., vi
self-actualization, 198
self-correcting, self-correction, 37, 43
self-determining, 38

self-governance, vii, 19
 and democratization, 96
self-observing systems
 See cybernetics, second order
self-optimizing, 19, 134–136
self-organization, 19, 37, 57, 118, 153–155
 animal groups, in, 161
 equivalence, requires, 180
 quality control and, 89–90
self-sufficient, 38
semi-autonomous, 118, 153, 154
separation of leading and measuring, 152
shareholders. *See* investors, investment capital
shipping crisis example, 60–62, 152–153, 233
Short-Term Measurement (STM), 136, 137
 See also compensation
Simon, Herbert, 73-74
 Administrative Behavior, 74
 "bounded rationality," 74
 cognition, 73
 computer simulations, 74
 Models of Man, 74
 satisfice, 74
Six Sigma, 86
social and political theory, 37–48
social impact of organizations, 132
social physics. *See* sociology
social responsibility of corporations
 and organizations, 127
socialism, viii, 46
sociocracy, 18–20, 29, 37–48, 115-124
 consultants, trainers, x, 119, 211
 democracy, differences from, 18
 history of, 37–48
 leadership, 115–124
 name, origin, vii, 18
 taught in college and university, ix–x
"Sociocracy" by Lester Frank Ward, 215–222
Sociocracy: A Reasonable Ideal
 by Gerard Endenburg 48
Sociocracy as Social Design
 by Gerard Endenburg, 48
"Sociocracy: Democracy as It Might Be"
 by Kees Boeke, 223–230
"Sociocracy for One," 239–242

by Sharon Villines
Sociocracy Group, x, 211
Sociocracy: The Organization of Decision-Making,
    by Gerard Endenburg, 48
sociocracy@groups.io, 210
Sociocracy.info, xv, 210
Sociocratic Centers & Resources, 211
Sociocratic Circle-Organization Method (SCM),
    xv, 47, 199
Sociocratic Consulting Group, 210
sociocratic organizational structure
    See circle structure
sociocratic organizations, 62, 102, 139–140 208
    engages self-interest, 127
    neighborhoods, 208
    owns itself, free organization, 140
    worker-manager-investor cooperative, 62
    schools, 208
Sociocratisch Centrum, x, 48
sociology, social theory, 18–19, 37, 39, 49,
staff meetings, 60, 89. 151
    See also operations leader
standards. *See* measurement
steering process. *See* circular process
stockholders. *See* investors
strategic planning process, 76, 120–124
    aims redefined during, 123
    war analogies and, 120–122
Sun Tzu, *Art of War*, 121–122
super–, supra-majority vote, 50, 59
SWOT analysis or matrix, 156
systems, systems theory, 19, 34, 57
    characteristics of strong, 57
    closed mechanical, linear 19
    dynamic sustainable, 19

                  T

tactics, 120, 124
tasks. *See* roles and responsibilities
Taylor, Frederick Winslow, 70
    Cheaper by the Dozen, 70
    scientific management, 70
    Taylorism, 70
Texas City, Texas
    See Deepwater Horizon oil spill

theocracy, theocratic, 38, 68–69, 75
The Republic by Plato, 53
time-and-motion study, 70
Tobacco Master Settlement Agreement, 126
top circle, 61, 138, 147–149
    composition, 112–114, 147–149
    budget decisions, 149, 199
    how time is spent, 148
    shipping crisis, 61
    See also circles
top management, managers, 135, 145
Total Quality Management (TQM), 87
trainers, internal, 147
    Also see implementation circle
transparency, 135–136, 130–131, 123, 124
    financial, 138
    organization records, 76
    proprietary formulas, 135
    proprietary information, 90

                  U

Umpleby, Stuart, 55
United Nations, vii

                  V

values, 17, 18, 21
variable compensation. *See* compensation
Veteran's Administration hospitals, 132
veto, 83–84
Villines, Sharon, xv, 27, 29–36
    about xv
    "Sociocracy for One," 239
    sociocracy@groups.io, 210
    Sociocracy.info, xv, 210
    Why We Need Another "-ocracy," 29–35
vision, vision statement, 93
vision, mission, and aim examples, 187

                  W

wages. *See* compensation
war and business analogies, 120–123
Ward, Lester Frank, 39–41, 43, 44, 49
    Comte's Positivism, 40
    father of American sociology, 40
    Psychic Factors of Civilization, 40

"Sociocracy" 215–222
   structure vs. control, 39
Weiner, Norbert, 53
   Cybernetics, 53
   education of, 53
Welch, Jack, 115, 119
Werkplaats Kindergemeenschap
   See Children's Community Workshop
Westerweel, Joop, 44
Wheatley, Margaret, 128
   communications, 128
   Leadership and the New Science, 128
"Why we need another -ocracy"
   Buck, John, 23–28
   Villines. Sharon, 29–36
Wilber, Ken, 118
worker commitment, satisfaction, 27, 66, 76
workers, employees, 92
   as equals, 59
   productivity, 47, 72
   protection for, 62
work process,
   "Designing the Work Process," guide for, 301
   See producing organization
World Bank, vii
Wright Brothers, 194
WW II, 37–48, 44–48

CPSIA information can be obtained
at www.ICGtesting.com
Printed in the USA
BVOW10s0954011117
499252BV00019B/863/P